Meetings: Ethnographies of Organizational Process, Bureaucracy, and Assembly

Journal of the Royal Anthropological Institute Special Issue Series

The Journal of the Royal Anthropological Institute is the principal journal of the oldest anthropological organization in the world. It has attracted and inspired some of the world's greatest thinkers. International in scope, it presents accessible papers aimed at a broad anthropological readership. We are delighted to announce that from 2014 the annual special issues will also be available from the Wiley Blackwell books catalogue.

Previous special issues of the JRAI:

MEETINGS: ETHNOGRAPHIES OF ORGANIZATIONAL PROCESS, BUREAUCRACY, AND ASSEMBLY

EDITED BY HANNAH BROWN, ADAM REED, and THOMAS YARROW

Library of Congress Cataloging-in-Publication Data

Names: Brown, Hannah, editor. | Reed, Adam, 1967- editor. | Yarrow, Thomas, 1977- editor.
Title: Meetings: ethnographies of organizational process, bureaucracy, and assembly/edited by Hannah Brown, Adam Reed & Thomas Yarrow.
Other titles: Journal of the Royal Anthropological Institute. Special issue.
Description: Chichester, UK; Hoboken, NJ: John Wiley & Sons, 2017. |
Series: Journal of the Royal Anthropological Institute Special Issue Series; volume 23(Supp) | Includes bibliographical references and index.
Identifiers: LCCN 2017009041 | ISBN 9781119405894 (cloth)
Subjects: LCSH: Meetings. | Bureaucracy.
Classification: LCC HD30.3 .M46 2017 | DDC 302.34–dc23 LC record available at https://lccn.loc.gov/2017009041

9781119405894

A catalogue record for this book is available from the British Library.

Journal of the Royal Anthropological Institute.
Incorporating MAN
Print ISSN 1359-0987
All articles published within this special issue are included within the ISI Journal Citation Reports® Social Science Citation Index. Please cite the articles as volume 23(Supp) of the Journal of the Royal Anthropological Institute.

Cover image: El Campo de Cebada, Madrid, May 2013 by Creative Commons BY-SA.

Cover design by Ben Higgins

Set in 10 on 12pt Minion by Aptara Inc.

Printed in Singapore by C.O.S. Printers Pte Ltd

1 2017

Contents

Notes on contributors

Simone Abram is Reader in the Department of Anthropology at Durham University and is a Director of the Durham Energy Institute. Much of her research has been on planning and bureaucracy. Books include *Rationalities of planning* (Ashgate, 2002; with Jonathan Murdoch); *Culture and planning* (Ashgate, 2011); and *Elusive promises: planning in the contemporary world* (Berghahn Books, 2013; with Gisa Weszkalnys). *Department of Anthropology, Durham University, Dawson Building, South Road, Durham DH1 3LE, UK. simone.abram@durham.ac.uk*

Catherine Alexander is Professor of Anthropology at Durham University. She has worked in Turkey, Kazakhstan, and Britain on bureaucracies and institutions; state/market/third-sector intersections; changing property regimes and wastes – from their management to how they escape being managed. *Department of Anthropology, Durham University, Dawson Building, South Road, Durham DH1 3LE, UK. catherine.alexander@durham.ac.uk*

Hannah Brown is Lecturer in Anthropology at Durham University. She has worked in Kenya and Sierra Leone. Her research explores how people care for one another through interpersonal relations and institutions, and how relations with animals and technologies shape possibilities for wellbeing. She is the co-editor (with Ruth Prince) of *Volunteer economies: the politics and ethics of voluntary labour in Africa* (James Currey, 2016). *Department of Anthropology, Durham University, Dawson Building, South Road, Durham DH1 3LE, UK. hannah.brown@durham.ac.uk*

Alberto Corsín Jiménez is Associate Professor in Social Anthropology in the Department of the History of Science at the Spanish National Research Council (CSIC). He is the author of *An anthropological trompe l'oeil for a common world* (Berghahn Books, 2013) and, most recently, editor of *Prototyping cultures: art, science and politics in Beta* (Routledge, 2017). His current work examines the relationship between forms of freedom, infrastructure, and the city. *Departamento de Historia de la Ciencia, Centro de Ciencias Humanas y Sociales, Calle Albasanz 26-28, Madrid 28037, Spain. alberto.corsin-jimenez@cchs.csic.es*

Adolfo Estalella is a postdoctoral researcher at the Spanish National Research Council (CSIC). He has an interest in the anthropology of knowledge and has done extensive fieldwork in urban activist contexts in Madrid, focusing his research on the study of digital cultures and grassroots urbanism. *Centro de Ciencias Humanas y Sociales, Calle Albasanz 26-28, Madrid 28037, Spain. adolfoestalella@gmail.com*

Gillian Evans is an urban anthropologist. She lectures at the University of Manchester and has held a RCUK Fellowship (2007-12). Gillian undertook a long-term ethnographic study of the planning of Olympic legacy in post-industrial East London. Her monograph on this subject – *London's Olympic legacy: the inside track* – was published by Palgrave Macmillan in 2016. *Department of Social Anthropology, University of Manchester, Manchester M13 9PL, UK. Gillian.Evans@manchester.ac.uk*

Maia Green is a Professor of Social Anthropology at the University of Manchester and works on issues of social transformation in East Africa. Her recent project explores new technologies of social organization in the form of civil society organizations and participatory institutions in Tanzania and internationally. *Department of Social Anthropology, University of Manchester, Manchester M13 9PL, UK. maia.green@manchester.ac.uk*

Bernard Keenan is a Ph.D. candidate at the London School of Economics and Political Science and a former immigration solicitor. His historically focused thesis links the legal form of the warrant to the strategies and visibilities involved in the secret interception of communication media, from the birth of the Post Office to the Snowden archive. *Law Department, London School of Economics and Political Science, 54 Lincoln's Inn Fields, London WC2A 3LJ, UK. W.B.Keenan@lse.ac.uk*

Nicolas Lamp is an Assistant Professor at the Faculty of Law at Queen's University. Prior to joining Queen's, he worked as a Dispute Settlement Lawyer at the Appellate Body Secretariat of the World Trade Organization. He holds a Ph.D. in Law from the London School of Economics and Political Science. *Queen's University, Faculty of Law, 128 Union Street, Kingston, Ontario K7L 3N6, Canada. nicolas.lamp@queensu.ca*

Morten Nielsen is an Associate Professor in the Department of Anthropology at Aarhus University and co-ordinator of the interdisciplinary research network Urban Orders (URO). Based on his fieldwork in Mozambique, Scotland, and, most recently, the United States, he has published on issues such as urban citizenship, time and temporality, urban aesthetics, materiality, infrastructure, and political cosmologies. *Department of Anthropology, Aarhus University, Moesgaard Allé 20, DK-8270 Højbjerg, Denmark. etnomn@cas.au.dk*

Alain Pottage is Professor of Law at the London School of Economics and Political Science. His research focuses on topics in the history and theory of property, especially intellectual property. *Law Department, London School of Economics and Political Science, 54 Lincoln's Inn Fields, London WC2A 3LJ, UK. R.A.Pottage@lse.ac.uk*

Adam Reed is a Senior Lecturer in the Department of Social Anthropology at the University of St Andrews. He conducts research in Papua New Guinea and Britain, and is the author of *Papua New Guinea's last place: experiences of constraint in a postcolonial prison* (Berghahn Books, 2003) and *Literature and agency in English fiction reading: a study of the Henry Williamson Society* (Manchester University Press, 2011). *Department of Social Anthropology, University of St Andrews, St Andrews, Fife KY16 9AL, UK. ader@st-andrews.ac.uk*

Annelise Riles is Jack G. Clarke Professor of Law in Far East Legal Studies and Professor of Anthropology at Cornell University. Her work focuses on the aesthetics and practices of legal knowledge in transnational contexts. She is the founder and director of Meridian 180, www.meridian-180.org, a non-partisan community of Pacific Rim intellectuals collaborating on transnational legal and policy issues. *Cornell Law School & Department of Anthropology, 120 Myron Taylor Hall, Ithaca, NY 14853, USA. ar254@cornell.edu*

Marilyn Strathern is Emeritus Professor of Social Anthropology, Cambridge University. Her ethnographic forays are divided between Papua New Guinea and Britain. Over the last twenty years she has written on reproductive technologies; intellectual and cultural property; and 'critique of good practice', an umbrella rubric for reflections on audit and accountability. *Girton College, Cambridge CB3 0JG, UK. ms10026@cam.ac.uk*

Thomas Yarrow is a Senior Lecturer in Social Anthropology at Durham University. His work mostly focuses on expertise and institutional knowledge, particularly through ethnographic engagements with architects, heritage professionals, archaeologists, and NGO workers. He is the author of *Development beyond politics: aid, activism and NGOs in Ghana* (Palgrave Macmillan, 2011) and the co-editor of volumes on *Archaeology and anthropology* (Oxbow, 2010; with Duncan Garrow), *Detachment* (Manchester University Press, 2015; with Matei Candea, Catherine Trundle & Jo Cook), and *Differentiating development* (Berghahn Books, 2012; with Soumhya Venkatesan). *Department of Anthropology, Durham University, Dawson Building, South Road, Durham DH1 3LE, UK. t.g.yarrow@durham.ac.uk*

Introduction: towards an ethnography of meeting

HANNAH BROWN *Durham University*

ADAM REED *University of St Andrews*

THOMAS YARROW *Durham University*

This introductory essay describes a novel approach to meetings in relation to broader literatures within and beyond anthropology. We suggest that notwithstanding many accounts in which meetings figure, little attention has been given to the mundane forms through which these work. Seeking to develop a distinctively ethnographic focus to these quotidian and ubiquitous procedures, we outline an approach that moves attention beyond a narrow concern with just their meaning and content. We highlight some of the innovative strands that develop from this approach, describing how the negotiation of relationships 'within' meetings is germane to the organization of 'external' contexts, including in relation to time, space, organizational structure, and society. The essay offers a set of provocations for rethinking approaches to bureaucracy, organizational process, and ethos through the ethnographic lens of meeting.

'Supporting materials': contexts of meeting

Before a meeting, it is usual to circulate the 'supporting materials' or the background documents that frame and contextualize the issues to be discussed. In this spirit, our opening section sets the context for the volume via a discussion of some key texts and literatures. In the borrowed vocabulary and form of meetings, subsequent sections set out our 'agenda', 'minute' key themes emerging from discussion of the essays, and put forward some concluding thoughts via the guise of 'AOB', or Any Other Business.

Meetings, as prescribed spaces for coming together, are important administrative, supervisory, and collaborative actions. Central to the life of formal institutions and many other organizations, including community and religious associations and political movements, meetings are instantiated through a range of typical forms including the gathering of committees and working groups, project meetings, stakeholder meetings, site meetings, annual general meetings, team meetings, and *ad hoc* or 'informal' meetings. Ubiquitous and diverse, these meetings act to order relations, understandings,

Journal of the Royal Anthropological Institute (N.S.), 10-26
© Royal Anthropological Institute 2017

and knowledge and thus to influence a range of 'conjured contexts' (Abram, this volume) beyond themselves. To the extent that meetings contain and animate social worlds outside the spatially and temporally demarcated arenas through which they take place, they offer novel vantage-points from which to consider a range of anthropologically significant concerns. In one sense composed through boringly, even achingly, familiar routines (see Alexander, this volume; Sandler & Thedvall 2016), including ordinary forms of bureaucratic conduct of seeming universal reach, they are in another sense specific and productive arenas in which realities are dramatically negotiated. Meetings, as the volume demonstrates, are not just instances that exemplify broader issues, but key sites through which social, political, temporal, spatial, and material circumstances are constituted and transformed.

In the social sciences, those seeking to define meetings in the contexts of such a broad array of activities have focused on attempting to characterize key features. Most well known, anthropologically speaking, is Schwartzman's definition of meetings as communicative events involving people who 'assemble for the purpose ostensibly related to the functioning of an organization or group' (1989: 7). Others have pointed to the fact that meetings tend to be planned in advance, are framed by particular kinds of documentary practice, and usually involve material objects such as tables and writing equipment (Asmuß & Svennevig 2009: 10-11); or have considered meetings to be defined primarily through what they seek to achieve, for example as the 'machinery by which group decisions are reached' (Richards 1971: 1; see also Bailey 2011 [1965]). Historically, the spread of this distinctive social form has been connected to the eighteenth-century 'meeting-ization' of society (van Vree 1999) – a series of linked transformations in Europe through which society was created as a distinct object of collective action, and meetings were increasingly standardized as the locus and embodiment of ideas of appropriate, transparent decision-making. The subsequent global spread of these standardized forms has been linked to colonialism and more recently to the actions of postcolonial governments and non-governmental organizations. This includes the prominence since the Second World War of meeting forms connected to the significant importation of models of 'good governance' and democratic speech technologies (see Hull 2010; Morton 2014). These historical factors are significant, as contributors variously demonstrate, but do not in any straightforward sense exhaust the complexity of meanings, actions, and relations now animated by this pervasive social form. Our own working definition, in some ways more expansive, in others more restrictive, is centrally ethnographic: the volume is an exploration of activities that are explicitly figured as 'meeting' from the perspective of those involved. In most cases these are activities that take a formally recognized organizational form. We deliberately eschew the analytic question of the 'modernity' of these activities while noting the range of ways in which, more or less explicitly, meetings are associated with this term (however that is defined) in many ethnographic contexts. Finally, our own comparative interests in meeting relate to the ethnographically significant sense in which organizational meetings also appear to those who participate in them as instances of a universal and ubiquitous practice.

Given their leading role in a range of institutions, it is unsurprising that meetings have featured prominently in literatures beyond anthropology. However, our approach marks a distinction from the more etic methodologies that predominantly characterize analyses of meetings in disciplines including sociology (e.g. Boden 1994; Goffman 1961), psychology (e.g. Volkan 1991), and business studies (e.g. Asmuß & Svennevig 2009), and from the search for generalized theories that pertain across contexts. It also marks, we believe, a shift in anthropological focus.

Meetings have of course been described in some classic accounts (Gluckman 1940; Richards & Kuper 1971), in particular in functionalist and structural-functionalist ethnography, in which interests displayed and negotiated in meetings have often been analysed in relation to questions of social organization. Indeed, 'traditional' or non-bureaucratic forms of indigenous meeting have continued to be important objects of ethnographic description: consider, for example, the well-known observations by Bloch (1971) on Merina councils or the work of Duranti (1981) on the village *fono* in Samoa. More recently, meetings, especially 'modern' meetings, have featured in a range of literatures, including in relation to documents (Riles 2006), speech acts (Atkinson, Cuff & Lee 1978; Brenneis & Myers 1984), organizations (Gellner & Hirsch 2001; Wright 1994), policy (Mosse 2005; Shore & Wright 1997), development (Brown 2013; Englund 2006; Li 2007; Riles 2000; Rottenburg 2009; Swidler & Watkins 2009; Yarrow 2011), politics (Graeber 2009; Haugerud 1993), and science and technology (Callon 1986; Dupuy 2000; Heims 1993; Law 1994). In various ways these literatures provide useful conceptual tools. And yet, notwithstanding some notable and significant exceptions (Abram 2011; Harper 2000; Moore 1977; Morton 2014; Richards & Kuper 1971; Sandler & Thedvall 2016; Schwartzman 1989), for all the many ways in which meetings figure in accounts orientated by other concerns, they have rarely been the subject of sustained ethnographic attention in their own right. Even within recent work on bureaucracy (e.g. Bear & Mathur 2015; Feldman 2008; Gupta 2012; Hull 2012; Naravo-Yashin 2012), meetings have not received the kind of detailed scrutiny that has been afforded to other kinds of bureaucratic tools and techniques, such as documents. Moreover, because attention to meetings has evolved within distinct and largely parallel literatures, this has precluded sustained exploration of the similarities and differences at stake in these various contexts. This volume starts from the premise that while existing accounts make important contributions to conceptualizations of the dynamics at play in 'meeting', a number of linked analytic assumptions have elided ethnographic description of key dimensions of these practices.

While the mid-twentieth-century interest in social order did not preclude detailed and insightful accounts of meeting, the analytic concerns of that time obscured important elements of these practices. In particular, an approach premised on the assumption of social order negated ethnographic attention to organization as an emergent quality of social practice (cf. du Gay 2007; Law 1994; Mol 2002). Indeed, as Hull (2012: 251) suggests, the ethnographic study of organizations was for many years animated by a sense of organizational culture that drew anthropologists to focus on informal aspects of organizations rather than the dominant formal dimensions of bureaucratic practice. We suggest that one explanation for this ethnographic intractability is, paradoxically, the very familiarity of the concepts and practices through which meetings operate. As with the documentary practices opened up by recent anthropological approaches to texts (see, e.g., Hull 2012; Reed 2006; Riles 2000; 2006), it is not simply that the mundane can seem uninteresting to a discipline conventionally concerned with elaboration of cultural difference, but that elements of practices are elided precisely because they work through categories and practices that overlap with those of anthropologists and social scientists. Anthropologists, like other academics, routinely participate in meetings, which are central to the organization of academic life, and to the very constitution of knowledge (a point that Mills [2014] makes in a thoughtful discussion of the history of meetings at the Annual Social Anthropology conference; see also Silverman 2002). Of course this volume, too, emerged from and was given impetus by various kinds of meeting, ranging from the regular informal meetings of its editors, to the conference at which initial papers were presented. In more or less explicit ways contributors highlighted how the forms that were ethnographically at issue were also those deployed in the drive to apprehend them.

In more recent accounts, the contextualizing logics of meeting have also been associated with ethnographic lacunae. Meetings, by definition, are socially delimited spaces that refer to contexts, interests, and agendas beyond themselves. As such they provide vital contexts for the exploration of a range of substantive and theoretical concerns. Although this interpretative strategy has proved insightful, attention to the contexts generated and represented through meetings has deflected attention from the routine procedures and forms through which context is constituted through meeting. As Schwartzman points out, 'The meeting frame itself contributes to this neglect because it suggests that it is what goes on *within* a meeting that is important' (1987: 287, emphasis in original); this frame actively misdirects participants from a look *at* the meeting.

Thus our approach extends the recent work of anthropologists of organizations and bureaucracy in suggesting that the forms (Lea 2002), aesthetics (Riles 2000; Strathern 2000), and material contexts (Hull 2012) through which meetings work are not incidental or subservient to the meanings and actions they produce.

'Agenda': arguments from ethnography

We have established that in various ways ethnographic attention has been diverted from key elements of meeting practices by methodological and theoretical assumptions that anthropologists have routinely brought to bear. We suggest that recovering a more thoroughly ethnographic orientation to the topic of meeting enables understanding of these forms as situated universals (Tsing 2005), highlighting the limitations of more generalizing analyses that have often characterized the approaches of cognate disciplines. We draw particular inspiration from earlier ethnographic accounts by Schwartzman (1987; 1989), specifically her concern to understand what is practically and conceptually at stake when people claim to 'meet'. It is significant that Schwartzman's insights have been under-developed in subsequent analyses of bureaucratic conduct, in which texts have more routinely drawn the attention of institutional analysis, as paradigmatic exemplars of the forms of knowledge that bureaucratic practices produce (but see Sandler & Thedvall 2016). We aim to recapture and recover the insights of this earlier literature in relation to specific ethnographic articulations, and to render these relevant to contemporary debates about institutional and bureaucratic knowledge.

We approach meetings ethnographically, seeking to understand, describe and explain how people conceptualize their own involvements in this mundane form. In various contexts contributors seek to examine how meetings are imagined, experienced, and practically realized through the ideas, actions, and pronouncements of those involved. Unified by this common approach, our commitment to ethnography entails an effort to confront a problem inherent in other forms of anthropology 'at home' (Jackson 1987; Strathern 1987). Insofar as meetings work through concepts, forms, and assumptions that have been central to academic thought and practice – in anthropology and beyond – the more routine problem of epistemic difference (how to render the 'strange' in 'familiar' terms) is confronted as an issue of epistemic over-familiarity. As meetings are instances of forms that are 'too familiar to approach with ease' (Riles 2000: 22), empirical understanding of their ethnographic entailments involves de-centring the analytic assumptions that have rendered these invisible. We are sympathetic to recent approaches in which ethnography is understood as a method for simultaneously understanding the ontological basis of others' categorical distinctions and for rethinking the theoretical basis of our own (e.g. Holbraad 2012; Viveiros de Castro 2004). However, our focus on meeting complicates actual or implied ideas of radical alterity as analytic-cum-methodological starting-point. As contributors variously show, meetings are spaces for the alignment and negotiation of distinct perspectives, and are constituted through the contextual interplay of similarity and difference. While multiplicity (e.g. of people, perspectives, knowledge) is often their point of departure, singularity (e.g. in the form of objective agreement) is often their achieved outcome. It follows that approaches that engender assumptions about the universal basis of sociality and those that assume radical difference are equally problematic positions from which to explore these articulations in which the relationship of similarity and difference is precisely at stake.

An ethnographic approach to meeting, defined in these terms, is not inconsistent with the selective incorporation of valuable insights from actor-network theorists – an approach which contributors to this volume engage in different, more or less direct terms – including through building on those in which meeting has figured (e.g. Bruun-Jensen & Winthereik 2013; Law 1994; Mol 2002). Such approaches open up important analytic perspectives, highlighting how meetings are sites in which people and materials are assembled as networks with more or less durability and differential capacity to act. The same approach inspires Hull to assess documents as 'mediators', things that 'shape the significance of the signs inscribed on them and their relations with the objects they refer to' (2012: 253). Indeed, we may ask whether it is helpful to judge meetings in the same light, and if so, to ask how we might study the translation or modification of 'the elements they are supposed to carry' (Latour 2005: 39). However, as other anthropological commentators have noted (e.g. Candea, Cook, Trundle & Yarrow 2015; Rabinow & Stavrianakis 2014), the analytic lens of 'practice' that orientates many actor-network-inspired accounts often acts to dissolve and displace the conceptual distinctions that actors present. Our own more conventionally ethnographic concern, by contrast, places actors' understandings of these practices as a central focus of analysis and as a source of theoretical insight. From this perspective, meetings can be seen as dynamic sites in which networks are extended but also cut (Strathern 1996), in situated articulations of people, documents, technology, and infrastructure. Theoretically the network allows for limitless analytic connection, but in various ways meetings entail categorical distinctions, including those relating to time and space. The ethnographies collected in this volume exemplify how meetings are defined in ways that are simultaneously conceptual, material, and social. Focusing on acts of cutting as much as connecting (cf. Myhre 2016), we ask: who is included and excluded? How are the 'internal' workings of meetings defined as distinct but related to specific 'external' contexts?

Recovering and extending the insights of earlier accounts of meeting becomes particularly pertinent in light of subsequent prevailing theoretical developments. Foucauldian approaches to institutional knowledge have generated vital insights, specifically in relation to the political implications of knowledge production, but have often been accompanied by a 'hermeneutics of suspicion' (Rabinow & Stavrianakis 2014), which can lead to ethnographically reductive accounts of institutional practice

Journal of the Royal Anthropological Institute (N.S.), 10-26
© Royal Anthropological Institute 2017

(see also Brown 2016; Mosse 2005; Yarrow 2011). As we elaborate further below, ethnographic attention focused on the ordinary forms and processes of meeting yields valuable insights, situating and extending interdisciplinary discussions of bureaucratic and institutional knowledge, and revealing new perspectives on a range of topics of broad and long-standing anthropological interest.

'Minutes': emergent themes

Our ethnographic approach focuses attention on what it takes to make a meeting; and on what it is that meetings make. In various ways, essays in this volume trace how these involve the assembly of specific people, things, materials, places, and ideas. A related focus is how relationships 'within' these spaces are linked to transformations beyond them, including of institutional structure, time, space, and society. Meetings, as contributors to the volume demonstrate, are not just about institutional and organizational practice, but also and indissolubly pertain to topics as various as time, space, politics, aesthetics, identity, scale, personhood, and the body. Essays reveal how the lens of 'meeting' situates and therefore variously extends understanding of these topics, as we outline below.

Meetings organize, collecting persons and things in compelling ways. They work through forms that elicit actions on their own terms. Meetings are full of capacity; at least this is what participants often wish to claim. It is evident from these accounts that the forms and aesthetic devices through which meetings proceed are generative of actions and understandings of various kinds. The power of the meeting form to draw out capacities and relations surfaces in many contributions, but is perhaps most dramatically illustrated in those instances when meeting is placed at the heart of social or political innovation and reform. Take the example of the Spanish Occupy movement provided by Corsín Jiménez and Estalella. As they illustrate from their ethnography of street gatherings in Madrid, it is the form of the assembly meeting itself that is employed to demonstrate the revolutionary potential of Occupy at the neighbourhood level. In fact, figured as a public demonstration of consensus-building and 'real democracy', the assembly form is imagined not merely as indicative but also as generative of socio-political transformation. Corsín Jiménez and Estalella report that the performance of assembly, which in many ways replicates conventional modalities of institutional gathering, is meant to capture the attention of passers-by, to draw them into local participation. Seen as a vehicle for political expression and mobilization, this example has obvious parallels with Nielsen's focus on the political aesthetics of collective meetings in Maputo, Mozambique. But what is of interest in this case is the persistence and continuing efficacy of a socialist procedural form of meeting after the collapse of the ideology from which it emerged (socialism ended in Mozambique in the mid-1980s). In this example, it appears that the assigned capacity of a meeting form can survive the demise of or even supersede what seemed to be its necessary context; as if socialism was a mere supplement to the mobilizing power of meeting itself.

These caveats about 'context' relate to a resistance to understand these spaces as subservient to (configured by) broader political processes. Rather, contributors reveal how 'meetings' are sites of political positioning and negotiation. For some, this may include, as Schwartzman (1989: 36-7) highlights, an attention to the ways in which values and social structure get 'bred into' the meeting form. However, this is accompanied by an awareness that through talk within meetings, and through the definitional boundaries through which the meeting space is circumscribed, power is not simply reproduced but also constituted in new terms. Abram makes this vividly evident in a discussion of Norwegian council planning meetings. Her account is concerned with meetings as spaces that act to order political life beyond these spaces, and highlights the precarious relationship that exists between decisions 'within' them and 'actions' beyond them. External contexts must be correctly evoked for the meeting to be effectual (i.e. it is through the performance of the former that the latter is made), and vice versa: the adoption of rituals, routines, performances, and 'consequential talk' is crucial to the establishment of authority that validates the link between internal decision and external 'action'. In her ethnography of the Olympic Park Legacy Company in London, Evans shows how meetings function as vehicles for circumscribed forms of empowerment, and do more than simply reproduce the kinds of interest they refract. Organizational meetings appear as fairly clear instruments of politics and strategy, at least from the perspective of East London local community petitioning parties. These meetings form mechanisms for negotiating conflicting actions concerning the same object of concern and appear as authoritative and 'polite' navigations of complex political fields. But at the same time, remainders of meetings leave a haunting legacy which only partly erases the antagonisms, conflicts, and emotions at stake within them. The meeting is here a heavily interest-laden object.

The everyday process of meeting aims to create order and organization of various kinds. Essays by Yarrow and by Brown and Green share a similar attention. In the latter case, a study of aid delivery in Kenya's health sector draws out the constitutive role of meetings in international development. Brown and Green argue that contemporary funding mechanisms have combined with concerns around capacity-building and participation in ways that render international development primarily into systems of meetings. These meetings enact the relations and senses of organizational scale that are necessary for the implementation of development. In Yarrow's ethnographic research at Historic Scotland (now known, since his research, as Historic Environment Scotland), meetings become a venue for the alignment of various forms of expert knowledge and in particular for techniques of heritage assessment objectivity. Essays by Evans, Yarrow, and by Brown and Green are unified by an acute sense of the precarious status of what the procedural device of meeting can produce. Whether viewed as a managerial process of 'stabilization', inside the Olympic Park Legacy Company, or as a technique that helps achieve a sense of much-valued 'consistency', in Historic Scotland, or as a technique of scale-making that 'enacts an architecture' for the structuring of international development in Kenya, the message is clear: that meetings are sites where subjects continually wrestle with resolution.

Institutional gatherings also usually occur as part of a series or hierarchy of meetings, figured in relation to various images of institutional structure and form. In Lamp's study of World Trade Organization meetings, there is even an explicit WTO theory of seriality, modelled on 'concentric circles'. This is unusual, but one does not have to look far in our contributions to find other references to the interconnection of meeting forms. In Historic Scotland, for instance, the office project meeting and the site meeting are conceived as closely interdependent. Keenan and Pottage, in their study of asylum case meetings, make clear the way one legal meeting can exist in anticipation of another kind; as does Abram, highlighting how codified, standardized forms of documentation tie these together. In Reed's essay on animal welfare bureaucracy, the team meeting seems to function as a form into which other meetings will eventually fold or at least in which they will be reported upon. Brown and Green make the point that health development meetings in Kenya only work because they are part of broader systems of meetings taking place at different 'levels' of organization.

Recent accounts within anthropology (e.g. Bear 2014; Miyazaki 2004) and beyond it (e.g. Lucas 2015) make explicit the extent to which analytic assumptions about the nature of modern time have been internalized in ways that render time as a container or 'envelope' (Lucas 2015) for social process. Accordingly these elide a more thoroughly empirical understanding of the practices through which temporality is socially and materially produced. Building on this work, contributors to this volume demonstrate how time is produced through forms, procedures, and practices of meeting. Meetings make time the subject matter for a gathering or the content for discussion. They are often orientated, for example, to resolution as a prerequisite to future social, political, or institutional action; or, as Riles points out in her reflections on Meridian 180, the avowedly non-partisan multidisciplinary community of academics, practitioners, and policy-makers that she helped establish, towards the achievement of 'outputs'. The latter, which involves subjects addressing themselves to strategic plans or work tasks, is a generative 'fiction' of the bureaucratic meeting that for her enables gatherings not just to be retrospectively recognized as such but also to prospectively proliferate into organized series. Meetings may include imaginaries of new organizational futures in relation to past activities and understandings. As Harper (1998: 214) describes in his analysis of International Monetary Fund meetings, the goal of these gatherings can be to both 'use the present to divine the future' but also to use 'reference to that future to further refine what the present might be'.

If meetings are therefore constitutive of time, in the elicitation of different forms of external context, they take place 'in' their own time, which can be variously ordered and experienced. Notwithstanding the pervasive framing of these through modern tropes of linear time, the relationship between 'internal' and 'external' temporalities is complex and specific. As several contributors identify, subjects often resent the minutes and hours that meetings take up. (Schwartzman [1989: 159] makes the point that in this regard meetings may be taken to 'select' for certain kinds of participants: i.e. those able to spare or devote the 'time' to attend a course of meetings.) This includes common complaints about the quality of that time, that it can, for instance, be dull or boring (see Alexander, this volume; Riles, this volume; Sandler & Thedvall 2016). Meetings often have very tightly designated start- and end-points: a meeting is usually a scheduled event and therefore expected to fit into a prescribed interval of time. In fact the meeting is a form of interaction that regularly ends abruptly, at the termination of the allotted hour. If a meeting 'runs over time', it can mean it is badly managed or alternatively that it is working too well. Meetings also regularly have fixed cycles; they can be scheduled over a period of months or years, or, as a core part of an organizational structure and calendar, be regarded as a constant, repeating form (see Abram, this volume). Such temporalities are a recurring theme in this volume, with contributors reflecting upon the quality and issues of time that are revealed through meetings, including the relationship between enactment of particular temporalities and the strategic or relational capacities of meetings.

Contributors to the volume variously show how ideas about consistency and objectivity emerge as regulatory ideals more than determining principles. This collective insight, that consistency and objectivity are often after the fact of practices that do not straightforwardly conform to these ideals, destabilizes widespread assumptions about the 'organized' nature of bureaucracy (see also Mol 2002). Essays by Yarrow and by Keenan and Pottage demonstrate an interesting inversion. While the former explores the achievements and struggles for consistency across diverse organizational meeting forms in a Scottish heritage body, the latter focuses on the animating role of 'inconsistency' in the example of asylum case conference meetings between barristers, clients, and their solicitors in London. In these conferences interaction develops around a close attention to the identification of contradiction and irregularity in the client's story; the meeting anticipates a later appeal meeting before a judge. But it also anticipates a professional ethics or legal code of conduct about coaching witnesses. Part of the challenge and tension of the case conference meeting is that inconsistency must be located without ever being spoken of; barrister and solicitor are constantly walking an invisible line (the code of conduct is vaguely defined in terms of what constitutes coaching) between ethical and unethical prompting.

Building on recent anthropological accounts (see Faubion 2011; Laidlaw 2013; Robbins 2007), a focus on the ethics of meeting highlights how bureaucratic encounters can involve indeterminately related ethical frames that relate to complex personal decisions. If the professional ethics of legal advice are bound up with and negotiated through the actual terms of engagement between barrister, solicitor, and client in the conference meeting described by Keenan and Pottage, the 'ethical' line of the Edinburgh charity described by Reed appears more straightforward. Indeed, participants come to team meetings and other organizational gatherings as fully formed ethical subjects; their involvement in those meetings is animated by a commitment to the principles of animal welfare. The meeting form is there to service or deliver the ethical mission of the organization. What both these examples also throw up is the convoluted and dynamic relationship between meeting ethics and organizational roles and offices. The case conference is formally an encounter between barrister, solicitor, and client; the code of conduct demands that legal officers respond professionally rather than 'personally' to the client. By contrast the client exists as an overly personal person, as someone whose biography or individuality needs to be cultivated to resolve or purify inconsistency. In the example of the Scottish animal protection charity, the expertise of role or office is valued as a facilitation of ethical goals. Participants in team meetings report from the perspective of office, and not that of individual person, but in the knowledge that this professional outlook is grounded in shared ethical sentiment. What emerges as an increasingly live tension in these meetings is the question of whether professionalism can function to perpetuate organizational ethical goals if there is no ethical individual subject behind the office-holder. The anxiety returns us to one of the initial orientating themes of the special issue, the recurring inquiry into the terms and nature of participation itself. This includes an exploration of the constitution of attendees, the composition of those persons who act and speak in the meeting.

For one needs bodies to make meetings happen. In a very literal sense, a meeting is often not formally enacted unless it achieves a quorum, a necessary number of counted persons in attendance. As a technology, meetings straightforwardly bring people together in one place, but, as an ethnographic focus on meeting highlights, the issue becomes what kind of bodies and persons are enrolled to make meetings happen. And how might they too, as artefacts of the process of meeting, undergo transformations? In part these are classic questions about the relationship between persons, roles, and offices (see Reed, this volume). But whereas in the structural-functionalist heyday these questions were linked to concerns with understanding what were assumed to be mechanisms for organizing and regulating society, the contributors here approach these as open and empirical questions. Essays in the volume reflect upon the kinds of person that meetings presuppose and the modalities by which people inhabit and convert these. In formal gatherings the individual person is often subsumed by the status of a technical role within the meeting (such as 'chair' or 'secretary' or 'minute-taker') or by a status as office-holder. Abram highlights how roles are performed as 'consequential talk' that makes the orator a concrete embodiment of a corporate entity. On the same logic that establishes this authority, the status of the 'personal' or 'individual' perspective may be thrown into doubt. Whether or not people speak as one or the other may be open to debate and is the focus of more subtle negotiations. With this in mind, many contributors have focused on the issue of 'who' precisely is present at meetings and in what moments. The emphasis here is on the oscillation between personal and role perspectives, the micro-dynamics of meeting interactions between persons but also within them.

These questions are intriguingly redirected in the ethnography of World Trade Organization meetings offered by Lamp, a legal scholar. Here participants represent member nations. The issue of who is present in these formal chamber meetings and who authors the official documents that accompany them is uncontroversial. More contentious is the issue of the meeting's visibility or publicness. The transparency of formal meetings and official documents, it would seem, can only achieve resolution if placed in tandem with informal meetings and papers that have an unofficial status. What is particularly thought-provoking in Lamp's example is the layered way in which techniques of formality and informality are elaborated by WTO participants into a whole set of principles for meetings practice. The contrast with the wholly public ambitions of the assembly meeting of the Spanish Occupy movement in Corsín Jiménez and Estalella's essay could not be more marked. But the WTO example can also be fruitfully compared with Alexander's examination of the transnational migration of one kind of public body project management process known as PRINCE and its accompanying meeting forms. Her essay focuses on the reception of this apparently transferable quality assurance package, which originated in Britain, in government circles in Turkey. More specifically, it describes a series of formal and informal meetings between an international lending agency, a Turkish government ministry, and international consultants. Here informality or *ad hoc* meetings seem to constantly undercut the ambitions of PRINCE to define parameters of engagement in an abstractable way.

As Lamp's contribution most dramatically illustrates, as well as bodies, meetings most obviously require documents, objects circulated before meetings, to which meetings are conventionally directed or sequenced. In fact it is documents that regularly give form to the order and time management of meetings. One need only think of the structuring role of the 'agenda', of 'discussion papers' and 'minutes' (see Abram, this volume). These papers are things participants are meant to have read before attending the meeting, artefacts that those leading the meeting are meant to refer to throughout the course of the meeting, and at the same time one of the most obvious outcomes of that meeting. In varying ways, all contributors ask themselves what the terms of this relationship might be. Is it perhaps more accurate to view meetings as artefacts or instantiations of documentation? How does the apparently inevitable interdependency between meetings and documents materialize between and across examples? Where do ethnographic subjects themselves place the emphasis? These questions are central to any exploration of the meeting form, to any emergent sense we might have of the artefactual status of meetings.

In both Lamp's and Alexander's essays, the issue of audience and the performative quality of meetings also comes to the fore. In formal WTO chamber meetings interaction is open to the gaze of a non-participatory audience, by contrast to closed informal meetings between member nations. Participants of these meetings are technicians of the difference; indeed, as Lamp invites us to think, the constitution of formal and informal WTO meetings is almost like moieties in a dual organization. They require each other to reproduce. In Alexander's narrative, international consultants are taken through a labyrinthine series of informal audiences with government ministers; these are also audiences for junior civil servants in the Turkish ministry, who are made to feel like these meetings are a test of their competency, set and assessed by those senior colleagues in attendance. Of course, the notion of audience also operates in the assembly meeting of Occupy examined by Corsín Jiménez and Estalella, but this time through the utopian idea that the public performance of consensus-building might capture the attention of the street. It is equally present in the example of the asylum case conference in Keenan and Pottage's essay. Barrister and solicitor may lead a dance around the coaching out of inconsistency in the client's story; however, all participants clearly view the meeting as a rehearsal for the next meeting, an anticipated audience with a judge.

Ethnographies of meeting also demonstrate how the mundane location of meeting matters. Mostly we tend to think of the 'modern' meeting as a form vitally attached to office space and to encounters around a table. Perhaps anthropologists and others too often take at face value the implicit basis of institutional knowledge in universal and placeless abstractions (Yarrow, this volume); the idea of meetings as 'non-spaces' may collude in this aesthetic, in ways that erase locality. But an interest in how what is known relates to where it is known and how place participates in the knowledge that is produced recurs across contributions. The examples provided by Corsín Jiménez and Estalella and by Nielsen aptly illustrate this. Meetings may take place outside, in public squares. Indeed, taking the meeting form out into the open and making it visible may be taken to reconfigure its capacities. This can also occur in less overtly politicized ways. Yarrow, for instance, demonstrates the significance of the shift for Historic Scotland staff between project meetings held in offices and those 'site meetings' which take place at the location of the historic building under restoration assessment.

The final essay of the special issue looks at one particular response to the perceived limits of bureaucratic gathering. Indeed, Riles tells us that the multidisciplinary and transnational collectivity of academics, practitioners, and policy-makers known as Meridian 180 emerged out of a historical failure of international bureaucracy and of its ambitions for the 'global meeting'. 'Gone is the faith in progress through deliberation in the global public square' (p. 182), a crisis that she identifies as entangled with a more general loss of faith in technocratic expertise and in the whole project of assembling the diverse political perspectives of nation-states in a singular global form. Meridian 180 aims to revive dialogue between experts but on a basis that bypasses the previous context for their dialogue, for instance as agents of the nation-state. It also aims to bypass what Riles identifies as some of the dominant fictions of the global meeting, such as the pressure to reach a recognized point of 'consensus' or the drive for subjects to address themselves to 'outputs' such as concluding texts. These were meetings, then, that actively resisted moves to instrumentalize dialogue and the relationality that was taken to both produce and emerge from it.

However, one of the unexpected outcomes of this experiment was precisely a renewed interest in the conventionalized forms of 'output' that drove international bureaucratic meeting. Riles recounts a gradual, sometimes reluctant but growing appreciation of the generative capacity of the 'one-pager', such as the press release or policy review document. So much so that for her Meridian 180 began also to become an experiment in *doing* output. In a perhaps less knowing way we see this shift repeated across ethnographic examples (it is worth highlighting that for Riles Meridian 180 is not principally an object of description, but a project of participatory enactment). Most obviously this occurs in the Spanish Occupy movement described by Corsín Jiménez and Estalella; for here a protest grounded in a total rejection of conventional order seizes on the bureaucratic procedure of consensus-building as an exemplification of renewal. Indeed, it is the intensification and elongation of that output, its continuing objectification across the assembly meeting, that demonstrates the difference that matters. While it would be quite wrong to imagine that these bold redeployments drive participants' relationship to outputs in more ordinary bureaucratic settings (such as project meetings at Historic Scotland, council meetings in a Norwegian local authority, or team meetings in the Kenyan health sector), the lesson remains. The mundane mechanisms of meetings can contain their own, sometimes unexpected, dynamic principles of action.

AOB: rethinking bureaucratic and institutional knowledge

It is conventional in many agenda-based forms of meeting to conclude with a call to Any Other Business, or AOB. Built into the structure of a thoroughly planned or structured event (at least on paper), the category ends a meeting by quite deliberately opening a space for unplanned and unexpected talk between participants. In these discussions, it is not uncommon for the chair to relinquish a degree of control over the direction of conversation, to let talk go. However, AOB is also part of the very technology of time management. It is the place where issues raised during the course of a meeting can be reassigned, if, for instance, a listed agenda items risks running on too long or unanticipated discussion points emerge that need to be curtailed to allow the completion of scheduled business to proceed (in reality, there is often no time to cover the issues pushed to AOB). Nevertheless, the potential acknowledgement of what is not predictable or what is indeterminate remains in condensed form. While we hope that this introductory essay lays out an argument for a convincing programme of scholarly work, and presents a provocative basis for reading emergent themes across the essays, it is also hoped that readers feel the constraint of the ordering of points imposed. In every essay, we believe, there is an opening or invitation to address unexpected business.

Our account, above, has in part been an attempt to exemplify how meetings express and resolve forms of complexity. Each essay in the volume speaks for itself, not simply as exemplifications of a singular stable form, but as a collective sense of the social complexity of its reproduction in these terms. That people in different parts of the world or within the same locale, occupying radically different organizational forms, animated by hugely different interests and understandings, can recognize their activities as instances of a form that others share is itself a product of the work required to make these forms appear the same. From this perspective the collection contributes insights about the paradoxically specific work required to make a form appear similar across scales, contexts, and places.

Journal of the Royal Anthropological Institute (N.S.), 10-26
© Royal Anthropological Institute 2017

Still, one might wonder what this all adds up to. Centrally our proposition is this: notwithstanding the many significant insights that anthropologists and others have brought to bear on questions of the nature of bureaucratic conduct and institutional knowledge, a methodological focus on texts has often been accompanied by discursive forms of analytic deconstruction that have tended to narrow horizons of ethnographic inquiry. Departing from this approach, recent ethnographies of documents have helped to open up a space for less textually reductive approaches that have resulted in a more complex picture, for example giving greater weight to the situated practices, social relations, and ethical complexities that are integral to the work of organizations. Still, this focus continues to reinscribe the importance of documents as the framing context from which other actions and ideas emerge and does not displace their central role as paradigmatic exemplars of modern knowledge.

A focus on meeting is not incompatible with acknowledgement of the vital role that documents play, not least as constitutive elements of the forms and procedures through which meetings emerge. It should be evident from our account that many of the insights developed in this volume build – in some cases very directly – on this work. Collectively, however, ethnographies centred on everyday processes and artefacts of meeting allow us to re-centre the analytical and methodological terms of inquiry (see Riles, this volume, for a direct reflection on how her own previous work on documents might be redirected by thinking through meetings). Just as documents produce meetings, so meetings produce documents, but the logic of production looks different depending on which of these artefacts one takes as the start of inquiry. To re-situate this dynamic through ethnographies of meeting, we argue, is both to highlight a set of practices that have received limited attention in existing literatures, and to rethink what it is that documents do and signify in these contexts. Meetings do not simply exemplify a set of understandings contained within documents (a point perhaps emphasized by the wayward status of AOB as both a category of documentary and meeting action); rather, they entail complexities that are not reducible to the textual accounts that organizations themselves produce.

Many of the central themes of the volume are also central to existing accounts of bureaucracy, but the focus of meeting leads to novel insights about the generative dynamics through which these are figured. Indeed, although meetings exist in the background of many descriptions of bureaucratic life, they tend to serve the purpose of illustrating what are perceived as broader organizational processes. The legacy of Weber is important here: meetings may be obvious exemplifications of rational-legal routinization, but they do not dominate his account of the stabilization of charisma into modern authority structures. To a certain extent, the absence continues in the more recent rise of anthropological accounts of bureaucracy (e.g. Bear & Mathur 2015; Feldman 2008; Gupta 2012; Hull 2012; Naravo-Yashin 2012), many of which are positioned as in some way responding to the Weberian legacy. However, we also identify interesting developments in that literature: in particular, when the Weberian argument is explored through an ethnographic focus on non-governmental, perhaps unexpected, forms of bureaucratization. The recent interest in describing Pentecostal organizations, especially in African contexts, has thrown up intriguing instances, for example, of meetings as comfortably bureaucratic-charismatic conjunctions, where respect for the recognized form and capacities of 'modern' meetings appears to go hand in hand with the need to ensure the active presence of divine inspiration. As Kirsch (2011) illustrates in his ethnography of the Spirit Apostolic Church in Zambia, this may involve elders and prophets undergoing fasting and contemplative isolation before a church meeting to ensure their contribution is charged with the authority of the Holy Spirit. Interestingly, for our purposes, one sign of that presence is precisely the unexpected or indeterminate element that gets registered during the course of participants' scheduled bureaucratic meeting, and which in their minds is in some ways anticipated by the blank spaces left on the agenda form (Kirsch 2011: 216). Here, instead of being pushed to the end of a meeting through a device such as AOB, surplus talk or the unscheduled event becomes the very source of the meeting's legitimation and power; it is what ultimately gives it agency or capacity.

Of the various insights that flow from our methodological-cum-theoretical move to re-situate understandings of bureaucracy, we also wish to highlight the indeterminate nature of many of the meetings described within the volume. Meetings may tend towards organization but are not *per se* organized, just as the move to resolution does not mean they are *de facto* resolved. Organizations produce systemic forms of knowledge, but the basis on which they do this is not as systematic as their own textual accounts – products of those ordering processes – might lead us to believe. Meetings are often attempts to tame, narrow, and contain uncertainty, including through efforts to align present and future circumstances (see Koselleck 2004). Insofar as these procedures are ways of regulating action, they do not conform to a concept of 'practice' in the sense in which this term is routinely deployed in academic discourse, to describe situated, specific, scattered, or non-systemic conduct as distinct from formal institutional structure. Meetings are spaces where practices are formalized and forms are practised, through performances that participate in, even as they reconfigure and extend, organizational imaginations. Still, as the essays in this volume highlight, procedures of partly indeterminate form are spaces of negotiation and transformation of various kinds.

ACKNOWLEDGEMENTS

We wish to thank the *JRAI* special issue committee, and especially Elizabeth Hallam, James Staples, and Jessica Turner, for their role in facilitating feedback and the stages towards proofing. In this introduction and across the essays of the volume as a whole, we are heavily indebted to Justin Dyer for his careful and insightful copy-editing, and to Nidhi Nagpal for her work on the cover pages and general production. We are also extremely grateful for the constructive comments and criticisms offered by the anonymous reviewers of this Introduction, and the author of the single whole manuscript review. Helen Schwartzman also offered a late and extremely helpful set of comments; hopefully she can see how valuable they have been. Finally, we should like to thank all of our volume contributors for their timely and patient response to our promptings and for the general enthusiasm with which they approached each stage of the process. This includes a thanks to those who gave papers at the original ASA Decennial Conference panel in Edinburgh and whose work for various reasons doesn't appear in the final volume.

REFERENCES

ABRAM, S. 2011. *Culture and planning*. Aldershot, Hants: Ashgate.
ASMUß, B. & J. SVENNEVIG 2009. Meeting talk: an introduction. *Journal of Business Communication* **46**, 3-22.
ATKINSON, M.A., E.C. CUFF & J.R.E. LEE 1978. The recommencement of a meeting as a member's accomplishment. In *Studies in the organization of conversational interaction* (ed.) J. Schenkein, 133-53. New York: Academic Press.

BAILEY, F.G. 2011 [1965]. Decisions by consensus in councils and committees: with special reference to village and local government in India. In *Political systems and the distribution of power* (ed.) M. Banton, 1-20. London: Routledge.

BEAR, L. 2014. Doubt, conflict, mediation: the anthropology of modern time. *Journal of the Royal Anthropological Institute* (N.S.) (Special Issue), 3-30.

——— & N. MATHUR (eds) 2015. Remaking the public good: anthropology of bureaucracy. *Cambridge Anthropology* (Special Issue) **33**: 1.

BLOCH, M. 1971. Decision-making in councils among the Merina of Madagascar. In *Councils in action* (eds) A. Kuper & A. Richard, 29-61. Cambridge: University Press.

BODEN, D. 1994. *The business of talk: organizations in action.* Cambridge: Polity.

BRENNEIS, D. & F. MYERS (eds) 1984. *Dangerous words: language and politics in the Pacific.* New York: University Press.

BROWN, H. 2013. 'Home-based care is not a new thing': legacies of domestic governmentality in Western Kenya. In *Making public health in Africa: ethnographic and historical perspectives* (eds) R.J. Prince & R. Marsland, 140-61. Athens: Ohio University Press.

——— 2016. Managerial relations in Kenyan health care: empathy and the limits of governmentality. *Journal of the Royal Anthropological Institute* (N.S.) **22**, 591-609.

BRUUN-JENSEN, C. & B.-R. WINTHEREIK 2013. *Monitoring movements in development aid: recursive partnerships and infrastructures.* Cambridge, Mass.: MIT Press.

CALLON, M. 1986. Some elements of a sociology of translation: domestication of the scallops and the fishermen of St Brieuc Bay. In *Power, action and belief: a new sociology of knowledge?* (ed.) J. Law, 196-233. London: Routledge & Kegan Paul.

CANDEA, M., J. COOK, C. TRUNDLE & T. YARROW 2015. Introduction: reconsidering detachment. In *Detachment: essays on the limits of relational thinking* (eds) M. Candea, J. Cook, C. Trundle & T. Yarrow, 1-31. Manchester: University Press.

DU GAY, P. 2007. *Organizing identity: persons and organizations 'after theory'.* Los Angeles: Sage.

DUPUY, J.-P. 2000. The Macy Conferences. In *On the origins of cognitive science: the mechanization of the mind* (trans. M.B. DeBevoise), 71-6. Princeton: University Press.

DURANTI, A. 1981. *The Samoan fono: a sociolinguistic study* (Pacific Linguistic Series B, Volume 80). Canberra: Australian National University.

ENGLUND, H. 2006. *Prisoners of freedom: human rights and the African poor.* Berkeley: University of California Press.

FAUBION, J. 2011. *An anthropology of ethics.* Cambridge: University Press.

FELDMAN, I. 2008. *Governing Gaza: bureaucracy, authority and the work of rule 1917-1967.* Durham, N.C.: Duke University Press.

GELLNER, D.N. & E. HIRSCH 2001. *Inside organizations: anthropologists at work.* Oxford: Berg.

GLUCKMAN, M. 1940. Analysis of a social situation in Modern Zululand. *Bantu Studies* **14**, 1-30.

GOFFMAN, E. 1961. *Encounters.* Indianapolis: Bobbs-Merrill.

GRAEBER, D. 2009. *Direct action: an ethnography.* Oakland, CA: AK Press.

GUPTA, A. 2012. *Red tape: bureaucracy, structural violence and poverty in India.* Durham, N.C.: Duke University Press.

HARPER, R. 1998. *Inside the IMF: an ethnography of documents, technology and organizational action.* London: Academic Press.

——— 2000. The social organization of the IMF's mission work: an examination of international auditing. In *Audit cultures: anthropological studies in accountability, ethics and the academy* (ed.) M. Strathern, 52-81. London: Routledge.

HAUGERUD, A. 1993. *The culture of politics in modern Kenya.* Cambridge: University Press.

HEIMS, S.J. 1993. *Constructing a social science for postwar America: the Cybernetics Group, 1946-1953.* Cambridge, Mass.: MIT Press.

HOLBRAAD, M. 2012. *Truth in motion: the recursive anthropology of Cuban divination.* Chicago: University Press.

HULL, M. 2010. Democratic technologies of speech: from WWII America to postcolonial Delhi. *Journal of Linguistic Anthropology* **20**, 257-82.

——— 2012. *Government of paper: the materiality of bureaucracy in urban Pakistan.* Berkeley: University of California Press.

JACKSON, M. 1987. *Anthropology at home.* London: Tavistock.

KIRSCH, T.G. 2011. *Spirits and letters: reading, writing and charisma in African Christianity.* Oxford: Berghahn Books.

KOSELLECK, R. 2004. *Futures past: on the semantics of historical time* (trans. K. Tribe). New York: Columbia University Press.

LAIDLAW, J. 2013. *The subject of virtue: an anthropology of ethics and freedom.* Cambridge: University Press.

LATOUR, B. 2005. *Reassembling the social: an introduction to Actor-Network Theory.* Oxford: University Press.

LAW, J. 1994. *Organizing modernity.* Oxford: Blackwell.

LEA, T.S. 2002. Between the pen and the paperwork: a native ethnography of learning to govern indigenous health in the Northern Territory. Ph.D. thesis, University of Sydney.

LI, T.M. 2007. *The will to improve: governmentality, development and the practice of politics.* Durham, N.C.: Duke University Press.

LUCAS, G. 2015. Archaeology and contemporaneity. *Archaeological Dialogues* **22**, 1-15.

MILLS, D. 2014. A 'joint meeting of the British Empire and the University of Chicago'? Scholarly meetings and the bounding of academic knowledge. Paper presented at the Meeting of the Association of Social Anthropology, Edinburgh, 21 June.

MIYAZAKI, H. 2004. *The method of hope: anthropology, philosophy and Fijian knowledge.* Stanford: University Presss.

MOL, A. 2002. *The body multiple: ontology in medical practice.* Durham, N.C.: Duke University Press.

MOORE, S.F. 1977. Political meetings and the simulation of unanimity: Kilimanjaro 1973. In *Secular ritual* (eds) S.F. Moore & B. Myerhoff, 151-72. Assen: Van Gorcum.

MORTON, G.D. 2014. Modern meetings: participation, democracy, and language ideology in Brazil's MST landless movement. *American Ethnologist* **41**, 728-42.

MOSSE, D. 2005. *Cultivating development: an ethnography of aid policy and practice.* London: Pluto.

MYHRE, K.C. (ed.) 2016. *Cutting and connecting: 'Afrinesian' perspectives on networks, relationality and exchange.* Oxford: Berghahn Books.

NAVARO-YASHIN, Y. 2012. *The make-believe space: affective geography in a postwar polity.* Durham, N.C.: Duke University Press.

RABINOW, P. & A. STAVRIANAKIS 2014. *Designs on the contemporary: anthropological tests.* Chicago: University Press.

REED, A. 2006. Documents unfolding. In *Documents: artifacts of modern knowledge* (ed.) A. Riles, 158-77. Ann Arbor: University of Michigan Press.

RICHARDS, A. 1971. Introduction: the nature of the problem. In *Councils in action* (eds) A. Richards & A. Kuper, 1-12. Cambridge: University Press.

RILES, A. 2000. *The network inside out.* Ann Arbor: University of Michigan Press.

――― (ed.) 2006. *Documents: artifacts of modern knowledge.* Ann Arbor: University of Michigan Press.

――― & A. KUPER (eds) 1971. *Councils in action.* Cambridge: University Press.

ROBBINS, J. 2007. Between reproduction and freedom: morality, value, and radical cultural change. *Ethnos* **72**, 293-314.

ROTTENBURG, R. 2009. *Far-fetched facts: a parable of development aid.* Cambridge, Mass.: MIT Press.

SANDLER, J. & R. THEDVALL (eds) 2016. *Meeting ethnography: meetings as key technologies of contemporary governance, development and resistance.* New York: Routledge.

SCHWARTZMAN, H.B. 1987. The significance of meetings in an American mental health center. *American Ethnologist* **14**, 271-94.

――― 1989. *The meeting: gatherings in organizations and communities.* New York: Springer.

SHORE, C. & S. WRIGHT (eds) 1997. *Anthropology of policy: critical perspectives on governance and power.* London: Routledge.

SILVERMAN, S. 2002. *The beast on the table: conferencing with anthropologists.* Lanham, Md: AltaMira Press.

STRATHERN, M. 1987. The limits of auto-anthropology. In *Anthropology at home* (ed.) A. Jackson, 16-37. London: Tavistock.

――― 1996. Cutting the network. *Journal of the Royal Anthropological Institute* (N.S.) **2**, 517-35.

――― (ed.) 2000. *Audit cultures: anthropological studies of accountability, ethics and the academy.* London: Routledge.

SWIDLER, A. & S.C. WATKINS 2009. 'Teach a man to fish': the sustainability doctrine and its social consequences. *World Development* **37**, 1182-96.

TSING, A.L. 2005. *Friction: an ethnography of global connection.* Princeton: University Press.

VAN VREE, W. 1999. *Meetings, manners, and civilization: the development of modern meeting behaviour.* London: Leicester University Press.

VIVEIROS DE CASTRO, E. 2004. Perspectival anthropology and the method of controlled equivocation. *Tipiti* **2**, 3-22.

Volkan, V.D. 1991. Psychological processes in unofficial diplomacy meetings. In *The psychodynamics of international relationships*, vol. II: *Unofficial diplomacy at work* (eds) V.D. Volkan, J.V. Montville & D.A. Julius, 207-22. Lexington, Mass.: Lexington Books.

Wright, S. (ed.) 1994. *Anthropology of organizations*. London: Routledge.

Yarrow, T. 2011. *Development beyond politics: aid, activism and NGOs in Ghana*. Basingstoke: Palgrave Macmillan.

Introduction : vers une ethnographie de la réunion

Résumé

Le présent essai introductif décrit une nouvelle approche des réunions, en relation avec diverses littératures anthropologiques et autres. Malgré les nombreux récits dans lesquels apparaissent des réunions, les formes concrètes que prennent celles-ci n'ont pas reçu beaucoup d'attention. En cherchant à concentrer clairement l'examen ethnographique sur ces processus quotidiens et omniprésents, les auteurs esquissent une approche qui élargit le champ de l'attention au-delà d'une vision étroite englobant simplement leur signification et leur teneur. Ils mettent en lumière quelques pistes innovantes qui naissent de cette approche en décrivant comment la négociation de relations « dans » les réunions s'apparente à l'organisation des contextes « externes », notamment par rapport au temps, à l'espace, à la structure d'organisation et à la société. Notre essai avance une série d'incitations à repenser les approches de la bureaucratie, du processus organisationnel et de l'éthique à travers le prisme ethnographique de la réunion.

1

Contradiction in contemporary political life: meeting bureaucracy in Norwegian municipal government

SIMONE ABRAM *Durham University*

Meetings are the apotheosis of contemporary bureaucratic life, containing dilemmas and contradictions that are at the heart of modernity. In particular, political and bureaucratic meetings (both state and civic) are ritual performances in which rules are enacted, ritual correctness is met with manipulative political game-playing, and formal transparency is intertwined with relational and informational secrecy. Meetings in bureaucratic government rely on a series of legitimating motifs, including the invoking of 'conjured contexts' to link bureaucratic practices to external action. This essay shows how meetings order political and bureaucratic life, and vice versa, and explores the materiality and embodiment of meeting practices, illustrating how a dominant global model of bureaucratic meeting is elaborated locally.

Helen Schwartzman's 1989 landmark volume brought a new focus to the practices of meetings in bureaucratic organizations. Her detailed ethnographic attention to the everyday production of meetings helped to illustrate how far the practice of meeting defines the organization, cementing the relationships between actors, and reproducing the effect of organization on a routine basis. Schwartzman comments that her focus on the meeting itself derived from her realization that the meetings she attended were not merely a means to understand the organization she was interested in; rather, 'meetings were the major form that provided participants in this setting with a sense of organization as well as a sense of themselves *in* the organization' (1989: 109, italics in original). Given this, her focus was on the way that meetings are framed, how they then frame the relationships between members of the organization and its clients, and the imaginary that is upheld of the enduring organization. Schwartzman offers a particular analytical perspective on the role of meetings in the self-reflection of its practitioners, with the focus primarily on the reproduction of the institution itself. In this essay, I draw attention to the role of the meeting, which also relates to the time spent on meeting protocols. Schwartzman sees these protocols as a guide to social relations of institutions, as they lay out the expectations of the institution, its members and its interlocutors, yet they are hardly straightforward, being a mélange of written, tacit, and improvised procedures. Based on ethnographic research on local government councils in the United Kingdom and Norway, I argue that the time spent in meetings discussing where and when to meet, which rules to follow, and how to behave in those meetings is seen by participants as wasteful not merely because attention to reproduction of the institution is experienced as less important than addressing matters of concern or decisions to be made in the meeting itself, but for reasons that provide the motivation and justification of the organizations' existence.

Participants in democratic local government councils, including elected representatives and public servants, as well as members of the public, citizens, observers, and so on, tend not to participate in debates for their own sake. A local politician in Sheffield who told me that local councillors were powerless, and he attended council because he 'liked a good debate', was doing so for shock value, precisely because this is the opposite of the usual reason put forward for participating in local government bureaucracy. Most of my ethnographic research in local government has related to planning issues, including planning for housing, forward planning, and community planning. In these contexts, council meetings are all about places that lie beyond the council chamber. For meetings to be successful, they must therefore conjure up external contexts as the object of their purpose. These '*conjured contexts*' are one way – and a particularly important way – that political and bureaucratic legitimacy can be upheld, but require all the technologies of modern government to sustain them. While the principles of what we might call 'government at a distance' (Law 1986) tend to be considered in relation to colonial powers, in fact all government is conducted at a distance. The distance between the council chamber and the local school already requires a set of governmental technologies that relate what happens in one to what happens in the other. In the council chamber, the school must be conjured up, imagined, and determined as an object on which action can be exerted, if the effect of 'government' is to be recognized as meaningful at all.

Meetings in government bureaucracy thus operate with a range of external correlates that must be correctly invoked for meetings to be effectual. While doing this, though, the participants also cover their tracks: that is, they underemphasize the fragilities in the links between speech and action, categorizing organizational work as (necessary) waste, and diverting attention away from the institution-building and ritual aspects of meeting practice. Instead, the focus is on the action that is supposed to result from the speech performed in the meeting. Brunsson (1989) has questioned these links, highlighting the disjunction between speech and action, which can make organizations appear to be hypocritical. In government committees, however, this link is essential, since it justifies the performance of the speech itself. Speech in a planning committee, for example, is largely focused on the plans linked to sites, even if these sites may be identified through principles of identification, only later to be tied to specific geographical locations. Speech in these contexts is clearly doing much more than defining, postulating, and passing judgements on external sites. This is to suggest not that participants deliberately or consciously mislead themselves or others about the purpose of meetings, but that the effectiveness of meetings seems to rely on this facility of distracting attention from their own bureaucratic workings towards the effects they might achieve in some other location. Another key element of committee speech is devoted to performing the authority of government, which is achieved by situated performances of ritualized speech. It is not only the speech itself that takes a ritual form, but the context in which the speech is delivered that is essential to its effectiveness.

In the particular context of municipal planning meetings, this plays out in relation to the indexical functions of planning documents, policies, and other references to some

Journal of the Royal Anthropological Institute (N.S.), 27-44
© Royal Anthropological Institute 2017

external place upon which regulation or government action should be exerted. Planning theorists have been very concerned with the ability of planners to enact the aims of planning, applying regulatory policies and exercising some form of rationality over the future, engaged in the symbolic construction of power as 'a means of defense against uncertainty and the self-destructive violence that always runs in a community's veins' (Mazza 1996: 9). Many planning theorists hence focus on the activities of planners, rather than tracing how the plan itself operates in practice (see Mandelbaum, Mazza & Burchell 1996). In our work on the anthropology of planning, Weszkalnys and I outline instead how a plan gains its authority from its invocation in appropriate contexts, that is, in certain kinds of meetings (Abram & Weszkalnys 2013). Looking back to the philosophy of Austin (1962) and Searle (1969), we argue that in order to achieve its status, a plan must be presented to the council as a formal document, and its acceptance must be noted with the appropriate, documented words, from the correct official persons (see also Riles 2006). Without the correct procedures, or where procedures are conducted without the trust and integrity that a true promise requires, plans might radically undermine the prospect of an orderly future. Indeed, as Baxstrom (2012) shows, infelicitous plans may lead those living on the ground that is 'planned-for' to feel that even the present is radically unpredictable, leading to a collapse in the horizon of the future (Guyer 2007). Infelicities may include a failure to conform to the rules of assembly, including the absence of key actors; failure to note decisions; failure to consult the requisite documents, regulations, or persons; or any other failure of due process related to the issue in question. All of the procedures often insulted as 'just ritual', or 'tedious bureaucracy', are those which remind the actors that they are not divinely empowered to govern others, but derive their power from a democratic process with checks and balances that allow for public accountability. Tedious as these procedures may be, they remain the only effective assurance of democratic practice that is widespread and relatively reliable. The fact that misuse is so frequently uncovered can be interpreted as an indication that these processes are quite a good means to maintain democratic structures.

In this essay, I consider these two key aspects of meeting practice in local government through the relation between meetings and their documentation, and the importance of felicitous performance of speech to the legitimacy of meetings and their broader context of government.

Which meetings?

If anthropological accounts have tended to focus on the subjects of plans rather than their authors and have prioritized the politics of government meetings, in this essay I attend to the bureaucrats and municipal administrators who bear much of the responsibility for producing the material in and of plans, in order to highlight some of the temporalities and imagined sites conjured in meetings (see also Abram 2014). Amongst bureaucratic meetings, planning meetings are perhaps the archetype of modernist practice. Municipal planning meetings, state and civic, are ritual performances in which explicit rules are enacted through tacit knowledge, where ritual correctness is met with manipulative game-playing, and formal transparency is intertwined with relational and informational withholding (see Garsten & Lindh de Montoya 2008). The formal meetings of a full municipal council are usually the arena for the confirmation of conclusions of longer series of work by sub-committees, or other working groups. They are, in other words, the occasion for the most explicitly ritualized political performance, the public communication of decisions prepared before and finalized at the council vote. They are the moment when the public may see that issues of concern have been discussed, but they are not the moment when such issues are actually considered. Instead, they can be understood both as the culmination of a long series of prior activities, as well as being a moment in the cyclical temporality of municipal life. Attention to prior activities thus informs the interpretations that are possible of a full, formal council meeting.

As an ethnographic example, I consider here one such prior activity, a two-day working seminar for senior administrators at a Norwegian municipality held in 2000 at a conference hotel near Hønefoss in southern Norway.[1] Norwegian conference hotels tend to be large, well-appointed hotels, with modern, well-equipped meeting rooms of different sizes, bedrooms that elsewhere would be considered most luxurious, and very high-quality dining. The invitation to participate in a 'seminar' at such a hotel was made attractive by the extremely comfortable accommodation, offered implicitly as compensation for giving up free or family time. Participants were invited by the Chief Executive to attend the meeting to work towards a revision of the holistic municipal plan that was due for publication in the following year. On 27 April 2000, the Chief Executive welcomed leading administrative staff to the seminar (this being both a kind of meeting and a collection of meetings in itself) to work up the new four-year plan that would later be presented as a proposal to the council. There had been some gossiping in advance among administrators about who had and had not been invited, with some key council staff pointedly not included. The municipality was concurrently going through a reorganization of its administration, a process that was proving divisive and stressful for many employees, with key figures in the administration being pushed out, and other emerging characters being promoted to senior positions. The tensions produced in working relations provide some of the background to this working party event, and the invitation in itself, as well as whether or not it extended to both days, including the overnight stay, or applied just to one of the days, was taken as some indication of the Chief Executive's evaluation of the importance of various members of staff.

With section leaders and other staff assembled around tables in a low-ceilinged conference room, the Chief Executive welcomed them with a kind of a pep talk emphasizing the importance of this phase of the four-year planning cycle. He outlined how the plan should be based on a vision and priorities, and identified the most important task for the working seminar as defining a direction and identifying concrete goals. 'It's easy to fill a plan with words', he said, 'but difficult to assess which are really important'. There had been several working groups already developing aspects of the plan in the preceding weeks and months, but now it was worth spending two days all together and travelling home with the priorities in place. The Chief Executive invited the Chief Planner to speak, and he outlined the planning process, adopting a much more technocratic tone, listing the legal requirements for a plan and how the current plan would differ from previous ones, and showing PowerPoint slides of the policies agreed so far and charts and diagrams to indicate the issues that should be addressed (demographic, economic, environmental). There was a vision for the district (thus conjured up as a presence in the discussion), that it should be a good place in which to live, but there were other themes that should be brought out. These had been discussed at a leader-group meeting on 6 April (and hence we can see a tie into another meeting that set the agenda for this one).

Journal of the Royal Anthropological Institute (N.S.), 27-44
© Royal Anthropological Institute 2017

The floor was then taken by the Director of the Technical Department, who discussed transport issues and the dangers of identifying specific interventions rather than broad aims, since the former sound more like lobbying for particular roads rather than vision-setting. His speech both tied the words of the vision to the prospective action in the world (through the potential of the vision to curtail future possibilities) and emphasized the need to comply with correct meeting procedure (in sticking to the agenda outlined in the vision document). Thus in the subsequent discussion, various leading administrators discussed what shape the plan should take and its role as a communicative document to be read by the inhabitants, invoking the future role of the document and the relation with the physical world of the council's constitutive district. Where previous plans were dry lists of policies, they wished the new plan to be a communicative handbook to guide the council in partnership with residents. Hence an imaginary figure of 'residents' (or a 'public') outside the meeting room was generated through the meeting talk. A senior officer proposed a tripartite categorization of the residents of the municipality organized by age (young, working, retired) according to a 'wheel of life'. Almost everyone agreed that this was a crude categorization that failed to acknowledge either cross-cutting needs (disability, unemployment, medical needs), specialist and general services (play and sports facilities, welfare services, social security, health services), or ethnic and/or national differences among the local population. Yet identifying each of these would create an unmanageable set of falsely discrete divisions, whereas the wheel was simple and all encompassing. The lack of surprise about the wheel proposal among senior staff indicated that it had already been discussed at a higher level (i.e. in other meetings, perhaps also informally), and it found its way through the discussions, despite widespread derision of the idea, as one means to bridge the discussions, documents, the organization of municipal services, and the municipality's population.

Throughout the discussions, various papers were circulated that had emerged from previous meetings and processes, including reference papers from leader-group meetings, previous plans, and maps. In contrast to political meetings, where administrators largely remain silent (see Abram 2004), the participants raised issues fairly freely, and as soon as they were devolved into smaller discussion groups, they engaged in lively conversation, throwing ideas back and forth and not hesitating to criticize municipal policy or party political ideas. From the start, in the joint discussions, the Chief Planner tried to steer the discussion, repeatedly, if gently, reminding the participants of the importance of identifying goals towards an agreed vision, and identifying strategies to achieve those goals.

Discussion soon turned to another preceding set of meetings known as the VOMP (Vision and Goal-Setting) planning process, which had included only the members of the council's cabinet and the administrative directors of the council. This series of meetings had been led by a consultant who had little understanding of the workings of the public sector and therefore made category errors in relation to the role of elected representatives, ignoring their role as representatives of diverse interest groups rather than autonomous individuals. He failed to abide by the ritualized aspects of public bureaucracy, precisely the elements of public practice that appear frustrating to business representatives, for whom chains of authority are often more direct. Recognizing that the consultant did not understand their procedures, the participants gradually abandoned the process, indicating their lack of confidence in it by withdrawing from meetings, or by going through the motions of the meetings but taking no decisions to avoid conducting politics outside the public arena (see Abram 2002). The outcome was a vision that was, to say the least, bland: that the municipality should be a good place in which to live. And now the administrators took up the criticism, saying that it could apply to any council, and such a safe slogan conjured up no emotion to motivate action. Quickly, Chief Planner Morten reminded the group that the council already had a vision, 'the municipality of opportunity', a vision that the municipality had used enormous resources to develop. The Chief Executive was surprisingly critical, in contrast to his public circumspection in criticizing the political arena, explaining that the council's existing vision was best, but that the politicians were a little sceptical since this was the adminstrators' vision and they wanted to have their own vision incorporated in the plan. If the cabinet was to throw out the new version, what should one do?

The Head of the Welfare Sector, Elia, stated that the council could not have one vision for the administration and another for the politicians, and Tone (Social Work) claimed the politicians dared not have a joint vision that muddied their individual party positions. The Chief Executive remarked that they shouldn't be afraid of dealing with political issues, and the Director of the Technical Department, Lars, pointed out that 50 per cent of what they did was political, since they were dealing with social politics all the time. The problem was to avoid the administrators being seen to engage in party politics. Their job was to bring people into focus, and take the residents seriously, as detailed in their existing visionary statement. A vision is a desired future, and this should not keep changing – the existing idea of a municipality of opportunity could be applied to many different things.

Through this set of arguments and the logic on which it relied, the administrators convinced themselves of the legitimacy of setting the vision and goals in the plan and then offering them to the politicians. Very quickly, it was clear that the administrators intended to salvage the vision they had carved out already, and write it back into the plan, over-writing or over-riding the weak visions that had been the outcome of the unconvincing joint administrative-political process. They would do this in a circumspect fashion, however, being careful to include some of the goals and themes in the VOMP papers, so that the politicians would recognize their own contributions to VOMP in the revised plan. One reason the politicians' vision was weak was because it was prepared as a consensus vision, not a political prospectus, so the administrators knew that many of the politicians were already sceptical about its value as a guiding text. Instead, the administrators wanted to see the plan's overall vision headed with the slogan already in use, 'the municipality of opportunity', and then discussion could revolve around how to define values such as quality of life, life-challenges, self-determination, and so on. Smaller groups each worked on separate themes towards a vision that was founded on the three fundamental qualities that were in the existing vision: fulfilment, security/care, and lifelong learning; or choice, independence, sustainable development, and good common solutions; or responsibility, community, and fulfilment. Much of the rest of the two-day workshop revolved around detailed discussions about how to define key terms and identify specific policies that could be used to achieve the aims identified. Arguments over the qualities of particular words gave way to outlines of strategic ambitions and formulations of idealistic ambitions.

In the frank exchanges such as those highlighted above, the different actors were both negotiating their own position (wishing to appear forthright and effective to the Chief Executive), establishing the role of the administrator through defining the boundaries of political action versus partisan action, and asserting their authority to produce texts that speak on behalf of the corporate entity that is the municipality through the person of the Chief Executive. As such, much of the meeting was indirectly devoted to the production of the institution, as Schwartzman has outlined, but also of the imagined internal and external world of the municipality beyond it. That is, a great deal of the discussion concerned the legitimacy of the administrators in developing, or rather derailing, the 'vision' that had emerged from VOMP. Such meetings can thus be shown to be powerful in their potential not only to reproduce the institution, but also to change it, possibly radically.

At this particular meeting, the administrators were also exercising an unusual freedom of expression that is normally quite absent in everyday administrative life. The two days appear as a moment of almost carnival-like reversal from the normal routine circumspection and formal technicism that characterize the administration's self-presentation. This sense was highlighted by the overnight stay at the hotel, where administrators met in the indoor-outdoor pool and the sauna, and gathered together for pre-dinner drinks in the bedrooms. At the end of the second day, the Chief Executive thanked all the participants for their hard work, and asserted that they had achieved together in two days what would have taken six months of separate working groups back at base. The Chief Planner and Chief Executive's thanks were met by general applause before the participants started to pack their things, engaging in general chat and meandering towards the exits, either to drive or, in at least one case, to ski over the mountains back home.

In this particular meeting, it was the exemptions from normal procedure that serve to highlight how 'normal' bureaucratic meetings function. The contrast illustrates the degree of constraint and ritualization that applies to municipal meetings, the rigidity of the roles of participants, whose stringency is said to require particular aspects of personality from the actors (see Abram 2004). Feeding the outcomes of this meeting required a considerable amount of subsequent work to translate it into the discourse of council business, as I will show below, again highlighting the means by which meetings must be shepherded and documented, legitimized and incorporated, before they can contribute to the reproduction of the institution. In contrast, the lack of attention to the legitimizing significance of electoral process in the VOMP meetings meant that the politicians could not participate, yet as the process had, in name, been proposed by the Chief Executive and approved by cabinet, they were bound to give the appearance of going along with it. Hence they played along, yet withheld their full participation and delegitimized the process, later ignoring the results too. In the next section, I offer a closer inspection of the formalized codification of these municipal meetings, to illustrate how diverse meetings are translated into standardized documents to meet the requirements of legitimate political action.

Codification

What eventually emerged from the two days of heated discussion and the argumentative construction of goals and visions described above was a document that was later presented with the composed veneer of officialdom to the political assembly, complete with technical-looking diagrams illustrating future scenarios, and formal charts outlining vague but clearly presented concepts of the 'life-wheel' of the citizenry (with its three phases: ages 0-20 years, 20-67, and over 67, corresponding roughly to school, work, and retirement). The lively and intense time at the hotel was thus translated back into the idiom of bureaucratic meetings, with its impression of generalizability derived from the very standardized form of the documents, minimizing both the degree of informality and the paradoxes that they might actually include. Documents associated with meetings thus have a number of roles. They serve to place the meeting within an institutional framework and offer navigational signals as to where in that framework the meeting fits, as well as recording formal decisions or statements. Hidden within them are the external context on which they purport to act. They are, thus, worthless as bits of paper without the surrounding paraphernalia of council ritual. Papers that are later not acted on are, indeed, described as worthless paper, as Vike (2004) has highlighted.

On first encounter, meeting papers appear so dry as to be almost illegible, and it takes some experience to divine the vehemence and idealism that may be hidden in the text.[2] Just as one must learn to navigate the meeting itself, one must learn to read its documents. This learning is entirely contextual, since even if one recognizes the coded language, one cannot know to what it refers without knowing the particular cases in question.

Meeting papers look something like the following. First there is a cover note, as shown in Figure 1, that lists all the issues to be discussed at the meeting. This is followed by a sizeable portfolio of notes that adopt the format shown in Figure 2.

The absolute standard codification of meeting papers has the effect of making all meetings appear equivalent and council procedure reliable and repetitive. To an outsider – a local resident, for example, new to council procedures – it would be difficult to ascertain which meetings are significant and which routine. Documents only provide information to a certain extent, and then only to those who know how to read them. Effective politicians are those who have learned how to read the papers and how to interpret the codes that link the papers to different cases, and who probably already know in advance which papers matter and what is to be in them. For really controversial topics, reading between the lines to discern the line to be taken by the administration, to see the missing statements, or to pre-empt decisions is a key political skill, and also an essential skill for administrators who wish to shepherd a particular policy through committee meetings (see again Abram 2014 for an example).

Speech and action

The two-day conference outlined above is a particularly strong example of the contrast between the narrow event of the meeting itself, from the call to order to the final business, and the formal minute or report that purports to record it. Each such event takes place not only in the context of a longer process and broader procedures, but in its immediate context of time and place, events preceded by others, and succeeded by immediate conversation, the coming together and dispersal of various participants. Codification is a means to an end – minutes link meetings together, sift the consequential talk from the circumstantial, and record only those elements of the meeting that identify actions to be taken, or points of principle to be recorded for future reference. It should be remembered that council minutes also constitute a legal record of decisions and statements that are written with a view to the council being held to account in the event of a future challenge.

It is worth knowing that when the papers from the two-day conference were presented back to the Planning and Development Committee, the response was mixed. One politician noted that there had been significant changes to the documents from the VOMP process that had been supposed to be the vision-setting exercise for the municipality, and asked, pointedly, 'was the administration in the same process?'

Journal of the Royal Anthropological Institute (N.S.), 27-44
© Royal Anthropological Institute 2017

INVITATION TO MEETING – Part 1

Organ: council

Date: 21.01.2014

Time: 18:00

Place: Town Hall

Deputies attending will be sent special invitations.

Notify valid absence by telephone 00 00 00 00 or Political.secretariat@municipality

Theme hour:

16:00-17:00: Ethics by Tor Jensen, [External Organization Name]

Dinner 17:00 for council members.

CASEMAP

Case	case number
	Content

14/1   13/2305

approval of protocol for council 12.12.2013

14/2   13/2937

scrutiny committee's calendar 2014

14/3   15/2435

negotiation reform. Status report October 2013

14/4   11/2534

status; profession and quality in health and care service

etc.

Municipality cabinet, [date]

Name (Sign.)

Mayor

Figure 1.

Journal of the Royal Anthropological Institute (N.S.), 27-44
© Royal Anthropological Institute 2017

```
┌─────────────────────────────────────────────────────────────────────┐
│ NAME OF MUNICIPALITY                                                  │
│                                                                       │
│                              L.no.:        89723/13                   │
│                                                                       │
│                              C.no.:        13/2345                    │
│                                                                       │
│                              Archive no.:  042//                      │
│                                                                       │
│                              Date:         08.01.2014                 │
│                                                                       │
│                              Caseoffcr.:   [Name]                     │
│                                                                       │
│ Council                                                               │
│                                                                       │
├─────────────────────────────────────────────────────────────────────┤
│ Handled by                      date          subcommittee case       │
│                                                                       │
│ Council                         23.01.2014    1/14 - PS               │
├─────────────────────────────────────────────────────────────────────┤
│                                                                       │
│ Approval of protocol for council 10.12.2013                           │
│                                                                       │
│                                                                       │
│ The Mayor recommends that Council take the following decision:        │
│                                                                       │
│ 1. Protocol from council meeting 10.12.2013 is approved as it is      │
│    presented.                                                         │
│                                                                       │
│                                                                       │
│ Attached is the protocol from the council meeting of 10.12.2013.      │
│                                                                       │
│                                                                       │
│                                                                       │
│ Name (sign.)                                                          │
│                                                                       │
│ Mayor                                                                 │
│                                                                       │
│                                                                       │
│                        Page 3 of 60                                   │
└─────────────────────────────────────────────────────────────────────┘
```

Figure 2.

Another noted that it was important that the process was open, and that it required a proper discussion. Clearly, politicians had got wind of the administrative event, and were sceptical about what appeared to be an attempt to over-ride the political leadership. The place for legitimate planning and decision-making was in the chamber, not in a private hotel with only administrators present (which could be seen as an infelicitous context). The Mayor, chairing the committee, was able to reassure members that this committee would not take decisions but make recommendations to the cabinet committee, thus casting the papers considered in this meeting as advisory, and as a preliminary to the cabinet. Ownership as well as authorship of meeting papers is thus clearly a significant attribute. The Chief Executive tried to gloss the changes as an informed editing of the VOMP outcomes (since the administration has responsibility for drafting papers), with the Mayor indicating that VOMP goals had to be aligned to the fifteen-year perspective required in plans. The committee members accepted that a series of further committee discussions would be held over the plan, and moved on to discuss the next issue: the relocation of post offices within larger shops. Hence, he steered the meeting away from the actual conflict between the politicians and the administration, negating the dilemmas this indicated, by defining the whole event as mere process, which need not provoke concern. In this context, the external referent for the meeting was in danger of being seen as the hotel seminar, and not the outside world of the residents and their interests, and the land upon which the plan would regulate action. Hence, a useful way to redirect the politicians' ire was to point them back to the content of the plan and its talk of houses, shopping centres, and schools. Conjuring this concrete context enabled the Chief Executive to point to a greater good, a more important concern, hence belittling the politicians' concern about due process and making it appear petty. Why worry about who said what, he appeared to be saying, when you should be worrying about the future of the municipality fifteen or twenty years hence. He was also indicating that their talk about the VOMP process and about the seminar were not purposive, an accusation that presses a sensitive nerve among municipal politicians.

Purposeless talk is not considered legitimate in municipal meetings, and participants are frequently urged to remain succinct and ensure that they address the issue at hand. This is materialized in the procedure for the municipal meetings of the full council, where speakers step up to a podium to address the council, or more correctly to address the Mayor chairing the meeting (beginning each speech with the single word 'Mayor'). A light on the podium shines green for up to four minutes for a first speech and two minutes for a rejoinder, and then shines red to indicate to both speaker and audience that their time is up (see Fig. 3).[3] If they continue, they are told abruptly by the Mayor to finish. Discipline is thus both materialized and internalized, as speakers conform to the requirements. I assert that much of the speech at full council meetings is performed to assert political positions, to ensure that voices are heard, or to demonstrate oratorical or political skill, just as Spencer (1971) described for English town councils in the 1960s. Looking through case papers in retrospect, it is clear that the links between talk, decisions, and actions tend to follow a prospective logic. It makes little sense to the participants to spend hours on detailed discussions if they do not promise to have any further purpose, since their aim is expressly to change things in the world outside the meeting room. Thus the various means of conjuring external contexts into the meeting room can be seen as an attempt to connect speech to action via external objects (be they sites or persons).

It is understood among the participants, therefore, that decisions are a precursor to action, of some kind, and preferably outside the town hall in the imagined municipality that is conjured up through various referents and indexes. Whether or not this action later happens is a known blind-spot in municipal planning, given that municipal forward plans are rarely evaluated *post-hoc* to ascertain which of the goals have been fulfilled; since plans are revised within the period they adopt for their actions, these are constantly shifting (Abram 2011). When a development takes place that is identified in a plan, it is possible to suggest that the plan led to the action. It is rare, though,

Figure 3. Asker municipal council chamber immediately prior to a full council meeting (1 April 2014 screenshot)

that actions identified in a plan that do not materialize are taken to indicate that the link between decision and action is fragile, to say the least. Implementation of council decisions is a complex arena that it is not possible to explore in detail here, but as any follower of politics should recognize, 'implementation' is a short word for a very unstable process in any organization, and nowhere more so than in government, local or otherwise. I suggest that, following Brunsson (1989), we reserve judgement about these links and treat them as ethnographic facts rather than policy evaluations or procedural inevitabilities.

Of all bureaucratic and political meetings, it is these full council meetings (as noted above) that are primarily routine performances, where objections to decisions proposed by the Mayor are unlikely to change the outcome of a vote if a council is dominated by a majority party or majority coalition. Only on rare occasions might there be a mutiny, and in this the situation is similar in most formal political arenas, from local council to government chamber. However, at smaller sub-committees there may be room to discuss details of cases or policies, and the papers presented by administrators (also known in Norwegian as 'case-handlers', *saksbehandler*) can alert politicians to areas of danger or potential controversy, and equally can hide them. However formal the textual format, the potential for manipulation remains. The formal codification of the papers disguises the personality of the (administrative) author, and appears to depoliticize (at least in a party-political sense) the issue for discussion. This depersonalization is an attempt to contrast with the political idiom and conform to the Weberian ideal of a united administration speaking with one voice. It enables the social politics of the administration to be concealed behind formal language and documentation, a concealment echoed by the administrators during political meetings, where they sit silently outside the political arena, waiting politely in case they are called to clarify an issue. The requirement to remain calm and appear disinterested is an essential quality for administrative staff, at least in this municipality (and, by all accounts, also elsewhere), and takes on the quality of a psychological trait required for the work (see Abram 2004). Public servants must embody a quality of obedience to the council that is temporally marked. While preparing case papers, administrators must be sure to include all the information they consider essential for a case to be properly evaluated and debated, since the discipline of a council meeting does not allow them to jump up and voice things they may have forgotten or chosen not to mention. Unless the chair chooses to invite them to contribute a clarification or requests further information – say, about the consequences of a particular decision (which may happen if an option is developed in the meeting that is not foreseen in the papers) – then administrators must remain outside the discussion. I argue that this phenomenon is one way in which the administration's purpose is conveyed as action upon the conjured contexts described in the papers, and not on its own internal politics. The administration is seen to speak with one voice (formally the Chief Executive's) in relation to the municipality outside, rather than being an assemblage of individuals engaged in internal power struggles or debates. Appearing to be impersonal is thus crucial to the effectiveness of administrators' roles in council meetings, an essential performance of the Weberian separation of powers that helps to uphold the legitimacy of the political process.

This embodiment of the separation of powers is echoed through the levels of the council hierarchy, although sub-committees may adopt slightly less formality than full council meetings. In all cases, though, a good administrator – one who wishes to have a long career, that is – will know to speak when spoken to, and to consider the response to any question cautiously to ensure it is not 'political' but administrative. So much was explained to me carefully by the pool during the seminar at the hotel, where administrators seemed to revel in the freedom to speak out as they desired on the issues to be discussed. Even so, they knew the Chief Executive was watching them (although, considerately, not at the pool), and that their performance would be subtly evaluated in the context of the administrative reorganization.

Such a close reading of these Norwegian public sector municipal meetings raises particular kinds of questions about meetings that may differ from those arising from business meetings, parochial meetings, educational assemblies, or protest actions. While it is common that much of the meeting may be taken up in organizing the meeting itself and its place in an ongoing series of events, the focus in this context is on the management of the separation of powers, distinguishing the roles of administrators and elected representatives, as played out through a concern with abiding by the rules of procedure. While much of the discussion appears self-referential in relation to the municipality's own procedures, policies, and practices, these are complemented by frequent reference to potential effects on the physical municipality and its population in relation to their perceived needs or demands. Reference is also made to national policies, laws, or current affairs, in placing the municipality's action into realms of legitimacy that span beyond particular meetings themselves, or the immediate concerns of the municipality. Yet in the Norwegian context, where the legitimacy of devolved local government is largely taken for granted, and the nature of political representation is generally respected (at least more than in other European countries, with Britain as a clear contrast), practices of legitimization are both routine and partial: routine, in the repetitive use of role-identifiers; and partial, in that what must be legitimized are particular policies or decisions, rather than the authority of the municipality to make them. What is not at stake in the meetings described here, for example, is the gender or clan affiliation of the council leaders (cf. Jones 1971), the presence or absence of secretive lobbying, the use of religious prayer, blessing, or language (Kuper 1971), or even the demands of frequent unremittingly long meetings and the sanctions applied to those who absent themselves, such as Howe (1986) documents among the Kuna of San Blas. So while one may argue that the form of the bureaucratic meeting is universalized, the particulars of the meeting practice are grounded in its implementation in each specific context. The ethnographic description above gives a detailed insight into the particulars of a Norwegian local council, while highlighting the general functions of meeting practices in bureaucratic democracies, and aspects of the legitimization of these practices through embodied performances and material practices of legitimization.

Conclusions

As performative actions, it is fair to conclude that meetings adopt ritual discourse and documentation to legitimize and give credence to their purpose and activities. These include the presence of appropriate participants – such as accredited elected representatives and a secretariat from the municipality's administration – as well as the trappings of municipal meeting-ness, such as codified papers, and in full municipal meetings the council chamber itself, with its constrained uses and peculiar decoration. As Schwartzman (1989) argues, the adoption of these rituals and routines not only lends credibility to the meeting but also brings into being the council as authoritative agent, and as corporate body (see also Robertson 2006). Here, I add that they lend the organization cumulative presence by establishing its existence over time as well, since the history of meetings along parallel streams that flow upwards through a hierarchy of generality and seniority provides a potentially infinite future for the municipality and its regular and repetitive nested calendar of meetings. Municipal meetings are thus embedded in processes and cycles, offering a set of temporalities that are both constituted by and punctuated by meetings. These meetings carry precedent and prior action, and reconstitute their authority at each turn. Meetings can collapse, and authority can fail, so strict adherence to disciplinary rules is often adopted to secure correct procedures that uphold the coherence of the municipal context and avoid the kind of 'infelicities' that Austin (1962) describes. Yet the by-product of all this legitimizing action is to smooth out the workings of the council to the outsider viewer. All meetings appear equivalent, and crucial issues can disappear into the standardized format of council action. Hence, understanding council business and process requires an investment in time, energy, and education before citizens can effectively participate. I do not argue that councils deliberately obfuscate as routine practice, but the effort that goes into legitimizing council meetings can have the effect of closing them off from external participants, who may then feel excluded from formal local politics. Yet this same structure serves to protect the legitimate activities of the state from prurient or irrelevant interference, enabling effective governance and representation. In this lies the contradiction at the heart of any democratic process, and this contradiction is performed through each meeting in its upholding of ritual procedures, while appealing to the electorate and conjuring up external contexts in the meeting chamber.

In the Norwegian context, central participants personify the council and its administrative body, embodiments that are enacted and acknowledged by the formal use of titles in meeting contexts. As noted, every speech addresses the chair, and the chair is explicitly named at the start of each participant's speech: 'Ordfører'. If the person who holds the office of mayor wishes to contribute to the debate, they must step down from their position and symbolically pass on their role to another person (usually their deputy), and when they stand at the podium to speak, they are addressed by their personal surname, and in turn begin their speech with 'Mayor' before speaking to the chamber. They later return to the chair's seat at the front table and resume the role of Mayor. The administration as a body is represented through the person of the Chief Executive (*Rådmann*), who is addressed by title both directly and indirectly. Policies proposed by the council are introduced as 'the Chief Executive's recommendation to council is . . .', so that all business appears to be conducted between the *Rådmann* and the *Ordfører*. Other participants adopt formal roles, becoming the corporate body through naming and through silence – the silence of administrators (public servants) at political meetings being a case in point. This elaborate stepping in and out of personas is itself an acknowledgement of – or an attempt to create – a separation between the personal and the political, and between the political and the administrative (in Weberian fashion), and remains necessary since the separation is always fragile. Constant reinstatement is required for formal structures to hold sway and not dissolve into personal interests or other potentially corrupt practices. Democracy is hard work, not least because the constant policing of correct procedure is both tiresome and necessary. But at the same time this hard work is seen as peripheral to the council's main purpose, which is to act on, and on behalf of, the physical municipal region and its populations, the council's electorate, its environment, and its economy (to name a few of the relevant external objects).

The papers that are circulated before and at meetings are not only essential equipment for furnishing the meeting and making its content meaningful, but they order the meeting in particular ways. Highly codified papers formalize and universalize the talk of previous and current meetings, as well as then providing a selective record for future meetings. Minutes of meetings are often the central legally accepted record of council proceedings, carrying weight precisely because their form is standardized and readable by non-participants. Even so, minutes and papers prepared by administrators carry coded meanings, and may disguise or provoke controversy or attempt to pre-empt particular discussions or encourage certain decisions (a role of the public servant that is well recognized in planning theory, e.g. Healey 1992). Given this codification, participants must learn the art of reading or interpreting meeting papers, just as administrators learn to be skilled in their writing. The papers materialize the corporation just as much as do the formal surroundings of the council chamber and the paraphernalia of the control of speech (the podium and its lights in the case presented here).

In the municipality, a major feature of committee meetings is that their legitimacy lies in the notion that they relate not only to their own procedure, but that meetings are primarily about something else, somewhere else. The defining and manipulation of context thus constitute much of the work that makes any decision or policy felicitous. But bringing the world into the committee room requires an array of techniques, including maps, images, charts, and texts, as well as verbal invocations. Reference to contexts provides a particularly important form of political legitimacy, but the connection is fragile – policies may fail to have the impact envisioned on that context conjured for the meeting, and even the effects that are desired may fail to make their way back to subsequent meetings, whose participants may be different, or for which conditions may have changed since the action was intended (see Abram 2014).

In the light of this summary of the ethnographic details of a Norwegian municipal meeting, what conclusions can be drawn about the meeting as an object of ethnographic inquiry, beyond the above conclusions about the due processes of (normal) municipal government? First, it should be noted that these municipal meetings are just one incidence of the more general principle of meetings as institutionalized gatherings. One of the advantages of taking the meeting as an object of inquiry is the opportunity to compare and contrast meetings held in different contexts, as in this collection. It becomes apparent, then, that the meeting form, while apparently universal, is flexible enough to be transformed in particular contexts. I can certainly travel to municipal meetings in different European countries, and recognize what kind of meeting I am in, but I will not understand the implications of discussions held there without a substantial degree of local knowledge too. What does that then tell me about the particularities of that context? In the Norwegian case, elements such as the public access to council meetings, public broadcast of those meetings, and availability of contact with participants reveal an entirely different set of assumptions about whom government is for than that found in the United Kingdom. Sitting in the segregated public gallery of a local authority in England recently, I was threatened with eviction for taking out a camera, accused of being a threat to security rather than being seen as a citizen with intense interest in the means by which I was governed. It is sometimes casually asserted that the Norwegian welfare state has more public credibility than the British, but such assertions are empty rhetoric if we cannot see how this supposed credibility is enacted. The publicly available, accountable meeting is one clear demonstration of the public accountability of the state.

Another is the content of the discussion, the scale of the budget, and the range of powers available to such an authority, as reflected in the decisions to be considered. Schwartzman implies that organizational meetings are the embodiment of the organization, yet in this case the meetings can be further understood to be the embodiment of the imagined state. Hence, it is to meetings that we should look for an enactment of what that state consists of, and how it is materialized. However, we must also ensure that this is complemented by an examination of the material context that is referred to in the meeting. Politicians may assert any number of narratives describing their achievements that may bear unpredictable comparison with material facts.

Finally, for the ethnographer of meetings, a challenge lies in the potential for discussions in municipal meetings to conceal as much as they reveal, since it is only possible to ascertain what is going on 'beneath the surface' of the documents and the meeting-speak through experiential knowledge of the council's history and the positions of different participants. This point echoes the acknowledgement that all meetings are moments in ongoing processes and relations, and their participants continue to learn throughout their lifetime how best to perform them. At the same time, the content of meetings often jumps from case to case, and is often referential, relating to other conversations, documents, or meetings. This makes it particularly difficult to write about meetings in a satisfyingly ethnographic way, since much of the speech is meaningless outside its web of relations, perhaps even more so than in other contexts. The documents, as illustrated above, are often dense and uncompromising, requiring extensive particular sited and temporal local knowledge to interpret them, despite carrying a paradoxical air of general transferability in their formal, generic format. Each section of a set of papers might require an hour's verbal elaboration to explain, making them also difficult to account for in ethnographic writing. The elements that can be explained or generalized lie either in the detailed consideration of the medium of personal relations, or at a meta-level, which may be less suited to contemporary ethnographic aesthetics. In brief, there is little to understand from particular instances

Journal of the Royal Anthropological Institute (N.S.), 27-44
© Royal Anthropological Institute 2017

of speech or text, since everything lies in the references, or is related to the conjured contexts invoked in the meeting, making it particularly difficult to write about meetings themselves without being attached to the content or banalized into the structure.

Debates about 'visions' and 'goals' may equally represent power struggles between politicians and administrators as local disputes about particular sites, or political conflicts between parties. The meeting form enables all of these varied points of contention to be managed and sculpted into the democratic process. The municipal meeting is a particular practice of bureaucratic organization that enables all of the complex and messy relations of governing to be ordered and managed, and which reveals itself as an extraordinarily malleable and amenable form that can be exploited at all levels of sophistication, from the straightforward to the Machiavellian. Seen in this way, bureaucratic governmental meeting practice offers an air of being both generalizable and highly particular. Whilst this ethnography is not an ethnography of a global organization (such as that by Campbell, Corson, Gray, MacDonald & Brosius 2014), its theoretical approach invites comparative ethnographic reflections from other bureaucratic state offices. In its potential to thus corral ethnographic examples from around the world alone, the meeting becomes a fascinating ethnographic moment.

NOTES

[1] I conducted ethnographic fieldwork in the municipality from January to August 2000, with return visits the following year. I should like to thank everyone who welcomed me into the municipality and shared their experiences and opinions. Note that pseudonyms are used in this text.

[2] This contrast is illustrated beautifully in Winifred Holtby's novel of local government *South Riding* (1936), which is framed entirely by the contrast between the dry coded language of meeting reports and the complex, messy relations to which they refer.

[3] Council meetings are public occasions, and are broadcast on-line: *http://www.asker.kommune.no/Politikk-og-samfunn/Lokalpolitikk/Video-fra-kommunestyret/*.

REFERENCES

Abram, S. 2002. Planning and public-making in municipal government. *Focaal* **40**, 21-34.
——— 2004. Personality and professionalism in a Norwegian district council. *Planning Theory* **3**, 21-40.
——— 2011. *Culture and planning*. Aldershot, Hants: Ashgate.
——— 2014. The time it takes: temporalities of planning. *Journal of the Royal Anthropological Institute* (N.S.) (Special Issue), 129-47.
——— & G. Weszkalnys (eds) 2013. *Elusive promises: planning in the contemporary world*. Oxford: Berghahn.
Austin, J.L. 1962. *How to do things with words*. Oxford: University Press.
Baxstrom, R. 2012. Living on the horizon of the everlasting present: power, planning, and the emergence of baroque forms of life in urban Malaysia. In *Southeast Asian perspectives on power* (eds) L. Chua, J. Cook, N. Long & L. Wilson, 135-50. London: Routledge.
Brunsson, N. 1989. *The organization of hypocrisy: talk, decisions and actions in organizations*. Chichester: Wiley.
Campbell, L.M., C. Corson, N.J. Gray, K.I. MacDonald & J.P. Brosius 2014. Studying global environmental meetings to understand global environmental governance: collaborative event ethnography at the Tenth Conference of the Parties to the Convention on Biological Diversity. *Global Environmental Politics* **14**, 1-20 (available on-line: *http://www.mitpressjournals.org/doi/pdf/10.1162/GLEP_e_00236*, accessed 5 January 2017).
Garsten, C. & M. Lindh de Montoya (eds) 2008. *Transparency in a new global order: unveiling organizational visions*. Cheltenham: Edward Elgar.
Guyer, J. 2007. Prophecy and the near future: thoughts on macroeconomic, evangelical, and punctuated time. *American Ethnologist* **34**, 409-21.
Healey, P. 1992. A planner's day: knowledge and action in communicative practice. *Journal of the American Planning Association* **58**, 9-20.
Holtby, W. 1936. *South Riding*. London: Collins.
Howe, J. 1986. *The Kuna Gathering: contemporary village politics in Panama*. Austin: University of Texas Press.

JONES, G.I. 1971. Councils among the central Ibo. In *Councils in action* (eds) A. Richards & A. Kuper, 63-79. Cambridge: University Press.

KUPER, A. 1971. The Kgalagari Lekgota. In *Councils in action* (eds) A. Richards & A. Kuper, 80-99. Cambridge: University Press.

LAW, J. 1986. On the methods of long-distance control: vessels, navigation and the Portuguese route to India. In *Power, action and belief: a new sociology of knowledge* (ed.) J. Law, 234-63. Keele: Sociological Review Monograph.

MANDELBAUM, S., L. MAZZA & R.W. BURCHELL (eds) 1996. *Explorations in planning theory*. New Brunswick, N.J.: Rutgers University Center for Urban Policy Research.

MAZZA, L. 1996. Designing a domain for planning theory. In *Explorations in planning theory* (eds) S. Mandelbaum, L. Mazza & R.W. Burchell, 3-9. New Brunswick, N.J.: Rutgers University Center for Urban Policy Research.

RILES, A. (ed.) 2006. *Documents: artifacts of modern knowledge*. Ann Arbor: University of Michigan Press.

ROBERTSON, A.F. 2006. The anthropology of grey zones. *Ethnos* 71, 569-73.

SCHWARTZMAN, H.B. 1989. *The meeting: gatherings in organizations and communities*. New York: Springer.

SEARLE, J.R. 1969. *Speech acts: an essay in the philosophy of language*. Cambridge: University Press.

SPENCER, P. 1971. Politics and democracy in an English town council. In *Councils in action* (eds) A. Richards & A. Kuper, 171-201. Cambridge: University Press.

VIKE, H. 2004. *Velferd uten grenser: den norske verferdsstaten ved veiskillet* [Welfare without limits: the Norwegian welfare state at the crossroads]. Oslo: Akribe Forlag.

La contradiction dans la vie politique contemporaine : bureaucratie des réunions dans les collectivités locales norvégiennes

Résumé

Les réunions forment l'apothéose de la vie bureaucratique contemporaine. Elles contiennent des dilemmes et des contradictions qui sont au cœur de la modernité. Les réunions politiques et bureaucratiques (au niveau national comme communal), en particulier, sont des rituels au cours desquels des règles sont mises en actes, le respect des rituels est assuré dans un jeu de rôles et de manipulations politiques et le secret des relations et des informations vient s'entremêler à la transparence de la forme. Les réunions des autorités bureaucratiques s'appuient sur des motifs qui les légitiment, notamment l'invocation de « contextes conjurés » qui font le lien entre les pratiques bureaucratiques et l'action externe. Le présent essai montre comment les réunions ordonnent la vie politique et bureaucratique, et réciproquement. Il explore la matérialité et la mise en œuvre des pratiques de réunion et illustre comment un modèle mondial dominant de réunion bureaucratique s'élabore à l'échelle locale.

2

Demonstrating development: meetings as management in Kenya's health sector

HANNAH BROWN *Durham University*

MAIA GREEN *University of Manchester*

International development operates as a system of meetings. This essay shows how meetings work within aid regimes to structure responsibilities for implementation, to situate projects within funding streams, and to realize the effects of scale. Where donor aid is increasingly allocated to support national plans which are the responsibility of recipient governments, the monitoring of outcomes requires the instantiation of project forms within and across existing state institutions. This involves the delineation of distinct sectors and their scale of operation, alongside the maintenance of relations with external funders. Drawing on ethnographic material from the Kenyan health sector, we show how development projects are realized as tangible social institutions through the structure of formal meetings. Meetings mark the temporality and trajectory of development as a set of planned activities contributing to specific targets. In the context of specific projects they become fora where commitment to development goals of participation, capacity-building, and effective management can be demonstrated.

Development finance makes a substantial contribution to Kenya's growing national economy, where net official assistance has stabilized at around US$2.6 billion annually.[1] The effects of this spending extend far beyond the confines of the projects and programmes that aid officially sustains. As in other countries where the presence of international development is significant, its organizational forms and the resources which accompany it are evident across Kenyan society, economy, and culture (e.g. Ferguson 1990; Green 2014). Signboards advertising small-scale projects are commonplace in densely populated urban areas and in remote rural locations. Offices of development agencies, from international organizations to local NGOs, are dispersed throughout the country. Along with projects and programmes directed at specific categories of beneficiaries, the development sector provides employment, opportunities for volunteers, and access to resources, as well as sustaining an expanding economy of support services, from consultancy to communications (Brown & Green 2015; Swidler and Watkins 2009). Meetings are integral to this economy and to development practice within it. Development workers in Kenya expect to spend a substantial proportion

Journal of the Royal Anthropological Institute (N.S.), 45-62
© Royal Anthropological Institute 2017

of their time travelling to and participating in various kinds of formal development meetings. This essay explores the central place of meetings in the organization of international development through an examination of meetings in the Kenyan health sector.

Meetings comprise a huge part of international development work, ranging from large multinational events within annual calendars to the numerous small-scale meetings that make up the 'project cycle' of appraisal, implementation, and evaluation (cf. Ferguson & Gupta 2002; Green 2003). From global summits to local stakeholder consultations and participatory workshops, these varied types of formal meetings enact the relations through which the social organization of international development as a system of politically motivated resource transfers is structured. Development interventions seek to direct outcomes through financial transfers that occur within designated time-frames. Accountability and temporality generate the architecture of development organizational forms. In contexts where vertically organized state structures become incorporated into development interventions, intricate lattices of audit and evaluation are created which aim to track multiple layers of accountability within different funding streams and time-frames. In Kenya, meetings embed the activities of numerous organizations and agencies involved in the delivery of aid into lateral relations with state organizations, integrating external agencies into the architectures of developmental governance. Meetings connect the different levels of a vertically and hierarchically structured state that extends down from the national level, encompassing the smaller administrative divisions of provinces, counties, and districts. Meetings enact the time, space, and relations of development interventions and are themselves ordered by these spatial and temporal visions.

Formal meetings, for example planning meetings between bilateral partners or appraisals between donor and beneficiary, have always been important in the social organization of development (e.g. Harper 2000). However, the structuring role of meetings in the development order has been transformed since the start of the twenty-first century with the inception of the development partnership aid regime. This regime is associated with the alignment of political objectives among certain donors, known as 'harmonization'; the increased devolution of spending to local 'partners'; and inclusion of a wider constituency of civil society and other stakeholders in development planning, evaluation, and implementation processes (Craig & Porter 2006; Green 2014). A greater proportion of development spending has been integrated, where accountability allowed, into national processes. These changes required a proliferation of meetings where debates about spending could demonstrate national ownership of and accountability for aid agendas. At the same time, with the agglomeration of aid into sector programmes and budgets, meetings become crucial as sites where the subsidiary projects within different sectors become visible. Meetings therefore enact the relations of 'sectors' and 'scale', which are the structural components of contemporary development infrastructure. These conceptual artefacts are the 'conjured contexts' (Abram, this volume) of meeting organization and practice. Meetings constitute the social space for the demonstration of other requirements of the development partnership funding regime: effective management, capacity-building, participation, and partnership.

Specialized forms of meetings have become established as essential to development infrastructures along with specific social categories of participant and attendee. Meetings enrol actors and agents who are situated at nodes of interface between different organizations or 'levels' of development as 'partners', 'stakeholders', and 'managers'.

The changing implementation, monitoring, and review processes articulated through meetings have implications for the practice of management within development and within the sectors and institutions supported by it. In the Kenyan health sector, the work of managers in the district health system is no longer only focused on managing the delivery of local health services. Significant effort must be put into managing relations with donor agencies as development 'partners' (Brown 2015). Development success partly rests on the management of expectations and the political context in which outcomes are deemed to be achievable (Mosse 2005). The management of development therefore cannot be accomplished 'at a distance' (Latour 1987; Miller & Rose 1990). In addition to the high volume of reports and specialized modes of audit and evaluation which script development success (see Tendler 1975) and which are an important component of extending development practices across different spaces through inscriptions of expertise, development management requires new social fora where relations can be nurtured, strengthened, and consolidated. This is achieved through meetings.

The everyday work of managers and staff in the Kenyan health system involves several kinds of meetings. Staff may request a meeting with a senior colleague to get advice or discuss an ongoing problem. They are likely to meet informally with colleagues when they travel to collect supplies or deliver reports. Managers carry out supervision visits which involve unscheduled but relatively structured meetings with front-line staff. Some meetings may anticipate future development interventions: for example, when NGO staff visit a senior government official, introduce themselves, sign a visitors' book, and say that they look forward to working together in the future. These meetings are part of everyday working life, but they do not make development infrastructure in the way that we are concerned with. The meetings we discuss in this essay are pre-planned events timed to coincide with development planning, implementation, and reporting cycles. They are documented through minutes and in reports to funders. They require the attendance of certain people who are accorded the capacity to act on behalf of a development constituency, either through professional office or through their position as representing a particular group, as when a member of a local civil society organization can act as a representative of beneficiary communities (Brown & Green 2015; Mercer & Green 2013). For Kenyan health managers, such meetings included weekly team meetings, monthly 'in-charges' meetings, annual planning meetings, and quarterly stakeholder meetings. Such meetings populate the encompassing development orders of sectors and vertical programmes with roles and duties, realizing the formal architecture of responsibilities outlined in project documentation as tangible social relations.

Meetings in development: the reorganization of international aid

Since the turn of the century, international development promoted by Northern agencies, including bilateral and multilateral organizations, has been increasingly concerned with scaling up isolated projects through sector-based interventions and harmonization of implementation, with donor funds aggregated within a single budget (Craig & Porter 2006; Harrison 2004). Ideologies of public management informed by neoliberal paradigms seek to reduce transaction costs, increase efficiencies, and devolve responsibility for implementation through a hierarchical structure of development 'partnerships' (Abrahamsen 2004; Brown 2015; Mercer 2003). These approaches are exemplified in the World Bank's Poverty Reduction Strategy approach, and in participatory approaches through which those defined as stakeholders are engaged in the design and implementation of development programmes (Green 2010; Lie 2015). Development interventions under this regime also contain capacity-building components that aim to enhance continuity, ownership, and sustainability after the project is ended with a view to improving processes of governance (Phillips & Ilcan 2004; Watkins & Swidler 2013). This organization of development required new modes of engaging those defined as stakeholders and a reconceptualization of the project as the vehicle through which aid spending produces development outcomes.

Previous aid regimes operated bilaterally and vertically through short chains of relationships between donor and recipient, with implementation undertaken by donor agencies themselves or their representatives. Development projects were discrete entities, often bundling in multiple activities in 'technical' interventions which operated as stand-alone endeavours in parallel to state structures (Hirschman 1967; Tendler 1975). Project employees were clearly differentiated from civil servants and government staff. Meetings and documentation played important roles in representing projects as managed interventions and constituting the political space through which objectives and agreements were negotiated (e.g. Harper 2000; Tendler 1975). The formal meetings through which social relations of aid were organized were limited to the dyad of donor and recipient in a bilateral relationship. Representatives of beneficiary groups and so-called 'stakeholders' did not generally participate in the formal social spaces through which development projects were assessed, monitored, and subject to management.

The current aid regime has different requirements. The 'good project' (Krause 2014) is no longer a stand-alone endeavour. Development requires changed forms of organization, which can demonstrate the progress of initiatives by making them visible as sets of activities which are internal to, and integrated within, national systems. Dyadic relations between donor and recipient have been replaced with complex latticed arrangements that enrol numerous different participants through processes of 'partnership', 'participation', and 'stakeholder involvement'. This is achieved through the official meetings that populate the global social order of international development: temporally, through progress markings against timelines of development targets within project and budget calendars (five-year plans, annual reviews, end-of-project reviews); territorially (country strategies, regional frameworks); and vertically (global visions).

In Kenya, the organization of development aid within the health system has followed a trajectory similar to that of other countries that have been in receipt of large amounts of foreign funding. In the period immediately following independence in 1963, there was a strong political will to extend health services (Maxon 1995: 132-4), including through 'harambee' self-help activities to which communities contributed labour or money (Holmquist 1984). Population increases and economic decline in the 1970s and 1980s, and a global political context where there was pressure to reduce state expenditure, meant that the government struggled to meet these goals (Barkan & Chege 1989; Throup & Hornsby 1998: 47). Since the 1970s, the Kenyan health sector has been heavily dominated by the influence of the international community and its funding priorities.

From the 1980s onwards, under the influence of the 'health for all' agenda of the declaration of Alma-Ata, which emerged from the 1978 International Conference on Primary Health Care, and the structural adjustment demands of the World Bank, funders emphasized the need for decentralization of government services and accountability to users. Responsibilities for the delivery of health and other services were shifted to local government authorities (Barkan & Chege 1989; Semboja &

Therkildsen 1996). Districts assumed responsibility for managing operational health services, subsidized through 'cost-sharing' (e.g. user fees for patients), which were legitimized through the narrative of community participation (Mwabu 1995; Mwabu, Mwanzia & Liambila 1995; Oyaya & Rifkin 2003: 115-16). District-level implementation was further formalized in 1994 through the introduction of District Health Management Teams. Throughout the 1990s, the attention to health systems reforms increased, as it did elsewhere (Therkildsen 2000), notably with the implementation of 'sector-wide approaches' (SWAps) aimed at improving the co-ordination of aid funding through a single centralized structure of management (Walt, Pavignani, Gilson & Buse 1999).

By the early 2000s, the direction of these changes was consolidated through a preferential shift among influential donors towards sector-based funding and budget support, alongside integration of funded projects into the routine activities of government ministries (Craig & Porter 2006). Funding for health care in Kenya now consists of both government budgets (which are themselves sustained by multi-donor support) and vertical interventions supported by different funders. These programmes have highly complex organizational structures. The US-funded PEPFAR interventions that support the majority of HIV/AIDS care and treatment in Kenyan public hospitals are a case in point. US implementing agencies such as the Centers for Disease Control and USAID are responsible for managing the distribution of HIV/AIDS funding in collaboration with the US-run office of the Global AIDS Programme, based in Nairobi. Smaller managing agents (which include NGOs and research agencies) compete with one another to gain contracts from these larger agencies and deliver services in different geographical areas.[2] Almost all service delivery takes place through Kenyan government structures (Brown 2015; Dietrich 2007; Ingram 2010).

Vertical interventions do not only target HIV/AIDS. They also include water and sanitation (WASH) projects, the national immunization programme, and tuberculosis and malaria control programmes. Each of these vertical programmes is supported by a different funding agency and each is concerned with different sets of development outputs. Funding from multiple donors and the implementation of projects inside the health system transform the role of some staff working within it, who, in addition to delivering health services to users of their facilities, have to deliver the outputs of projects to their various funders outside it. This particularly affects health managers within district or regional management teams, whose responsibility is to represent their district as a deliverer of health services to users as beneficiaries of aid transfers, while reporting on what is delivered, and who has paid for it, to management and development partners further up the system. Managing in this context thus becomes more than the management of health facilities and outcomes. It is fundamentally concerned with the management of development relationships and expectations.

This is not a small undertaking. The district health managers whose work is described in this essay worked with a total of nineteen partner organizations of varying sizes at the time of fieldwork. The 'harmonization' of development activities within the health sector has had the paradoxical effect of increasing complexity as external projects are brought into the sector to be managed but remain separate in terms of their social relations, implementation, and reporting processes. In these reconfigured health systems which incorporate vertical streams of donor funding, a key task of managers is to demonstrate responsibility for development. This is achieved through reporting and monitoring on project progress and through the demonstration of professionalism.

Journal of the Royal Anthropological Institute (N.S.), 45-62
© Royal Anthropological Institute 2017

Official meetings constitute the social fora where these responsibilities can be enacted and the demands of partnership can be managed.

Meetings and management

In 2011 Hannah Brown spent around eight months carrying out ethnographic fieldwork with a District Health Management Team in western Kenya. This group consisted of between ten and twelve mid-level managers who worked within a tiered system of management. Above them were provincial managers (with whom they interacted occasionally) and national managers (with whom they rarely or never interacted). Below them were the 'in-charges' of rural health facilities. In-charges in turn line-managed front-line health workers and supervised the day-to-day running of health facilities of varying sizes.[3] The managerial team that participated in this research managed health services across a rural district with a population of approximately 150,000. The district included twenty-one health facilities ranging in size from two to fifteen staff members, each led by an 'in-charge'. Development funds and resources were distributed through these managerial structures, with monitoring and management required at each level.

The District Health Management Team spent most of their time in meetings. The board outside their main offices listed planned activities for the month ahead, revealing a working life structured almost entirely around meetings of different kinds: monthly in-charges meetings with health workers; budgetary planning meetings with NGO partners; weekly team meetings; quarterly review meetings for various projects; and stakeholder meetings that brought together providers, funders, and recipients of health care in the district. Indeed, health managers spent so much time in meetings that it was hard, if not impossible, to imagine work without meetings. Managers used meetings to maintain working relationships with partner organizations. At meetings, they met the facility in-charges and gave formal updates about ongoing interventions while in-charges reported 'up' from their facility. Meetings were opportunities to demonstrate professional expertise in development and ensure the proper management of health systems, whilst engaging agendas of capacity-building, partnership, and participation. Meetings also instantiated development as the delivery of projects within the health system. For district health managers as interstitial actors between development funders and service users, participation in health system meetings enhanced one's capacity as a manager and as an agent of development (cf. Pigg 1997; Watkins & Swidler 2013).

An 'in-charges' meeting

It is almost 9.30 a.m. and around fifty people have gathered for a meeting in a large hall in a small market town, little more than a cluster of buildings around the main road, approximately 70 kilometres from the regional capital Kisumu. The hall is a recent addition to a popular local hotel where people with disposable income, including wealthy men and those with salaried employment, come to drink beer and eat *nyama choma* (roasted meat), perhaps staying overnight in one of the small self-contained rooms. The hall was built specifically to capitalize on the growing business opportunities for hosting development meetings in the town, but local residents also make use of the facilities for weddings and other events. Participants at the health meeting include the District Managers and other senior Ministry employees based at the nearby government hospital, representatives from 'partner organizations', and the 'in-charges' who manage the smaller health facilities in the district. Despite the hot weather, men are dressed in jackets and ties. The women wear tailored suits and have salon-styled hair,

Journal of the Royal Anthropological Institute (N.S.), 45-62
© Royal Anthropological Institute 2017

demonstrating professionalism and a business-like demeanour. The managers who lead the meeting are differentiated from attendees by their sitting positions at the front of the hall next to the main part of the stage. Tablecloths and a display of plastic flowers next to them further emphasize the seniority of the managers and the special status of the meeting.

When participants arrive, they sign in on a printed form that will be used to organize the payment of transport and attendance allowances. They are provided with a copy of the agenda for the meeting, a bottle of drinking water, a notebook, and a pen. Once the hustle and bustle of greetings has died down, and all participants have taken their seats, the meeting is formally opened. On the programme this task is allocated to the District Medical Officer, but she is late to arrive and a senior manager does this on her behalf, welcoming the participants and asking one of the female managers to lead a word of prayer before the meeting begins. The meeting starts with management presentations. Managers are mostly in their forties or fifties and consist of women and men who are trained in different areas of public health, clinical medicine, and nursing. They are a confident and charismatic group. Managerial behaviour at meetings is a taken-for-granted set of high-status skills and experience, underlined by confidence and familiarity with the social conventions of meetings. Managers carry laptop bags or fabric cases branded with logos from higher-level development meetings which they have previously attended. Meetings at this level are held in English and participants, particularly managers, employ a wide range of technical development terms. This month there is a presentation from the District Disease Surveillance Officer, who gives an update on epidemic reports and reminds in-charges of the alert protocol if they see cases suggestive of particular diseases, such as measles.

Then the Reproductive Health Manager takes the stage. 'I don't have a presentation for you today', she says, 'but I am requesting you all for something. Data on family planning is still a problem. We don't reflect exactly what we are doing in the facilities. We have changed now to a monthly reporting tool; however, some of the reports are not complete. How am I expected to give my reports to provincial level?', she complains, underlining how in-charges' reports are embedded in a larger system of reporting that extends upwards. She brings up a copy of the reporting form on her laptop, which is projected onto the wall at the back of the hall, and explains how to complete it. 'Let's make sure we are reporting properly', she emphasizes.

There is a break for tea and snacks: hard-boiled eggs and small doughnuts. People move outside to enjoy the cool fresh air and collect their food. By now, the District Medical Officer has arrived, her late arrival giving the impression of busyness and her interruption to the meeting underlining the power and status of her position. She is not expected to queue for food, and one of the younger female nurses is sent to fetch tea and snacks for her while she sits down next to the other managers. When people gather in the hall again she addresses them, discussing the overall strategy for the district, new facilities that will be opened, and upcoming initiatives. She informs attendees that a partner organization funding HIV care and treatment will be calling health workers to a training course on how to use their new reporting frameworks. In-charges are told to expect invitation letters and to select appropriate participants from their facility. The following week there will be a refresher course on TB management as part of the national HIV/AIDS and Tuberculosis strategy. This will take place over three days in Lakeside Hotel in Kisumu. Both training events seek to educate health workers on the use of standardized modes of clinical practice and reporting. These

Journal of the Royal Anthropological Institute (N.S.), 45-62
© Royal Anthropological Institute 2017

training programmes constitute evidence for the organizations contracted to deliver them – who also have to report back to their own funders – that they are 'working through government structures' and 'building capacity' (cf. Swidler & Watkins 2009).

The District Medical Officer's interruption to the meeting is followed by an update from the District Records Officer. He gives an extended presentation about the district's overall performance against its health indicators, which are pegged against the Millennium Development Goals for health. He points out areas where 'we are not doing well' and selects other targets for special attention: 'Please can dispensaries [the smallest category of health facility] remember that you should be aiming to do ten deliveries per month, and please everyone try hard with the measles vaccine as we are almost there on that target'. As well as presenting data about the district's performance, he uses the meeting as an opportunity to educate in-charges about their own data collection obligations. He tells participants, 'With voluntary male circumcision, I have an issue: reports are not coming to the district, and we agreed that facilities would forward circumcision reports alongside others'.[4] He puts up a PowerPoint slide which shows the reporting responses of each facility. 'It would be good to know the difficulties that hinder these reports', he says, diplomatically. The effect of his presentation is, again, to highlight the embeddedness of the health facilities within larger developmental systems and to show the importance of 'reporting up' in management practice, as well as to visibly demonstrate his own management of reporting processes. After he sits down, his presentation is praised by a Japanese aid worker present at the meeting who is leading a national health-systems strengthening and capacity-building programme, and who takes the presentation as an opportunity to further the agenda of his own project. Standing up he tells everyone, 'Let me congratulate the District Records Officer on an excellent presentation! I encourage you to share it with the whole management team and to use it for planning so that you can then visit the weak points'.

By now it is lunchtime. People pile their plates high with chicken stew, roast beef, fish, rice, chapatti, and *ugali* (a Kenyan staple made from maize). They sip their favourite sodas as they engage in lively banter and relax in the shade outside. In-charges' presentations follow lunch. Unlike the senior managers, many of these presenters are nervous; some are visibly shaking when they take the stage, clearly worried about making mistakes. Meanwhile, managers demonstrate empathy towards their junior colleagues by training them in professional meeting comportment (cf. Brown 2016). As the facility in-charges are preparing to speak, the District Public Health Nurse gestures to the wall where the order of presentation is listed on a piece of flip-chart paper and says, 'It is good that you people are organized because you can be each getting ready when the first one is presenting'. After the first presentation, which is a verbal report, another manager praises the presenter for his time-keeping but then says, 'It would have been better if you had made a copy of your presentation on flip-chart paper. Let those who have written on a flip-chart paper go first, during which time others can be preparing', and the order of presentations is revised.

In-charges' presentations each follow a similar format. First, presenters remind the audience of the size of their health facility and the population they are serving. This information is fed into a formula that they use to calculate numerical targets for health service delivery in their facility. Like the district targets, these are informed by a national plan that relates to the global Millennium Development Goals for health. Then they describe how they are performing against these health indicators, including, for example, the number of under-5s receiving immunization, the number of women attending four antenatal appointments, the number of women having safe deliveries, and so on, embedding their development work within a global knowledge economy centred on metrics and indicators (e.g. Adams 2016; Merry, Davis & Kingsbury 2015; Rottenburg, Merry, Park & Mugler 2015).

Once the in-charges have described their 'performance' in this way, they turn to a list of the 'challenges' that they face during the delivery of services. These usually include infrastructure and staffing issues, lack of equipment, and so on. One health centre mentions as challenges a lack of funds owing to an accounting error; the lack of an ambulance; and high expenditure on non-pharmaceuticals. Finally, the in-charges list their 'achievements', which include the partnerships they have established, funds they have received, improvements to specific forms of service provision, and the creation of strong and committed management teams. Sometimes in-charges use their description of achievements as a way to praise the management team or the District Medical Officer for their leadership. This format is typical of performance management cycles and development projects. Meeting presentations are therefore not only about presenting the outputs of interventions. They are also a presentation in aptitude and familiarity with modes of developmental governance and the technical language of development projects.

By now, many participants are beginning to feel tired, because it is hot under the corrugated iron roof, even though the hall is large and the sides of the building are open to the breeze. This is not a high-status development meeting. The hall in this small district centre lacks the fans and air-conditioning found in the hotels in the provincial capital where the more senior managers have their meetings concerned with higher tiers of the system. The relatively low-status surroundings indicate that this is a development event which is lower down the scale, a meeting that is itself reaching out into the even less-developed rural areas of the district. One of the district managers is currently engaged in a business venture to build a competing meeting hall and is convinced there is a potential in the town for something more upmarket, but that venue will not open until some months in the future. A generator rumbles loudly in the background, serving both the hall and, intermittently, the *posho* (an electric mill for grinding maize) in the building next door, which is also owned by the hotel proprietor, which further underlines the semi-rural nature of the location. In town, people don't grow maize that needs to be ground at the *posho*; they buy it ready-ground in the supermarket. Similar points of scale and understandings of how the developmental is constituted are reiterated in many of the community-level meetings held in the district, which take place not in hotels but in school classrooms or churches, with food cooked on open fires on the ground outside by local women's groups or community health workers. As one of the managers once jokingly put it, 'There are those who can sit under a tree [for a meeting], and those who cannot'. The physical surroundings of meetings reflect their imagined space in the developmental order.

The in-charges' meeting is not yet over. There is afternoon tea, with more snacks, and then it is time to hear presentations from representatives of donor agencies. Development partners fund the in-charges' meetings (as they do many of the meetings that are part of the managerial calendar). These contributions are agreed in the district's Annual Operational Plan (previously set out through its own process of meetings). Meetings therefore strengthen lateral relations with partners by integrating these external organizations in scaled and sector-based development activities, in this case at the interface between district management and health facility in-charges. When stakeholder representatives take the stage, they emphasize without fail the way that their project activities are nested within broader government strategies and structures, and their close working relations with the Ministry of Health.

At this meeting there is a presentation from a representative of a US government-funded NGO promoting male circumcision. Targets for male circumcision are part of the national HIV/AIDS strategy, and at the time of this fieldwork the district is working towards these targets through a partnership with this organization. The partner group manages the project logistics, but circumcision operations are held in government health facilities and carried out by government health workers who have been trained as part of the programme. This is described by the presenter as 'working through government structures'. At this meeting, the project manager gives a presentation about the overall goals of the organization, showing PowerPoint slides about their funding sources and intervention strategy. Then he presents the progress of the district against these population-based targets. Finally, he draws attention to difficulties in reaching targets across the district. He asks staff to be more committed, and emphasizes that even small facilities could achieve success if the staff are dedicated to this project.

Stakeholder meetings

In-charges' meetings are an example of what are categorized as Stakeholder meetings in the development sector. 'Stakeholder' is a politically constituted category pertaining to those who have a stake in an intervention. Key stakeholders include representatives of powerful institutions with direct interests in a project as well as beneficiaries or their representatives, a position in the current constellation of development frequently accorded to community-orientated civil society organizations (Mercer & Green 2013). Because the stakeholder category encompasses funders, implementers, and recipients of development aid, the practical inclusion of stakeholders necessitates a system of representation. In the Kenyan health context, all members of a beneficiary community were considered to be stakeholders in development projects, but not all were invited to stakeholder meetings. Similarly, all health workers in the district were considered stakeholders in the delivery of health services, but again, not all were invited to meetings. At meetings, stakeholder categories became individual roles enacted by people with the capacity to stand in for others either as managers, leaders, or formal representatives of groups such as the recipient community. In stakeholder meetings in the Kenyan health sector, the abstract architecture of development represented as a matrix of sectors and scales of intervention was made real through individualized, interpersonal relations between development actors.

The form by which stakeholders were engaged through meetings was stylistically different depending upon the 'level' of development at which they took place. This further enacted the scaled architecture of development. For example, although there is a similar managerial aesthetics of planning and reporting in the District Record Officer's interaction with stakeholders at a community stakeholders' meeting, consider the difference in style and tone.

He greets the participants in the national language, Swahili, 'How are you? I don't have a lecture, but I want to discuss one or two things. This morning we started immunization. Where is it done?', he asks rhetorically, 'In the hospital. And where do those people being immunized come from? From the community. And this meeting is called what? Stakeholder meeting ... so you people have a stake in health services delivery. For that reason I would like to thank you for what you are doing, because you are doing something to promote health'.

'Now, this is how we are doing in terms of service delivery performance', he says, as he attaches an indicator chart to the wall with masking tape. 'What I'm showing is the data that we have from July 2010 to April 2011. Under-1-year vaccination against measles from those dates was expected to be 4,830 and we achieved 3,741. That is 77 per cent. That means 23 per cent have not been covered. Measles is one of the viral diseases for which we have no cure but luckily enough we have the vaccine. If this continues, by next month we will still have more who have not been covered and soon we will be attacked by a measles outbreak'.

'My question is, as stakeholders, how do you find these indicators? What do you say? Are we doing well? Are we not able to do something to improve this? *Wanyalo timo gimoro* [can we do something]?' he repeats in Luo, the local language, for emphasis. 'Yes!' the participants shout back. 'This is my appeal: please let us encourage community members to bring children for these services. Community members are not maximizing use of the facilities'.

Facilitation has assumed a special role within development practice as an instrument of training and community participation in which facilitators assume temporary positions of authority and leadership (Green 2003). These kinds of skilled oratorical practices and facilitation skills realize the relationships that enable development systems to be produced in practice. In East Africa the directive practices of facilitators build upon a rich indigenous tradition in which public oratory is an important signifier of status in meetings of various kinds, ranging from political meetings to those organized by groups of kin and community groups, including funerals (e.g. Moore 1977; Parkin 1978). In this context, facilitation entailed assuming a leadership role, giving formal presentations, and educating others on how to act at meetings and carry out development activities, but also explaining key development concepts to participants, like the notion of the 'stakeholder'. The District Records Officer was a highly skilled facilitator, drawing upon different techniques and approaches in his work with stakeholders at different 'levels' of the development architecture. His facilitation drew different significant actors into the structured order of development and built the relationships that were required to deliver development. His work was viewed as exemplary management. During a return visit in 2013 it transpired that he had been promoted to a senior position in the new county-level administration. His colleagues described how proud they were of him and how deserving he was of this promotion.

Internal meetings

Unlike the in-charges' meetings and stakeholder meetings, which often had large audiences and were more public events, the Monday Morning Brief was a team meeting for members of the District Health Management Team that took place in the privacy of the District Medical Officer's office. This was a small room in a dilapidated building that had once served as staff accommodation, which was repurposed to hold the management team offices when the district was formed as a breakaway from a larger district in 2009. In contrast to better-appointed offices in other districts, the poor repair and small size of this office underlined the relative youth of this hospital as a centre for health administration and the lack of financing for material infrastructure that had followed the introduction of new management structures and the arrival of a new managerial class of staff. The room was empty apart from the District Medical Officer's wooden desk and a large plastic table that had been pushed up alongside it, around which chairs were placed for the meeting. The room was so small that there was barely enough space for all the team members to sit comfortably.

This internal meeting was in many respects more informal than most other meetings that the managers attended or facilitated. The office cleaner made tea, boiled eggs, and buttered bread with margarine, which she sold to those present for a few shillings each. These were consumed during the meeting itself rather than in a designated break. There was a sense of camaraderie during these meetings as people caught up with each other's personal news and lives. Nevertheless, the meetings were pre-planned and formally minuted. In the minutes, health workers were referred to by their office rather than by their personal names. These weekly meetings were an important feature of managerial work.

At one meeting, the agenda was as follows:

1. Feedback and planned activities.
2. Select participant for JICA [Japan International Cooperation Agency] meeting on quality service management.
3. Planning for supportive supervision.
4. Select Community Strategy focal person.
5. Date for stakeholder meeting in August.

The primary focus of the Monday morning brief was communicating among the team and organizing managerial activities. Each member shared with the others what she or he had been doing in the previous week, and any problems they were having. Managers verbally documented shortages of supplies that had affected their work. Problems encountered during visits to health facilities were discussed at these meetings, including absenteeism or disagreements between health workers. Managers requested fuel to travel to specific health facilities if there was a situation that required their attention. These discussions were important. However, much of the work of these weekly meetings involved reporting on meetings which staff had attended and making plans for future meetings. This included deciding when other meetings would take place and who would attend them. Because it was minuted and formally reported, this meeting demonstrated that the managers who participated in it were part of a functioning health system within which people with different kinds of professional expertise performed appropriate roles. A key feature of these weekly internal meetings was that they allowed managers to organize their work and representation within a larger system of meetings.

Meeting development expectations

Both kinds of meetings described above – participatory/stakeholder meetings and team meetings – have a double (and somewhat paradoxical) role within development architectures that has become typical of development meetings: they are at one and the same time part of processes of delivering development and also demonstrative evidence of developmental outputs (see also Green 2003: 134). The format of the in-charges' meeting centred on its role in demonstrating the devolution of management from the district to the health facility level and in nesting the activities of health workers within broader development targets and activities. It was an important site for making this devolution of development work visible through the public demonstration of outputs linked to different health system priorities, highlighting the managerial expertise of those who were positioned at different levels of the health system, and demonstrating the delivery of development outputs. The presentation from the external agency organizing a male circumcision intervention mirrored exactly the presentations by government managers and in-charges. This alignment of reporting and organizational forms enabled discrete development projects to be practically and representationally folded into state structures through a shared aesthetics of development reporting. These kinds of stakeholder meetings rendered participatory and managerial relationships visible and tangible, and were thus able to act as proof that development was being delivered through appropriate relationships, maintaining and legitimating the social architecture of development organization.

Development projects have evolved as sets of bounded activities and procedures that combine modes of accountability and predictability in attempts to intervene upon society (Rottenburg 2000). Under both previous and contemporary aid regimes, project success has been measured as much through the proper execution of procedures as by the actual effects of projects (Ferguson 1990; Mosse 2005). Particular tools such as the 'logical framework' (Green 2003; Krause 2014: 70-91) and other forms of development practice and reporting have become of central importance to development implementation. Meetings take on a similarly central role in the delivery of contemporary development projects because of their capacity to instantiate projects and development relations.

The management work that takes place in meetings makes development relationships visible. The causal relationship of development projects, between spend and output, is demonstrated through meetings as much as through reports. Whereas reports are documentary acts of closure that 'sign off' a development intervention, meetings are active modes of reporting. Meetings demonstrate the relationship between spend and output whilst it is in process, as an ongoing and controlled set of activities. Meetings act as validations of project spending because they are calendared occasions marking the temporal progress of projects, where participants visually and verbally present development outputs and achievements. Moreover, because meetings are nodes of interface that bring together actors situated in different organizational positions within developmental architectures, these outputs and achievements can be reported 'up' to higher levels of the state and made visible and tangible to funders. Meetings thereby programmatically situate development projects within national sectors and in terms of lateral relations with donors.

The capacity of meetings to situate development actors within a network of relations is key to understanding the importance of meetings in engaging agendas of partnership and participation. Literature on participatory meetings in development studies and in the anthropology of development has focused primarily on engagements between community recipients of development and project or agency employees (e.g. Marsland 2006; Mosse 2005). In recent years, as seen in our ethnographic description, meetings have become a visible demonstration of participation, idealized as stakeholder partnership and enacted at all scales of development architecture. The participation of actors who are positioned as stakeholders validates partnership relations. It is only when embedded in the professional spaces that are created by meetings that developmental capacity can be demonstrated.

Meetings also engage development agendas of capacity-building. The smaller weekly internal meetings described above helped to enact development as a system of meetings by planning and organizing future meetings. The very existence of these meetings was translated into a performance of good management and evidence of increased managerial capacity. The management of meetings (through smaller internal meetings) had become a demonstrable output of a strengthened health system.

Development meetings are in this respect embedded within processes of 'responsibilization' (Rose 1996; 2007) which involve handing over some managerial responsibilities for the delivery of development from funders to national managers. In practice, as Rose and others have argued, this entails reduced levels of governmental control over the detail of implementation. Monitoring and evaluation, including a range of reporting mechanisms, come to be significant domains of development practice in such systems.

We agree with others who have analysed processes of 'governing at a distance' that indicators and targets are central to systems of meetings-as-development, that these forms of audit can act as proxies for the achievement of policy visions (Harper 2000; Power 1997; Strathern 2000), and that they play a key role in extending networks of developmental governance as standardized objects of inscription that can travel back to funders' 'centres of calculation' (cf. Latour 1987; Miller & Rose 1990). However, we argue that because meetings are also sites for enveloping the participation, partnership, and capacity-building agendas, this particular form of 'governing at a distance' can only be achieved through the enrolment of new forms of intimacy, professional connection points, and interpersonal spaces. Distance from one perspective necessitates closeness from another. Meetings rely upon people who become development actors and agents, 'stakeholders' who have professional relationships with one another. It is these relations which enable development projects to be instantiated within existing organizational structures.

Health management is not only about the delivery of health care, but also about managing and sustaining relations between different parts of the development system. The role of health managers is thus extremely important in maintaining impressions of capacity and effective implementation. International development, within and outside the health sector, is therefore linked to the emergence of new forms of professionalism, including a figure which conflates the roles of the civil servant/government manager and development professional. It also includes positions such as the 'volunteer' who works at the interface of formal organizations and local communities (Brown & Green 2015; Prince 2015; Prince & Brown 2016). These professionals take on the roles of managers or leaders at different 'levels' of development systems. Development meetings, in Kenya and elsewhere (Harper 2000; Mosse 2005; 2011; Riles 2000), highlight the professional competencies and capacities of managers responsible for achieving project objectives in the areas under their control. Professionalism is demonstrated in part through proper meeting behaviour, which has become synonymous with the effective delivery of development.

Conclusion: governing at a distance

Meetings are not the same everywhere. Moreover, whilst meetings are certainly productive in their capacity to enact particular kinds of organization (e.g. Boden 1994; Law 1994; Schwartzman 1987), they are also to some degree responses to particular administrative and governmental regimes. Meetings have proliferated in their current forms within the health sector in western Kenya because of intersections between the historical legacies of health system reforms and the specific social forms of contemporary development funding and implementation. Development cannot be proved or enacted simply through projects, documentation, and reports. It requires the new social relations of meetings. The ethnographic material presented in this essay highlights that although meetings are widespread and familiar forms of contemporary organization, there is important diversity in their form which partly relates to the nature of the administrative systems and context in which they emerge.

Our ethnographic material highlights an important paradox within development conceptualized as partnership through which implementation is managed at a distance. Theorists such as Nikolas Rose see the kind of devolution of responsibility that is assumed in the involvement of representatives of recipient governments as stakeholders and partners in the delivery of development aid as central to advanced liberal forms of governmentality (e.g. Rose 1996; 2007). In such processes, Rose and others have argued that managers become part of the new authorities for supervising the 'conduct of conduct' within systems which explicitly seek to utilize and create the vertical relations which enable the devolved responsibilities essential to 'governing at a distance' (Miller & Rose 1990). In the Kenyan health system, funders aim to make implementing governments and their representatives key actors and partners in development. National managers and other actors placed in significant spaces of interface within organizational infrastructures are viewed as able to represent recipients of development aid by virtue of their office. Capacity-building and delivering development through government structures means that development is devolved to people who can be given managerial responsibility for monitoring development. In-charges of rural health facilities who mediate between the District Health Management Team and the staff and clients at these health centres, and managers who mediate between higher and lower levels of the health system, become highly significant roles in these kinds of systems.

However, while this creates a system where responsibilities for governing are handed down and internalized by managers at different levels of the health system, these actors are at the same time not trusted to deliver development effectively without careful oversight and monitoring. What is performed at stakeholder meetings are therefore relations with other development actors and managerial capacity. Because this is achieved through meetings, meetings proliferate. Whilst it is true that from the perspective of the funders implementation is taking place at greater 'distance', the requirements for monitoring the delivery of development have the effect of folding this distance back in upon itself from the perspective of managers. This causes a proliferation of management, as managers must make their expertise in managing development constantly visible to funders, managing 'up' as well as 'down', whilst also enrolling those whom they manage (e.g. in-charges and community leaders) into the networks that make development management work visible.

In development architectures, then, the paradox of 'governing at a distance' is that it requires more diverse involvement of stakeholders and the creation of new organizational structures. This not only allows those positioned as distant governing actors (such as international agencies) to act as enabling partners in development, but also provides opportunities for them to see the effective implementation of others. Performing management at meetings becomes a means of delivering development by proxy. Whilst our analysis has focused on meetings in the Kenyan health sector, such effects may well not be limited to African contexts. Accounts of neoliberal governmentalities and modes of governing at a distance risk conflating theorizations of governance with models of the systems that governmental bodies seek to achieve. What Rose and others describe are primarily visions of governmental agencies and

Journal of the Royal Anthropological Institute (N.S.), 45-62
© Royal Anthropological Institute 2017

their rationalizations for particular forms of intervention and control. Ethnographic analyses of how such systems operate show the unpredictable effects and contradictions of such governmental forms. In development architectures, where results must be proven and outputs made visible, meetings operate as a performance of oversight where management professionalism and participation can be displayed as a proxy of effective implementation.

NOTES

Hannah Brown would like to thank the District Health Management Team who participated in this research, and colleagues at KEMRI (Kenya Medical Research Institute), especially John Vulule and Pauline Mwinzi. Fieldwork was funded by the Leverhulme Trust under a research leadership award held by Wenzel Geissler (F/02 116/D, 'Trial Communities'). She would like to thank the director of KEMRI for granting ethical approval for the original study (SSC1991) and for approving this publication. Ethical clearance was also obtained from the London School of Hygiene and Tropical Medicine. Hannah also acknowledges the financial support of the ESRC (ES/L010690/1), the British Institute in East Africa (small grant award), the London School of Hygiene and Tropical Medicine (departmental fellowship), and Durham University.

[1] *http://data.worldbank.org/indicator/DT.ODA.ALLD.CD* (accessed 16 January 2017).

[2] For an example of how development contracting relations play out further upstream, see Roberts (2014).

[3] The organization of health-care delivery and other public services has undergone a major revision in Kenya since this fieldwork was undertaken, with the scrapping of provinces and the introduction of the county system. This has also devolved larger amounts of funding to the forty-seven different counties. Mid-level managers remain important actors in the new system.

[4] Voluntary male circumcision was part of a suite of HIV/AIDS interventions introduced after research undertaken nearby showed that male circumcision greatly reduced the risk of HIV transmission. In Western Kenya this intervention was funded by an NGO that was a spin-off from the research consortium that carried out the original study.

REFERENCES

ABRAHAMSEN, R. 2004. The power of partnerships in global governance. *Third World Quarterly* **25**, 1453-67.
ADAMS, V. 2016. *Metrics: what counts in global health.* Durham, N.C.: Duke University Press.
BARKAN, J.D. & M. CHEGE 1989. Decentralising the state: district focus and the politics of reallocation in Kenya. *The Journal of Modern African Studies* **27**, 431-53.
BODEN, D. 1994. *The business of talk: organizations in action.* Cambridge: Polity.
BROWN, H. 2015. Global health partnerships, governance, and sovereign responsibility in western Kenya. *American Ethnologist* **42**, 340-55.
——— 2016. Managerial relations in Kenyan health care: empathy and the limits of governmentality. *Journal of the Royal Anthropological Institute (N.S.)* **22**, 591-609.
——— & M. GREEN 2015. At the service of community development: the professionalization of volunteer work in Kenya and Tanzania. *Africa Studies Review* **58**, 63-84.
CRAIG, D. & D. PORTER 2006. *Development beyond neoliberalism: governance, poverty reduction and political economy.* London: Routledge.
DIETRICH, J.W. 2007. The politics of PEPFAR: the President's Emergency Plan for AIDS Relief. *Ethics and International Affairs* **21**, 277-92.
FERGUSON, J. 1990. *The anti-politics machine: 'development', depoliticization, and bureaucratic power in Lesotho.* Cambridge: University Press.
——— & A. GUPTA 2002. Spatializing states: toward an ethnography of neoliberal governmentality. *American Ethnologist* **29**, 981-1002.
GREEN, M. 2003. Globalizing development in Tanzania: policy franchising through participatory project management. *Critique of Anthropology* **23**, 123-43.
——— 2010. Making development agents: participation as boundary object in international development. *Journal of Development Studies* **46**, 1240-63.
——— 2014. *The development state: aid, culture and civil society in Tanzania.* Woodbridge, Suffolk: James Currey.

Harper, R. 2000. The social organization of the IMF's mission work: an examination of international auditing. In *Audit cultures: anthropological studies in accountability, ethics and the academy* (ed.) M. Strathern, 52-81. London: Routledge.

Harrison, G. 2004. *The World Bank and Africa: the construction of governance states.* London: Routledge.

Hirschman, A.O. 1967. *Development projects observed.* Washington, D.C.: Brookings Institution.

Holmquist, F. 1984. Self-help: the state and peasant leverage in Kenya. *Africa: Journal of the International African Institute* **54**, 72-91.

Ingram, A. 2010. Governmentality and security in the US President's Emergency Plan for AIDS Relief (PEPFAR). *Geoforum* **41**, 607-16.

Krause, M. 2014. *The good project: humanitarian relief NGOs and the fragmentation of reason.* Chicago: University Press.

Latour, B. 1987. *Science in action: how to follow scientists and engineers through society.* Cambridge, Mass.: Harvard University Press.

Law, J. 1994. *Organizing modernity.* Oxford: Blackwell.

Lie, J.H.S. 2015. *Developmentality: an ethnography of the World Bank-Uganda partnership.* New York: Berghahn Books.

Marsland, R. 2006. Community participation the Tanzanian way: conceptual contiguity or power struggle? *Oxford Development Studies* **34**, 65-79.

Maxon, R. 1995. The Kenyatta era 1963-78: social and cultural changes. In *Decolonization and independence in Kenya: 1940-93* (eds) B.A. Ogot & W.R. Ochieng, 110-47. London: James Currey.

Mercer, C. 2003. Performing partnership: civil society and the illusions of good governance in Tanzania. *Political Geography* **22**, 741-63.

——— & M. Green 2013. Making civil society work: contracting, cosmopolitanism and community development in Tanzania. *Geoforum* **45**, 106-15.

Merry, S.E., K. Davis & B. Kingsbury (eds) 2015. *The quiet power of indicators: measuring governance, corruption, and rule of law.* Cambridge: University Press.

Miller, P. & N. Rose 1990. Governing economic life. *Economy and Society* **19**, 1-31.

Moore, S.F. 1977. Political meetings and the simulation of unanimity: Kilimanjaro 1973. In *Secular ritual* (eds) S.F. Moore & B.G. Myerhoff, 151-72. Assen: Van Gorcum.

Mosse, D. 2005. *Cultivating development: an ethnography of aid policy and practice.* London: Pluto.

——— (ed.) 2011. *Adventures in Aidland: the anthropology of professionals in international development.* New York: Berghahn Books.

Mwabu, G. 1995. Health care reform in Kenya: a review of the process. *Health Policy* **32**, 245-55.

———, J. Mwanzia & W. Liambila 1995. User charges in government health facilities in Kenya: effect on attendance and revenue. *Health Policy and Planning* **10**, 164-70.

Oyaya, C.O. & S.B. Rifkin 2003. Health sector reforms in Kenya: an examination of district level planning. *Health Policy* **64**, 113-27.

Parkin, D. 1978. *The cultural definition of political response: lineal destiny among the Luo.* London: Academic Press.

Phillips, L. & S. Ilcan 2004. Capacity-building: the neoliberal governance of development. *Canadian Journal of Development Studies/Revue canadienne d'études du développement* **25**, 393-409.

Pigg, S.L. 1997. 'Found in most traditional societies': traditional medical practitioners between culture and development. In *International development and the social sciences: essays on the history and politics of knowledge* (eds) F. Cooper & R. Packard, 259-90. Berkeley: University of California Press.

Power, M. 1997. *The audit society: rituals of verification.* Oxford: University Press.

Prince, R.J. 2015. Seeking incorporation? Voluntary labor and the ambiguities of work, identity, and social value in contemporary Kenya. *African Studies Review* **58**, 85-109.

——— & H. Brown (eds) 2016. *Volunteer economies: the politics and ethics of voluntary labour in Africa.* Oxford: James Currey.

Riles, A. 2000. *The network inside out.* Ann Arbor: University of Michigan Press.

Roberts, S.M. 2014. Development capital: USAID and the rise of development contractors. *Annals of the Association of American Geographers* **104**, 1030-51.

Rose, N. 1996. Governing 'advanced' liberal democracies. In *Foucault and political reason: liberalism, neo-liberalism and rationalities of government* (eds) A. Barry, T. Osborne & N. Rose, 37-64. London: Routledge.

——— 2007. *The politics of life itself: biomedicine, power and subjectivity in the twenty-first century.* Princeton: University Press.

Rottenburg, R. 2000. Accountability for development aid. In *Facts and figures: Economic representations and practices* (eds) H. Kalthoff, R. Rottenburg & H. Wagener, 143-73. Marburg: Metropolis.

————, S.E. MERRY, S.-J. PARK & J. MUGLER (eds) 2015. *A world of indicators: the making of governmental knowledge through quantification*. Cambridge: University Press.

SCHWARTZMAN, H.B. 1987. The significance of meetings in an American mental health center. *American Ethnologist* **14**, 271-94.

SEMBOJA, J. & O. THERKILDSEN 1996. *Service provision under stress in East Africa: the state, NGOs and people's organizations in Kenya, Tanzania and Uganda*. Portsmouth, N.H.: Heinemann.

STRATHERN, M. (ed.) 2000. *Audit cultures: anthropological studies in accountability, ethics and the academy*. London: Routledge.

SWIDLER, A. & S.C. WATKINS 2009. 'Teach a man to fish': the sustainability doctrine and its social consequences. *World Development* **37**, 1182-96.

TENDLER, J. 1975. *Inside foreign aid*. Baltimore, Md: Johns Hopkins University Press.

THERKILDSEN, O. 2000. Public sector reform in a poor, aid-dependent country, Tanzania. *Public Administration and Development* **20**, 61-71.

THROUP, D. & C. HORNSBY 1998. *Multi-party politics in Kenya*. Oxford: James Currey.

WALT, G., E. PAVIGNANI, L. GILSON & K. BUSE 1999. Health sector development: from aid coordination to resource management. *Health Policy Plan* **14**, 207-18.

WATKINS, S.C. & A. SWIDLER 2013. Working misunderstandings: donors, brokers, and villagers in Africa's AIDS industry. *Population and Development Review* **38**, 197-218.

Démontrer le développement : la réunion comme mode de gestion dans le secteur de la santé au Kenya

Résumé

Le développement international fonctionne comme un système de réunions. Les auteures montrent comment, au sein des régimes d'aide, ces réunions contribuent à structurer les responsabilités d'exécution, à situer les projets dans les flux de financement et à réaliser les effets d'échelle. À l'heure où l'aide des bailleurs de fonds va de plus en plus vers des plans nationaux gérés par les gouvernements bénéficiaires, le suivi des résultats nécessite le déploiement de formes de projets au sein des institutions nationales existantes et entre celles-ci. Il faut alors délimiter des secteurs spécifiques et déterminer l'échelle de leur action, tout en entretenant les relations avec les bailleurs de fonds externes. À partir de matériaux ethnographiques recueillis dans le secteur de la santé au Kenya, ils montrent comment, à travers la structure de réunions formelles, les projets de développement revêtent la forme d'institutions sociales tangibles. Ces réunions marquent la temporalité et la trajectoire du développement comme un ensemble d'activités planifiées, contribuant à réaliser des objectifs spécifiques. Dans le contexte de ces projets, elles deviennent des forums où peut se manifester l'engagement en faveur des objectifs de participation, de création de capacités et de gestion efficace pour le développement.

3

The receding horizon of informality in WTO meetings

NICOLAS LAMP *Queen's University*

The essay starts from the observation that attempts to formalize negotiations in the World Trade Organization (WTO) have consistently spawned new forms of informality, such as the holding of meetings as 'chairperson's consultations' which do not require the adoption of an agenda, or the emergence of new types of 'unofficial' documents. The essay sketches the resulting layers of formality/informality and attempts to account for the survival of informality in the WTO. The most commonly offered explanation for the persistence of informality in WTO negotiations is that it serves to facilitate and disguise the exercise of power. The essay argues instead that formal and informal meetings serve essentially different functions. Informality can provide opportunities for productive interventions, alliances, and performances that are precluded in more formal settings. Gradations of formality/informality offer different avenues for WTO Members to talk to each other and to their domestic and international audiences.

Meetings of the Dispute Settlement Body (DSB) of the World Trade Organization (WTO) can be dreary affairs. The DSB is composed of representatives of the WTO's member states and administers the WTO's dispute settlement system – it establishes panels to rule on disputes between member states, adopts the panels' reports, and surveils the implementation of panel rulings. To a large extent, what happens at a DSB meeting is predictable. The agenda has been circulated in advance; almost every agenda item concerns an official WTO document, such as a status report on the implementation of a panel ruling, a request to establish a panel, or a panel report, which have also been circulated in advance. Not only the structure of the meeting, but also the exchanges that take place among delegations under each agenda item, are largely foreseeable. At the time of my field research, everyone who had attended a DSB meeting before knew that, after the first agenda item, in which the United States would report (what amounted to) non-compliance in a then-thirteen-year-old dispute, the Cuban representative would launch into an extended speech deploring the effects of US non-compliance on the credibility of the WTO's dispute settlement system (WTO 2015*a*: 2-3; 2015*b*: 2-3; 2015*c*: 2-3). After Cuba's intervention, a few dozen other representatives would speak in support of Cuba. In fact, this pattern had become so predictable that the chair of the DSB had taken to preface this agenda item with a reminder of Rule 27 of the Rules of Procedure for DSB meetings, which stipulates that repetition of 'full debates' should be avoided (WTO 2015*a*: 2; 2015*b*: 2; 2015*c*: 2). For years, this reminder, which had at that point itself become somewhat predictable, was to no avail. Where the DSB had to take a decision on an item of the agenda, the outcome was also virtually pre-ordained by the applicable decision-making rules.

While the ritualized character of formal meetings at the WTO can make them tedious for the participants, it is to a large extent a desired feature of those meetings. Official WTO meetings are predictable *by design* – the rules of procedures and applicable decision-making rules leave little room for surprises. In fact, when surprises do happen, they create a considerable amount of anxiety. A WTO Member who fails to report on implementation activity in a dispute in which other Members do not consider that it has achieved compliance can expect to earn a sharp rebuke (WTO 2014*a*: 23-4; 2014*b*: 19-20). And a Member who raises an issue that has not been inscribed on the agenda under 'Other Business' will invariably be reminded that no substantive issues should be discussed under this agenda item (WTO 2014*a*: 24; 2015*a*: 15).

There are also meetings of another type at the WTO: informal meetings. These range from consultations between the chairperson and individual delegations (so-called 'confessionals') and 'small group' meetings comprising no more than six Members to 'informal open-ended meetings' that are open to the entire membership and mainly serve to update the membership on the state of play in the more exclusive negotiating formats. A particularly (in)famous type of informal meetings are so-called 'Green Room' meetings, which the Director-General of the WTO (and previously the Director-General of the General Agreement on Tariffs and Trade, GATT) holds with the heads of (what he perceives as) the key delegations and which used to be a forum where crucial decisions were made over the heads of the rest of the membership (Jones 2009: 349; Kwa 2003: 15).

The notoriety of 'Green Room' meetings – so named for the colour of the conference room in which they used to take place – and of other backhanded tactics that have historically been employed by developed countries to promote their agenda in the trading system has profoundly shaped the terms in which WTO Members and commentators perceive and discuss the role of formality/informality in the WTO. Pursuant to these terms, formality is associated with transparency and egalitarian decision-making, whereas informality is seen as facilitating the improper exercise of power. I say 'historically', because it is widely acknowledged that the operation of the WTO has become more transparent and inclusive. The membership is now kept abreast of developments in smaller group negotiations, which themselves have become more permeable. Commentators have also commended the WTO's efforts to make more documents available to the public, especially through its website. At the same time, they continue to urge that more be done in this regard (Charnovitz 2004: 679; Roberts 2004: 413-14). Some are troubled by the existence of an 'unofficial' document series (the so-called 'JOB' documents) that is not systematically published, or express puzzlement at the lack of documentation on negotiations that are known to be going on, sometimes for years, without leaving any publicly accessible paper trail (Charnovitz 2011). The sometimes implicit, but often explicit, explanation for the persistence of informality in WTO negotiations that emerges from these writings is that it simply serves to facilitate and disguise the exercise of power.[1]

Journal of the Royal Anthropological Institute (N.S.), 63-79
© Royal Anthropological Institute 2017

The present essay seeks to explore the theme of the formality/informality of WTO meetings and documents from a different angle. The hypothesis that I will advance is that formal and informal formats are not simply two versions of the same thing – with the former more conducive to egalitarian decision-making, the latter more conducive to power plays – but can serve essentially different functions. Gradations of formality/informality need to be taken seriously as offering different avenues for WTO Members to talk to each other and to their domestic and international audiences. Statements at formal meetings are largely made 'for the record'; they are primarily addressed to an audience that transcends the meeting room both in time and in space. It is precisely because of this wide potential reach of statements made at formal meetings that they are carefully choreographed. Formal meetings therefore do not lend themselves to the exploratory, spontaneous, and creative exchanges that are required to achieve agreement in negotiations. I will also argue that formal meetings serve purposes that have little to do with communication *per se*. For example, formal meetings often serve as occasions for rituals and symbolic performances in which little of substance is communicated. Informal meetings, by contrast, allow for a genuine back-and-forth between the participants; surprises, to the extent that they take the form of an innovative negotiating proposal or an unexpected convergence in positions, are welcome and necessary. Given the different functions that formal and informal formats serve, attempts to formalize informal meetings and documents are bound to be futile, because new forms of informality will inevitably emerge: attempts to formalize WTO meetings and documents will simply let the horizon of informality recede.

One respect in which the difference between formal and informal meetings becomes apparent is the manner in which the formality/informality of meetings is intertwined with the production of documents. The intimate relationship between meetings and document production has so far not received much attention in the anthropological literature (an exception is Riles 2006a: 71). In the WTO context, a key distinguishing feature of 'formal meetings' is that they are recorded in an 'official' document, namely in minutes, whereas informal meetings are meetings 'with no official record' (WTO 2015d). As noted in my description of DSB meetings above, documents also play an important role as anchors for different agenda items in formal meetings – without the predictability produced by heavy reliance on formal documents, which are accessible to all WTO Members, meetings could not proceed as orderly and predictably as they do.

I conducted the research presented in this essay while I was working as a lawyer in the Secretariat of the WTO from 2012 to 2014. In that capacity, I had the opportunity to observe some sessions of the ongoing negotiations on the revision of the WTO's Dispute Settlement Understanding, to interview a number of WTO Secretariat officials and delegates from WTO Members about their experience with WTO negotiations, and to encounter and work with WTO documents in various contexts. I also regularly observed meetings of the DSB and reported on developments in these meetings (a task that was greatly facilitated by their predictability). While I cannot reveal the content of the discussions in the informal meetings that I observed, the statements made at formal meetings are in the public domain, in the form of minutes published by the WTO.

In the following, I will begin by discussing 'formal' meetings of WTO bodies, as well as the features of 'official' WTO documents and their role in WTO negotiations. I then turn to the properties and role of unofficial documents and informal meetings of negotiating

Journal of the Royal Anthropological Institute (N.S.), 63-79
© Royal Anthropological Institute 2017

bodies. Finally, I discuss the particularly telling example of the formality/informality of interventions by chairpersons in WTO negotiations.

Formal meetings and official documents

The meetings of the DSB that I described at the beginning of this essay exemplify an important feature of formal meetings: at the time a DSB meeting takes place, virtually all information of consequence – the content of a status report on the implementation of a panel ruling, the substance of a panel request, the results of a panel ruling – has already been communicated through official documents. I noted in the introduction that DSB meetings are predictable by design: given the publicity of formal meetings, no delegate wants to be put in a position where she has to react spontaneously to new developments without having the opportunity to carefully vet a response with officials back in her capital. One may wonder, then, why these meetings are held at all. One answer to this question is that the public character of formal meetings, which makes them a risky venue for unscripted exchanges, at the same time allows them to serve as occasions for the performance of a number of rituals. A first ritual performed at DSB meetings is the multilateral 'surveillance' of the implementation of panel rulings, in which the delegates of a non-compliant WTO Member are subjected to what amounts to an exercise of public shaming: the indignity of being lectured by their colleagues about the dangerous implications of their country's behaviour for the credibility of the multilateral trading system. Only if we understand multilateral surveillance as a ritual rather than a substantive exchange of information can we make sense of the fact that, for a period of years, the first forty-five minutes of every DSB meeting were taken up by repetitive statements concerning the same case.

Another ritual performed at DSB meetings allows WTO Members gradually to escalate a trade dispute: at the first meeting at which a WTO Member requests the establishment of a panel to adjudicate a dispute, the responding party can withhold its consensus, forcing the complainant to present its request again at the following meeting, at which point different decision-making rules apply, so that a panel is invariably established. The ritual of the rejection of the first panel request gives the complaining Member an opportunity to show its seriousness, and gives the respondent an opportunity to publicly present a defence and demonstrate its resolve to defend its position.

While DSB meetings serve the administration of the WTO's dispute settlement system, formal meetings also take place in the context of another of the WTO's functions: serving as a forum for trade negotiations. The semi-official description[2] of the relationship between formal and informal meetings in the context of trade negotiations employs the metaphor of 'concentric circles'. The WTO website defines 'concentric circles' as follows:

> a system of small and large, informal and formal meetings handled by the chairperson, who is at the centre. The outer 'circle' is the formal meeting of the full membership, where decisions are taken and statements are recorded in official minutes or notes. Inside, the circles represent informal meetings of the full membership or smaller groups of members, down to bilateral consultations with the chair. Members accept the process as they all have input and information is shared (WTO 2015e).

This description of the negotiating process in the WTO already indicates that the primary purpose of 'formal' meetings is to serve not as a forum for negotiations, but rather as the place 'where decisions are taken and statements are recorded'. The actual negotiations in which substantive agreement on the decisions is reached take place elsewhere – in informal meetings. A first function of formal meetings in the context of trade negotiations is thus *ceremonial*, and in some cases *celebratory*:[3] they serve to ratify the consensus reached in other fora.[4] Where a consensus has not been reached by the time a formal meeting, such as a Ministerial, takes place, it is still sometimes possible to achieve a consensus at the formal meeting itself – the Ministerial Meeting in Bali in December 2013 is a case in point. However, in these instances the outlines of a final accord are usually fairly clear, and the WTO Members withholding their consensus do so primarily to generate a maximum of attention for their negotiating position. At the Bali Ministerial, Cuba and some of its allies withheld their consensus on legal language in a (thinly veiled) attempt to draw attention to the injustice of the US embargo of Cuba. While the legal concessions that they ultimately extracted were purely cosmetic (language reaffirming established principles of WTO law, whose validity no one had ever called into question), the act of withholding consensus at a formal meeting allowed them to make a point in a way that would have been impossible in the informal negotiating process. This effect was a function of the ceremonial and celebratory role of formal meetings – withholding consensus at a formal meeting allowed Cuba to disrupt the ceremony (and, quite literally, 'spoil the party' that was to go ahead had agreement been reached), which is considerably more spectacular than the everyday occurrence of deadlock in substantive negotiations. After the Bali Ministerial, a negotiator who was still furious about the hold-up caused by Cuba noted that the Cuban delegates would not be invited to any parties anytime soon.

Sometimes a formal meeting is called even though no substantive consensus is in reach. This phenomenon draws attention to another function of formal meetings: to serve as *deadlines*. Calling a formal meeting is a way of putting pressure on delegations to intensify efforts to reach a consensus, so as to avoid the embarrassment of arriving at a formal meeting empty-handed. In a way, then, formal meetings do not simply serve to ratify decisions; they are also intended to force decisions. This strategy rarely works, which is why many formal WTO meetings, and ministerial meetings in particular, are remembered as spectular failures (Montreal 1988, Brussels 1990 [Paemen & Bensch 1995: 177], Seattle 1999, Cancún 2003, and Geneva 2008 [Wolfe 2010] come to mind). The frequent failure of formal meetings to function effectively as deadlines should not be surprising: unless a decision to withhold consensus is designed from the outset as a publicity stunt, WTO Members are unlikely to abandon their positions in the publicity of a formal meeting. As a US representative has characterized it, scheduling meetings as deadlines 'is a bit like making hotel reservations at a nice resort while not making the reservations to get there' (WTO 2011*a*: 34). A formal meeting is an opportunity to take a stand when the world is paying attention – a feature that makes formal meetings particularly unsuited to reaching consensus. One indication of how much easier it is to reach consensus in more informal settings is that several of the issues that led to the failure of ministerial meetings were subsequently resolved in low-profile negotiations in Geneva.[5]

This function of formal meetings – to provide WTO Members with an opportunity to take a (public) stand – is already alluded to in the above-quoted description of the 'concentric circles' metaphor, which states that formal meetings allow Members to have 'statements ... recorded'. This function of formal meetings is brought out even more clearly in a statement by a chair of a negotiating group, which describes the division of labour between formal and informal meetings as follows. The chair suggested that the group first hold meetings 'in an open-ended, informal setting, to allow Members to discuss the proposals among themselves openly and frankly and to make as much progress as possible in covering all elements of the substance'. The purpose of a later meeting 'in formal mode', by contrast, would be 'to allow delegations to make any statements they might wish formally for the record' (WTO 2005: 38-9). Similarly, another chair of a negotiating group announced that he would 'consider convening a formal session' of the group 'at which views and ideas could be put on record' (WTO 2013: 7). For these chairs, the *only* purpose that a formal meeting serves is to 'record' statements, whereas informal meetings serve as occasions where negotiators can discuss and 'make progress'.

In fact, substantive discussions are seen as inappropriate at formal meetings. For example, when a debate regarding a controversial request for a waiver from WTO obligations by a major WTO Member developed into a back-and-forth between the delegations concerned, the chair implored the delegations to 'try to avoid at this formal meeting entering into a lengthy debate, repeating positions of the various parties which were well known to all' (WTO 2000: 20). In response, one of the delegations suggested that the Council 'declare itself in informal session' given the disagreements among Members on how to proceed (2000: 21). A formal meeting was not seen as the proper site to resolve substantive differences. The discussion at formal meetings is tightly controlled by the chairperson, whereas 'during informal meetings it would be in the hands of all Members to decide the breadth of the discussion' (2000: 2).

A final example of the use of formal meetings to make a public point is Georgia's decision in 2006 to block all formal meetings of the Working Party negotiating Russia's accession to the WTO (*Inside US Trade* 2006). As a matter of WTO practice, all decisions, including the adoption of the agenda of a formal meeting, are taken by consensus. By withholding its consent to the adoption of the agenda of any formal meeting of the Working Party, Georgia could prevent such meetings from taking place. Georgia's posture did not prevent the actual negotiations from progressing – the WTO Secretariat advised the chair that these could instead be held in the format of informal chair's consultations which did not require the adoption of an agenda (Jóhannesson 2013).

In sum, formal meetings are not primarily intended to communicate with one's negotiating partners (who would be familiar with one's position anyway as a result of informal negotiations). Rather, they are intended to communicate with the outside world, and with posterity. This recording function of formal meetings is facilitated by the central role that *official documents* play in such meetings.

Official WTO documents are distinguished from other texts that are produced in the course of WTO negotiations – such as NGO briefs, press releases by member states, press reports, or academic articles – by certain formal features. Some of these features are the same in all official documents and lend them *uniformity*, thereby signalling their embeddedness in a larger context of texts. Thus, all official documents carry the label 'World Trade Organization' and the logo of the WTO in the upper left corner, and a document number and date in the upper right corner (Fig. 1). Moreover, all official documents are produced in a uniform font. The document number and the date, while uniform features of all documents, also lend each document *singularity*, in that they make every document unique and thus unambiguously identifiable. The document number, or document 'symbol' in WTO parlance, is the DNA of the document, and no two documents can have the same symbol.[6]

Journal of the Royal Anthropological Institute (N.S.), 63-79
© Royal Anthropological Institute 2017

WORLD TRADE
ORGANIZATION

(14-4944)

Dispute Settlement Body
18 June 2014

RESTRICTED

WT/DSB/M/346

28 August 2014

Page: 1/25

Figure 1.

The symbols of WTO documents situate these documents both within the areas of activity of the WTO and in relation to other documents. Official WTO documents are organized into 'collections' and 'series'; they are classified by type and numbered in sequential order (Mesa 2001: 247-8). There are six collections reflecting the different types and areas of activity of the WTO (WT for 'World Trade Overseeing Bodies'; TN for 'Trade Negotiations'; G for 'Trade in Goods'; S for 'Services'; IP for 'Intellectual Property'; and OFFICE for administrative matters of the Secretariat). There are a larger number of series, which further specify the area of activity (e.g. WT/DS/ ... for 'Dispute Settlement') and often mirror the organizational structure of the WTO. Finally, there are different document types,[7] and a document can be a revision (Rev.) of, or an addendum (Add.) or supplement (Suppl.) or corrigendum (Corr.) to, another document. For example, the document symbol TN/AG/W/4/Rev.4 tells us that we are dealing with the fourth revision (Rev.4) of a working paper (W) produced in the course of trade negotiations (TN) in the Committee on Agriculture (AG).

A further aspect of the uniformity of official documents is the series of standardized operations that they trigger. Whenever a WTO Member sends a communication to the WTO Secretariat with the request that it be circulated as an official document, or whenever the WTO Secretariat itself produces such a document, the document will be assigned a document symbol, translated into the WTO's three official languages (English, French, and Spanish), archived, and 'dispatched to over 15,000 addresses in Geneva and all over the world' (Mesa 2001: 246).

The production of official documents has a number of profound effects. To begin with, it records, validates, disseminates, and amplifies whatever a WTO Member wishes to communicate. Thus, the communication is *recorded* by aquiring a specific materiality (be it in the form of paper, microfiche, or an electronic database [Mesa 2001: 246]) that is designed to allow its preservation for eternity. Moreover, the trappings of an official document *validate* what the Member has to say. This validation cuts both ways. On one hand, the document validates the status of its author, in that it embodies an acknowledgement by the WTO of the author's 'right' to have its position or communication recorded in an official WTO document. On the other hand, however, the author – by choosing to circulate it as an official document – also validates and, in a sense, assumes responsibility for the content of the document. Except in the most mundane and routine contexts (e.g. notifications or status reports), to circulate an official document is to make a point. Issuing an official document has a certain definiteness; it is irreversible. An official document can subsequently only be qualified through further documents: addenda, revisions, or, in the worst case, corrigenda. Apart from this validating effect, the translation and wide distribution of WTO documents have the effect of *disseminating* and *amplifying* what the Member has to say.

A further feature that communications aquire by becoming official documents is that they become referenceable. This is a function of their preservation through archiving, and their individualization through the assignation of a unique document symbol. Owing to their accessibility and identifiability, official documents lend themselves to the incorporation into chains of references. As Anneliese Riles has observed, '[D]ocuments anticipate and enable certain actions by others – extensions, amplifications, and modifications of both content and form' (2006b: 21).

The production of official documents also has symbolic effects that are independent of the specific content of any one document. First, official documents demarcate the line between insiders and outsiders of the WTO. Only a strictly circumscribed circle of entities has the right to have its position disseminated and its views recorded in official WTO documents, namely WTO Members, organs of the WTO (councils, committees, working parties, negotiating groups, as well as the chairpersons of such organs), and, in certain circumstances, the WTO Secretariat. Corporations, NGOs, non-member states, private individuals, or other international organizations are not entitled to have their views recorded and disseminated in official WTO documents. Second, the production of official documents is strictly egalitarian: while the communications by different WTO Members that are circulated as official documents differ in length, quantity, and style, no document is formally more significant than any other, and each occupies a unique spot in an order that is exclusively governed by chronological sequence. Official documents thus partake in the legal construction of the sovereign equality of WTO Members.

The symbolic effects of official documents were also at stake in the above-mentioned conflict between Georgia and Russia in the course of Russia's accession to the WTO. Georgia not only blocked formal meetings of the Working Party, but also withheld its consent to the 'formal publication and circulation of a revised [Working Party] report' in 2008 (Jóhannesson 2013). Instead of publishing the report as an official WTO document entitled 'Revision 4 of the Draft Working Party Report', the WTO Secretariat ended up making the report available to WTO Members in the unofficial JOB document series (to be discussed below) as a 'Consolidation of Texts Registered since the Circulation of Revision 3 of the Draft Working Party Report' ('JOB(08)/36') (Jóhannesson 2013). As in the case of Georgia's opposition to formal meetings of the working party, this move made little difference to the substantive negotiations. However, by blocking the convening of formal meetings and the publication of official documents, Georgia made sure that there was no official recognition on the part of the WTO of progress in Russia's accession negotiation until Georgia's demands were addressed, as they eventually were in 2011.

Informal meetings and unofficial documents

Virtually all formal meetings in the WTO are complemented by informal meetings and exchanges between WTO Members. Informal meetings are particularly prominent in the context of WTO negotiations. In the negotiations that I observed, there were four different types of informal meetings. A week-long negotiating session would start with a meeting in a so-called 'G-40' format. The G-40 group comprised approximately forty WTO members (out of a total of 150 at the time). The chairperson decided which countries to invite to these meetings; however, he made sure that, along with the largest trading nations, all major groups and coalitions of WTO members were represented. The G-40 essentially served as a steering group for the negotiations. Apart from the

Table 1. The formality/informality continuum: meetings.

Formal meetings	Informal open-ended meetings	G-40 meetings	Small group meetings/chair consultations/'confessionals'
– Agenda	– Agenda	– Agenda	– No agenda
– Translation	– Translation	– No translation	– No translation
– Minutes	– No minutes	– No minutes	– No minutes
– Open to all Members	– Open to all Members	– By invitation only	– By invitation only

G-40 meetings, the chairperson also held so-called 'small group' meetings, comprised of no more than six Members (see Table 1). The small groups comprised those Members who had submitted (competing) proposals on a particular issue. The goal of meeting in a small group format was to allow the proponents to agree on a compromise proposal that could then be presented to the G-40 for discussion. At the end of the week, the chair held an 'informal open-ended meeting' open to the entire WTO membership, in which he updated the Members not present in the more exclusive negotiating formats about the progress in the negotiations.

As I noted in the introduction, informal meetings have become less controversial since transparency has been improved. Pascal Lamy, the Director-General from 2005 to 2013, takes credit for the 'innovation' of 'explicitly let[ting] everyone know ... that these various concentric groups existed' (WTO 2009: 24). Previously, in Lamy's telling, '[t]hese were non-meetings, as there are non-papers and non-conversations' (2009: 24). The central change compared to previous decades is that other members find out what happens in the Green Room meetings. As Lamy explained in relation to a negotiating session held in July 2008, 'I spent hours in G-7 meetings and then hours in a G-30, followed by more hours in a G-153 [i.e. the entire WTO membership at the time] in order to explain to the G-30 what the G-7 had done, and to the G-153 what the G-30 had done' (2009: 25).

In order to underline the need for different types of meetings in order to conclude a WTO negotiation successfully, Lamy introduced the concept of a 'cocktail approach' to meetings (WTO 2010a: 2). He identified three ingredients of the 'cocktail': chair-led negotiations in negotiating groups on specific issues in various configurations (so-called 'variable geometry'); contacts among WTO Members outside the context of negotiating groups; and 'horizontal' consultations held by the Director-General himself '[w]ith the aim of maintaining an overview of the entire negotiating landscape' (2010a: 2). Some delegations applauded the Director-General's proposal, noting that it was 'easier to have a frank discussion ... among ten or fifteen people than among 153' (WTO 2010b: 11). At the same time, there has also been a lingering concern on the part of some delegations that, despite the Director-General's best efforts, they would be unable to follow what was happening in all areas of the negotiations; as one delegate put it, the process was 'so opaque and confused that his delegation had difficulty following it' (2010b: 11). Overall, however, the debate about the 'cocktail approach' showed that most WTO Members recognized that the negotiations could not succeed if they were restricted to any one format.

In particular, WTO Members acknowledged the crucial role of informal meetings in small groups. As the Colombian delegate put it, 'substantive discussion in small groups' gave members 'the opportunity to stand back from our position for a moment, to listen to the problems of the others involved, to measure the magnitude of our differences, and to exchange ideas on possible approaches to a solution' (WTO 2010*c*: 31). The Indian delegate noted that the 'informal process' held the promise of 'real engagement' and of 'creative discussions', and expressed hope that the formal negotiations would 'benefit' from the 'flow of new ideas' (2010*c*: 32-3). In a similar vein, the US delegate emphasized that 'small, informal meetings' were 'intended to supplement and to catalyze the work of the multilateral negotiating groups', not supplant it (WTO 2010*d*: 32). Several months later, the European Union observed that the 'small group process had been instrumental in kick-starting the negotiations' (WTO 2011*b*: 9). In one area, the 'small-group process' and 'discussions in informal settings' had led to 'openings and convergences ... on a number of key elements' (WTO 2011*c*: 4). Another concept often invoked in relation to informal meetings was the idea that these meetings allowed the participants to 'brainstorm' (WTO 2010*d*: 2-3, 24-30; 2011*d*: 22).

In sum, informal meetings allow WTO Members to interact in a way that is fundamentally different from the carefully scripted exchanges that are the hallmark of formal meetings. Since they are only communicating with their negotiating partners, without their statements being disseminated to the world at large, they can explore ideas, ask questions, and signal flexibilities in a way that would be very difficult to do in the public eye. This is not to deny that informal meetings may also allow the more powerful members of the WTO to exert a disproportionate influence on the outcome of negotiations. My argument is that explaining the persistence of informality in WTO negotiations simply as an attempt to disguise the exercise of illegitimate power misses a big part of the picture – even WTO Members who remain sceptical of the Director-General's efforts to maintain full transparency and inclusiveness of the negotiations tend to recognize that informal meetings are necessary to achieve progress in the negotiations.

Like formal meetings, informal meetings are intertwined with documents, though in distinctive ways. To begin with, informal meetings are sites where negotiators actually *work on* documents: they go through draft texts line by line, compare alternative formulations, and attempt to eliminate some of the numerous 'brackets' that mark off parts of the texts that are not yet agreed (see also Riles 2006*a*). A written negotiating proposal can also serve as an entry ticket to the more exclusive negotiation settings: a WTO Secretariat official shared with me his impression that some delegations submit negotiating proposals not so much because they have a substantive contribution to make, but because they hope to be invited to the small group consultations regarding a particular issue. If a delegation has submitted a proposal on an issue, it will be hard for the chair not to invite them to the small group meeting regarding the issue in question.

The documents submitted to and produced in informal meetings are often not official documents, but rather more informal texts, such as 'working papers' and 'non-papers'. Informal documents have always played a role in multilateral trade negotiations. As early as 1948, at the first session of the Contracting Parties, there is a reference to a 'working paper' as 'Miscellaneous Job 6166' (GATT 1948: 6). According to a WTO Secretariat official, informal papers were initially given a 'Job' number in order to facilitate their translation into other official languages. Since the founding of the WTO in the mid-1990s, 'JOB' documents appear to have proliferated and have become their own 'unofficial', 'informal' document series (WTO 2015*f*). Initially, the symbols of this document series had none of the sophistication of the official document series – they simply consisted of the JOB symbol and a number. In 1999, however, the Secretariat began to organize JOB documents by year. For example, one can find (though not access) the document JOB(99)/1799 concerning preparations for the 1999 Ministerial Conference through the WTO website search engine. While this facilitated situating the documents chronologically, it did not differentiate them by type or area of activity. This system for organizing JOB documents was employed until 2009. From 2010 onwards, JOB documents have been organized by areas of activity with symbols that largely mirror the symbols of official document series (e.g. AG for 'agriculture', MA for 'market access', etc.[8]).

More recently, another unofficial document series – the so-called 'room documents' – has made its appearance. Room documents have always existed as informal papers that circulated in meeting rooms. With the WTO's transition to electronic document distribution, which was implemented in order to achieve cost savings in document production, it became necessary to assign these informal papers a document number. One delegate described the emergence of room documents to me as follows: after a negotiating session, someone goes around the room and picks up all the pieces of paper that the delegations have left behind, assigns them a number, and archives them electronically. The cover page of room documents makes it plain that the document number is not supposed to fulfil the *validating* functions of official document symbols. Instead, the cover page of every room document cautions that these documents 'are not official WTO documents', that they are 'intended for use in the WTO meeting rooms' only and are assigned an 'unofficial symbol' for 'archiving purposes only'. The only functions that the formalization of room documents appears to serve, then, are recording and referencing. Room documents have from the outset been organizd by subject area, with symbols that correspond to those used in the JOB document series (i.e. there are JOB/AG/* documents and RD/AG/* documents, JOB/DEV/* documents and RD/DEV/* documents).

On the WTO website, both JOB documents and room documents are described as 'informal restricted documents' that are accessible only to WTO Members and not to the general public. The main difference between JOB documents and room documents is that the latter are usually only available in their language of submission and are not systematically translated into the other working languages of the WTO. Moreover, the distribution of room documents is even more restricted than the distribution of JOB documents. There are two types of room documents. Documents with the symbol RD/* are by default accessible to all WTO Members, although the WTO Secretariat can restrict access to 'specifically authorized users' only. Documents with the symbol RD/INT/* are by default accessible to the Secretariat only; they can be distributed in meetings in paper form (see Table 2). Room documents thus clearly do not have the *disseminating* and *amplifying* functions of official documents.

What explains the persistence of 'unofficial' and 'informal' documents in the WTO? It is worth recalling that these documents share some features with official documents, in particular their materiality, unambiguous identifiability, and hence referenceability. With respect to these features, unofficial documents have arguably become more similar to official documents in recent years. In particular, the move to symbols indicating the subject matter of informal documents (such as AG, MA, DEV) has made it easier to identify documents pertaining to a particular issue area. Through inclusion in the WTO's electronic documents database, informal documents have become searchable and accessible (if only to WTO Members and the Secretariat, and, in the case of

Table 2. The formality/informality continuum: documents.

Official documents	JOB documents	Unofficial room documents I (RD/*)	Unofficial room documents II (RD/INT/*)
– Usually unrestricted – Issued in all official languages – Organized by collection and series – Available on-line to the general public	– Usually restricted – Issued in all official languages – Initially organized by year – Now organized by series – Available electronically to WTO Members and Secretariat	– Always restricted – Issued only in language of submission – Organized by series – Available electronically to WTO Members and Secretariat by default – Possibility to restrict access to specific users	– Always restricted – Issued only in language of submission – Organized by series – Available only to Secretariat by default – Available to WTO Members only on paper in meeting rooms

RD/INT/* documents, only the Secretariat), just like official documents. The features of official documents that unofficial documents do not share relate primarily to the validating, disseminating, and amplifying effects of official document status. Unofficial documents are disseminated primarily among the WTO's Members. To be sure, a good number of JOB documents find their way to the general public, either because the WTO decides to publish these documents itself (usually with some delay), or because officials of WTO Members with access to them leak them to the media, NGOs, law firms, or other interested parties. It is thus plausible to assume that one reason why WTO Members and chairpersons may choose to circulate documents as unofficial rather than official documents is to avoid the validation, dissemination, and amplification that official document status entails.

Why, in turn, would they want to avoid these effects? Understandably, some commentators find this suspect. Referring to the lack of publicly available documentation on accession negotiations, Steve Charnovitz (2011) has speculated that

> [t]he WTO's lack of transparency on accession is due, I believe, to the WTO's desire to impose applicant WTO-plus conditions on applicant countries. By keeping the WTO's demands secret before the WTO Council votes on accession, the WTO can more easily assure that the public does not become aware of any inappropriate demands by the WTO being made on applicant countries.

One may wonder, however, whether the desire to keep dubious practices out of the public eye can explain so widespread and systematic a phenomenon as that of unofficial documents in the WTO. Perhaps an episode from the Uruguay Round negotiations (1986-94) can illuminate this issue further. During discussions in one of the Uruguay Round negotiating groups, the representative of Switzerland distributed a 'non-paper' to his fellow delegates. While it is not clear whether the 'non-paper' survives, the representative explained, in comments that were recorded in the official Secretariat note on the meeting, why the format of a 'non-paper' had been chosen:

> The reasons for presenting a non-paper rather than a formal submission were threefold: the paper was intended to be a discussion paper rather than a full-fledged proposal; the paper contained elements

which had not been of major concern to Switzerland but which seemed to correspond to the general
will of the Group; and the text was not yet at a stage of full maturity (GATT 1990: 3).

The reasons given by the representative of Switzerland do not have anything to do with
the desire to avoid publicity for its proposal – at the time, even a formal submission
would not have been made available to the public. Rather, they appear to reflect a
reluctance on the part of Switzerland to *validate* the content of its communication
through the form of an official document: because the communication was designed
to stimulate and structure discussion rather than reflect the Swiss position, and tried to
capture an emerging consensus rather than address elements of concern to Switzerland,
the Swiss delegation simply did not want to be *associated* with the contents of its
communication in the way that it would have been in the case of a formal submission.
Finally, the text was still at an early stage of development; the solution expressed in it
was thus *tentative* rather than definite. It made much more sense, therefore, to give it
the form of an informal non-paper that would be forgotten (as the Swiss paper has
indeed been) than to record it as a formal document for eternity.

Being able to say something tentatively is of great importance in WTO negotiations.
It allows WTO Members to float ideas without wedding themselves to them, and to
gauge the reaction of other Members without entrenching their own position. The very
definiteness of official documents is in tension with this. Changing a position that a
Member once held sufficiently strongly to record it in an official document inevitably
looks like a retreat, an admission of error, or of defeat. This is not true to the same
extent with unofficial documents. Unofficial documents have the feel of something
provisional, transient, temporary, and unfinished. They serve to take snapshots of
ongoing developments, and to signal that a position or negotiating outcome is still
open to revision. It is unsurprising, from this perspective, that JOB documents are
often used by the chairpersons of negotiating groups to record the state of play of
negotiations. If such documents were perceived as authoritative and definite, they could
ossify and paralyse the negotiations, as any change to the language in the document
would be perceived as akin to an amendment of an agreed text. Reportedly, something
like this happened to the draft modalities in the now-abandoned Doha Round of
negotiations, which remained unchanged after December 2008. These modalities, as
one delegate put it, had become 'mystified', and even though they were not agreed among
the membership, any change to them would have been perceived as a 'big deal'. The
modalities were – perhaps not coincidentally – contained in official WTO documents.

The formality/informality of chairpersons' interventions

Chairpersons of negotiating groups play a crucial role in WTO negotiations, but one
that is very difficult to navigate. On the one hand, the intervention of chairpersons
is sometimes needed to move the negotiations forward: a chairperson may have to
propose compromise language in order to bridge the gap between participants. On
the other hand, chairpersons need to be extremely careful to maintain their authority
and the trust of all sides. If they make proposals that are perceived as imbalanced or
as exceeding their mandate, their authority may be fatally undermined. The following
anecdotes from the history of GATT/WTO negotiations show how chairpersons can
use the formality or materiality of their intervention to minimize these risks.

In one case, the chairperson, after long consultations with the parties, sought to
break the deadlock in the negotiations by telling the assembled negotiators that he

Journal of the Royal Anthropological Institute (N.S.), 63-79
© Royal Anthropological Institute 2017

had a solution to the problem on a paper in his pocket, but that he would only show it to them if everyone agreed in advance to accept it (Lacarte Muró 2011: 112). After some handwringing, the negotiators agreed to go along with the proposal. While the chairperson's text was finely calibrated to achieve a compromise between the parties' positions and solved the problem to everyone's satisfaction, the chairperson prevented the negotiators from picking it apart by withholding it from them until he had secured their agreement to accept it.

In another case, the Director-General of the WTO handed out copies of a compromise proposal to the assembled delegates, but insisted that they return all copies to him at the end of the meeting. In other words, the delegates were supposed to read the proposal, reflect on it, discuss it, but were not allowed to keep the paper on which it was written. The Director-General thereby achieved the opposite effect of that associated with the issuance of an official document: his proposal would not be archived, validated, disseminated, and amplified, but instead would only have a fleeting, temporary, transient material existence. It could be talked about and considered, but not referenced and passed around as the 'Director-General's proposal'.

A final strategy was mentioned to me by a WTO Secretariat official who used to work closely with the chair of a negotiating group. This entailed making any document containing compromise language proposed by the chair look sloppy, for example by including punctuation and minor grammatical errors and not properly formatting the document. The idea was to make it look as though the chair had just done some brainstorming, had not taken particular care in formulating the proposal, and did not take it very seriously, even though he had in fact thought very long and hard about every word in it. This strategy served two purposes. The first was to avoid the impression that the chair was making a formal proposal, which the Members might have perceived as him overstepping his authority. The second was to minimize the fallout if his proposed language was rejected; if the proposal was perceived as just an idea that the chairman had had on the fly, there would be no serious repercussions for his credibility. In other words, the purposive informality of his proposal allowed him to say what he wanted to say, while at the same time allowing him to keep some distance from his own proposal.

Conclusion

I have argued that the persistence of informality in WTO meetings cannot simply be explained as an attempt to facilitate and disguise the exercise of illegitimate power. Instead, I have tried to show that the features of formal meetings and the properties of official documents render them unsuitable as productive venues for negotiations. Formal meetings serve a number of other purposes: they are sites for the performance of rituals, they fulfil ceremonial and sometimes celebratory functions, and – being recorded in official and publicly available minutes – they provide opportunities for WTO Members to speak to the world at large and to posterity. They are carefully scripted occasions for WTO Members to speak 'for the record'. Negotiations, by contrast, require that WTO Members be willing to move away from their established positions, genuinely attempt to understand each other's perspectives, and be open to exploring points of convergence. This can only happen in a setting where they are able to express ideas tentatively – in exchanges that are not recorded and in unofficial documents that are not published. Informality is a particularly valuable tool for the chair of the negotiations, who is not expected to make formal proposals, but can provide informal suggestions that nudge the negotiations forward. While these are exercises of power, there is nothing that is necessarily improper about them – the need for informality arises not because what is done is illegitimate, but because the type of exchanges that are required to move negotiations forward can only take place if the validating, disseminating, and amplifying effects of formality can be avoided.

NOTES

An earlier version of the essay was presented at the Decennial Conference of the Association of Social Anthropologists, Edinburgh, 19-22 June 2014. I would like to thank the participants, and in particular Marilyn Strathern, Adam Reed, and Thomas Yarrow, for their comments. I would also like to thank the editors, Véronique Fraser, and two anonymous reviewers for their helpful comments and suggestions on earlier drafts of the essay. I am grateful to Erin Crochetiere and Theo Milosevic for research assistance.

[1] The almost universal call for 'more formality' in the WTO is an interesting contrast to the context of domestic bureaucracies, which have long been under pressure to become more informal and flexible (du Gay 2005).

[2] The description is semi-official in that, while not embodied in any legal texts or formally adopted decisions, it is often invoked by WTO officials and chairpersons and is provided on the WTO website.

[3] One example of a celebratory function of meetings was the adoption of the WTO Agreement, which had been finalized in Geneva, at a meeting of ministers in Marrakesh, Morocco. The formal title of the WTO Agreement is the 'Marrakesh Agreement Establishing the World Trade Organization', in honour of this meeting. Some commentators have perceived it as ironic that a package of agreement that is widely seen to pay little regard to the interests of developing countries was formally adopted in a developing country.

[4] The ceremonial role of official meetings is reinforced by the WTO practice of taking all decisions by consensus; although voting is foreseen in the WTO's constitutive documents, it virtually never happens. WTO Members will ascertain in advance of a meeting whether a decision is capable of attracting consensus; where this is not the case, the decision will usually not be put on the agenda.

[5] Examples include the delayed adoption of results of the 1988 mid-term Ministerial in Geneva in April 1989 (following the failure to reach agreement in Montreal in December 1988) and the adoption of the July framework in 2004 following the failure of the Cancún Ministerial in 2003.

[6] In the 1960s, the newly formed Committee on Trade and Development started issuing its documents with the symbols TD/1, TD/2, and so on. When the GATT Secretariat found out that the 'TD' symbol was also being used by the United Nations Conference on Trade and Development (UNCTAD) – a different international organization – it decided to change the symbol for the Committee's documents from 'TD' to 'COM.TD' (GATT 1965).

[7] M for 'Minutes', N for 'Notification', R for 'Report', W for 'Working Paper' (Mesa 2001: 248).

[8] The correspondence is not always exact: for example, official documents issued by the Committee on Trade and Development bear the symbol WT/COMTD/... or TN/CTD/... (depending on whether the Committee sits in regular or special [i.e. negotiating] session), whereas all unofficial documents issued by the committee bear the symbol JOB/DEV/...

REFERENCES

CHARNOVITZ, S. 2004. The WTO and cosmopolitics. *Journal of International Economic Law* **7**, 675-82.
——— 2011. WTO transparency remains poor. International Economic Law and Policy Blog, 28 October (available on-line: *http://worldtradelaw.typepad.com/ielpblog/2011/10/wto-transparency-remains-poor.html*, accessed 17 January 2017).
DU GAY, P. (ed.) 2005. *The values of bureaucracy*. Oxford: University Press.
GATT 1948. First Session of the Contracting Parties. Summary Record of Seventh Meeting. Held at the Capitolio, Havana, Cuba, on 13 March 1948 at 6.00 p.m. GATT/1/SR.7 (15 March).
——— 1965. Committee on Trade and Development. Committee Documents. COM.TD/3 (26 February).
——— 1990. Group of Negotiations on Goods, Negotiating Group on the Functioning of the GATT System. Meeting of 25-26 June 1990, Note by the Secretariat. MTN.GNG/NG14/18 (9 July).
INSIDE US TRADE 2006. Russian pork barriers still an obstacle to WTO deal. *Inside US Trade*, 20 October.
JÓHANNESSON, S. 2013. The role of the WTO chairperson beyond the gavel. Unpublished manuscript, on file with author.

JONES, K. 2009. Green room politics and the WTO's crisis of representation. *Progress in Development Studies* **9**, 349-57.

KWA, A. 2003. *Power politics in the WTO*. Bangkok: Focus on the Global South.

LACARTE MURÓ, J. 2011. Wielding the gavel. In *Managing multilateral trade negotiations: the role of the WTO chairman* (ed.) R. Kanitz, 109-21. London: Cameron May.

MESA, J. 2001. Legal and documentary research at the WTO: the new documents on-line database. *Journal of International Economic Law* **4**, 245-59.

PAEMEN, H. & A. BENSCH 1995. *From the GATT to the WTO: the European Community in the Uruguay Round*. Leuven: University Press.

RILES, A. 2006a. [Deadlines]: removing the brackets on politics in bureaucratic and anthropological analysis. In *Documents: artifacts of modern knowledge* (ed.) A. Riles, 71-92. Ann Arbor: University of Michigan Press.

——— 2006b. Introduction: in response. In *Documents: artifacts of modern knowledge* (ed.) A. Riles, 1-38. Ann Arbor: University of Michigan Press.

ROBERTS, A. 2004. A partial revolution: the diplomatic ethos and transparency in intergovernmental organizations. *Public Administration Review* **64**, 410-24.

WOLFE, R. 2010. Sprinting during a marathon: why the WTO Ministerial failed in July 2008. *Journal of World Trade* **44**, 81-126.

WTO 2000. Council for Trade in Goods. Minutes of the Meeting. Held in the Centre William Rappard on 7 July and 16 October 2000. G/C/M/44 (30 October).

——— 2005. Negotiating Group on Trade Facilitation. Summary Minutes of the Meeting. Held in the Centre William Rappard on 25-26 July 2005. TN/TF/M/7 (16 September).

——— 2009. General Council. Minutes of Meeting. Held in the Centre William Rappard on 29-30 April 2009. WT/GC/M/119 (23 June).

——— 2010a. General Council. Minutes of Meeting. Held in the Centre William Rappard on 4 May 2010. WT/GC/M/126 (22 June).

——— 2010b. General Council. Minutes of Meeting. Held in the Centre William Rappard on 20 October 2009. WT/GC/M/122 (26 February).

——— 2010c. General Council. Minutes of Meeting. Held in the Centre William Rappard on 29 July 2010. WT/GC/M/127 (6 September).

——— 2010d. General Council. Minutes of Meeting. Held in the Centre William Rappard on 21 October 2010. WT/GC/M/128 (18 November).

——— 2011a. General Council. Minutes of Meeting. Held in the Centre William Rappard on 22 February 2011. WT/GC/M/130 (5 April).

——— 2011b. General Council. Minutes of Meeting. Held in the Centre William Rappard on 14 December 2010. WT/GC/M/129 (16 February).

——— 2011c. Committee on Trade and Development. Note on the Meeting of 13 January 2011. TN/CTD/M/43 (28 February).

——— 2011d. Council for Trade-Related Aspects of Intellectual Property Rights, Special Session. Minutes of Meeting. Held in the Centre William Rappard on 28 October 2010. TN/IP/M/27 (5 January).

——— 2013. Trade Negotiations Committee. Minutes of Meeting. Held in the Centre William Rappard on 7 December 2012. TN/C/M/31 (18 February).

——— 2014a. Dispute Settlement Body. Minutes of Meeting. Held in the Centre William Rappard on 18 June 2014. WT/DSB/M/346 (28 August).

——— 2014b. Dispute Settlement Body. Minutes of Meeting. Held in the Centre William Rappard on 22 July 2014. WT/DSB/M/348 (23 September).

——— 2015a. Dispute Settlement Body. Minutes of Meeting. Held in the Centre William Rappard on 18 November 2014. WT/DSB/M/352 (30 January).

——— 2015b. Dispute Settlement Body. Minutes of Meeting. Held in the Centre William Rappard on 17 December 2014. WT/DSB/M/353 (13 February).

——— 2015c. Dispute Settlement Body. Minutes of Meeting. Held in the Centre William Rappard on 26 January 2015. WT/DSB/M/356 (6 March).

——— 2015d. Entry 'Formal/informal'. WTO Glossary (available on-line: *https://www.wto.org/english/thewto_e/glossary_e/glossary_e.htm*, accessed 17 January 2017).

——— 2015e. Entry 'Concentric circles'. WTO Glossary (available on-line: *https://www.wto.org/english/thewto_e/glossary_e/glossary_e.htm*, accessed 17 January 2017).

——— 2015f. Entry 'Job document'. WTO Glossary (available on-line: *https://www.wto.org/english/thewto_e/glossary_e/glossary_e.htm*, accessed 17 January 2017).

L'informalité dans les réunions de l'OMC : un horizon qui s'éloigne

Résumé

Cet essai part de l'observation que les tentatives de formaliser les négociations au sein de l'Organisation mondiale du commerce (OMC) ont toujours donné naissance à de nouvelles formes d'informalité telles que les « consultations du président » qui ne nécessitent pas l'adoption d'un ordre du jour, ou l'apparition de nouveaux types de documents « non officiels ». Il décrit les strates de formalité et d'informalité qui se forment ainsi et tente d'expliquer la survie de l'informalité dans les négociations de l'OMC. L'explication la plus fréquente de sa persistance est qu'elle facilite et masque l'exercice du pouvoir. L'auteur avance que les réunions formelles et informelles ont, dans les faits, des fonctions différentes. L'informalité peut créer des occasions d'interventions productives, d'alliances et de réalisations qui sont empêchées dans un cadre plus formel. Les niveaux de formalité ou d'informalité offrent aux membres de l'OMC différents moyens de se parler les uns aux autres et de s'adresser à leurs auditoires nationaux et internationaux.

4

The meeting as subjunctive form: public/private IT projects in British and Turkish state bureaucracies

Catherine Alexander *Durham University*

Drawing on meetings within structured project environments in Turkey and Britain, this essay explores how and if this kind of highly rational, instrumental meeting travels and why so much frustration is typically expressed by British participants in such meetings. Meetings held in the Turkish senior government bureaucracy did not conform to expectation: they embraced formal and informal relations and were spectacles and tournaments of skill. I suggest that expectations of what constitutes a proper meeting are shaped by a specific British genealogy of common sense and technologies of fact creation, neither of which necessarily have purchase elsewhere. Nor is their applicability 'at home' straightforward, despite the fact that 'common sense' is often treated as simply commensurate with cultural systems as practical action: how one gets things done. Rather, the meeting, as shaped by this tradition, appears as a subjunctive form, a fiction of selective relationality where the meeting and project are treated as if they were set-aside spaces, participants act as if they had single formal roles cut from a web of internal and external relations, and highly summarized information allows discussion towards a shared goal.

I made the mistake once of observing to a colleague (in another time and place) that the two events that created a sense of a collective, indeed an effervescence, were the weekly research seminar and a good department meeting. I have not forgotten the look of amazed contempt. The error, I think, was to make explicit that meetings *can* engender something over and above minutes unread until the next such assembly. My observation was prompted by a sense of the affect of successful meetings, together with notes from colleagues that they had found a meeting enjoyable and/or productive; observations that were never publicly made. For if it is received wisdom that meetings are held in order to do things communally, then it is equally accepted that meetings, particularly those in institutionalized settings, are rituals devoid of purpose. This latter view is well illustrated in Mervyn Peake's *Gormenghast*, where days are filled by esoteric ritual signifying nothing but the status of those who maintain due form, in an isolated castle quite divorced from any connection to the world outside.

Over twenty-five years ago, Schwartzman observed that 'whereas meetings appear to be everywhere, they are almost nowhere in the research literature ... because meetings are so basic and pervasive ... in American society that their significance as a

Journal of the Royal Anthropological Institute (N.S.), 80-94
© Royal Anthropological Institute 2017

gathering in these settings has not been recognized' (1989: 4). Only now are meetings beginning to attract attention as things in themselves worthy of study. Otherwise they have typically been the background to things that pique anthropologists' interest, and though increasingly (e.g. Riles 2006) attention has been focused on the artefacts of such key moments of social ordering and what they do, the interactions that produced them are often but aetiolated traces in the documentary remains. Schwartzman juxtaposes an American grassroots organization's meetings with political speech in traditional communities, theorizing meetings as communicative events through which political relations of domination are performed. The comparison is intended to enact the customary manoeuvre of ethnographic defamiliarization; she quotes the definition by Marcus and Fischer: 'Disruption of common sense ... placing familiar subjects in unfamiliar contexts ... to make the reader conscious of difference' (1986: 137, cited in Schwartzman 1989: 5). Common sense here is equated with cultural norms. In the current essay, however, I follow a different tack in exploring the meeting form.

My approach is this. A certain kind of highly structured and structuring meeting has proved a very exportable form. Via international corporations or development agencies, 'the project' as a mechanism to order time, social actions, and relations, and generate legitimate knowledge and action, has taken firm hold, as Kuzmanovic (2012) describes for the NGO world in Turkey. Meetings are a vital part of such projects to monitor progress, and discuss and resolve problems. The project methodology of PRINCE2 (PRoject management IN a Controlled Environment), originally developed in 1980s Britain, is the most successful of these structured approaches, and is often used for IT developments. The key element is the staging, allowing progress to be assessed at critical points and for a project to be stopped if the justification for continuing it is too weak. PRINCE2 is free of content; it provides a sequence of processes, techniques (e.g. Critical Path Analysis), and documents (Strategy, Scoping, Project Initiation, etc.), into which almost anything can (theoretically) be fitted.

Thus, on IT projects, data-gathering meetings are succeeded by analysis, which includes plotting relationships between data and erasing duplications. Having one instance of each datum, linked to all processes that use it, enables what is known as referential integrity in a relational database: stand-alone data can easily fall out of synch so that different versions of the same datum coexist. Ideally, an organization is similarly streamlined, each part contributing to the endeavour of the whole; there is no excess or duplication. There is a reductive elegance about a well-designed database that can panic people when they realize that informal tweaks have no place in this formal abstraction. One way round this is to regularize and include the informal. The interplay between what is formally included and informal 'workarounds' characterizes both the process of developing IT systems and project management meetings that assess progress against schedules and make formal, joint decisions.

PRINCE2 emerged at the same time as New Public Management (NPM), which was inspired by the belief that private sector methods and goals should be transplanted into what had hitherto been called public administration, in the interests of greater efficiency, which accountability and transparency were now made to serve. Hood (1991) observes that this was a very Anglo-Saxon vision. There have been copious critiques, to which I add here, of just how useful the notion of transparency has been in the pursuit of effectiveness and efficiency. Nonetheless, these ideas continue to underpin ideas of good governance, apparently made visible through audit procedures. PRINCE2 flourished first as a mechanism for achieving the 'projectization' of public administration itself

Journal of the Royal Anthropological Institute (N.S.), 80-94
© Royal Anthropological Institute 2017

and then as a means of managing Public/Private Partnerships, which later morphed into Private Finance Initiatives (PFIs). The rationale behind these partnerships is to inject private finance into large public infrastructure projects, offloading set-up and operational risks onto the private sector. The benefit for the private partner is assured income. Theoretically, a sound contract overwrites tensions between long-term public good and short-term profit,[1] but PFI meetings can struggle with the notion of a common aim enabled through partnership when public and private goals are inimical (Alexander 2009).

Here I examine PRINCE2 meetings during a World Bank-funded IT project in the Turkish Treasury partly to see if that vision travels. But this is only part of the story. There can be considerable ambivalence about the function of meetings in the very place that gave rise to them in this shape. If this is what people like to call 'anthropology at home', then this is an uncanny home indeed. The opening example shows a familiar polarity: depending on context, a common-sense approach might variously take meetings to be either an efficient way of achieving things or pointless. I suggest that part of the reason for these differences are the antecedents of the meeting form, which continue to both mould and baffle anticipation; just because a form is inherited does not mean it always makes sense to its legatees. The meeting is a learned form the contours of which some navigate with dexterity but others regard with bemusement. I therefore also present PRINCE2 meetings in the context of a PFI project for a British government agency in order to explore what can happen when supposedly playing by home rules. I worked on both projects as an IT consultant who had been trained as an anthropologist.[2] As I show below, I was not the only one occupying multiple positions.

The use of sense and common sense in the preceding paragraphs is deliberate. Geertz (1975) nailed common sense for anthropology as a cultural system determining practical action. But I suggest that recovering the eighteenth-century meaning of common sense,[3] which draws on the simultaneity of individuals, roles, and a collective, would enhance understanding of a culturally specific form that has gone global and might explain why certain meetings do not run as expected; that particular, unarticulated idea of common sense failing to find purchase. Common sense is not always synonymous with cultural systems; it is also one specific cultural system embedded in early eighteenth-century philosophy. The familiar phrase of a meeting's chair embarking on a summation or recommendation after discussion, 'My sense of the meeting is . . .', draws directly on an inflection from that period suggesting an empathetic capacity.

Nor is this the only assumption that partly underscores such meetings and may not be easily translated to other settings: the technologies and protocols associated with the formal production of knowledge also help to explain why something so familiar causes so much exasperation. I am not claiming that meetings replicate laboratory protocols or rehearse Stoic philosophy, merely that these ways of ordering and understanding relationships may act as a heuristic for the meeting form.

My contention is that these kinds of meetings make, or are intended to make, time and sociality through the rational choreography of coexistent temporalities, scales of activity, and social relations. For the meeting, in this frame, is essentially relational. As Schwartzman notes, 'Meetings may be examined as individual or related events because what is clear from the cross-cultural literature . . . is that meetings always produce more meetings' (1989: 37). There is usually a pre-meeting to give legitimacy to the opening meeting. Subsequent meetings are poly-temporal in their references; multi-scalar in terms of tying together broader events, working groups, tasks, sub-tasks, milestones, deliverables, and so on; and recursive in the sense that pre- and post-meeting briefings rehearse the same content and form, and minutes return as agenda items to later instantiations of a meeting. Social relations are nominally ordered within the space of a meeting as potentially separate elements: persons and roles are brought together and, if not fused into one voice, then combined into a group with a common direction. And each of these modes of being exists in relation to other roles outside the meeting space/time but still within the bounded world of 'the project'.

But that boundedness is leaky; it doesn't hold.

These structured processes, mapped out in PRINCE2 manuals and protocols, typically exist *as if* they are delimited in space and time: isolated castles. While internally relational, they ignore related events and social relations outside the world of the project, which invariably spill in. Even within the imaginary, internal, closed system there are associations that are visible and invisible, permitted and unpermitted. To put it another way, the material documentary traces of meetings erase the informal, cumulative relationships that develop around and through these projects – muddying transparency and variously acting to impede, or enable, the agreements and outcomes that the meeting is there to generate.

Meetings perform this selective relationality through techniques of ordering events and time beyond the meeting, together with the ordering elements of a meeting itself: minutes, reports, and agendas with their commands to consider, receive, discuss, recommend, approve. In an effort to orchestrate debate further, some agendas (somewhat hopefully) attach duration to each item. Information to be discussed is filleted to digestible summaries,[4] raising further questions about the transparency of such meetings (see also Barry 2013). Complexity is cut to enable orderly progress; the tension between the selective 'as if' and the infinite 'is' perhaps contributes to familiar frustrations with meetings. The subjunctive form in these contexts eclipses the relations that variously enable or frustrate the meeting.

PRINCE goes international

Under Turgut Özal's premiership (1983-9), Turkey embraced economic liberalization. But political instability in the country, caused by successive coalitions, high inflation, economic crises, and internal war, meant that whereas it had been the 'darling of the [World] Bank' in the late 1980s, by 1993 its 'portfolio was considered the [World Bank's] weakest' (Kavalsky 2006: 7), requiring tighter fiscal management to support broader structural adjustments. An improved macroeconomic database was seen as essential for the Treasury's economic data analysis, enhancing the NPM virtue of increased transparency underpinning rational management. The IT project was intended both to enable good governance and to operate as an example.[5] The British company, which won the contract, specified PRINCE2 as their way of meeting this latter condition.

As an employee of the company, I spent eighteen months over a two-year period in the Turkish Treasury, joined by analyst or economist colleagues for different phases. The Turkish state bureaucracy at this time had a series of specific features (Alexander 2002). First, it was politicized, in the sense that each successive political coalition brought in a wholesale change to senior civil servants. Second, in order to cut through a complex and often sclerotic bureaucracy, Özal had introduced what was almost a privileged parallel structure of bright young things well versed in the latest economic and management theories. These officials were nicknamed Özal's little princes (or princesses) by disgruntled colleagues. The rapidity with which senior officials were replaced meant that many of the Treasury's staff were young and, whether or not they were little princes, in the absence of experienced colleagues in their economic area, they would constantly consult the university professors who had taught them on their undergraduate degrees.

We were given an office in the IT Department but reported to Emine,[6] the formidable Director-General (DG) of Economic Research, who lost her job, shortly after the project described below, when the Minister of Economy changed. In line with PRINCE2 protocols, we started by drawing up a Gantt chart, or workflow schedule. This shows graphically: (1) elapsed and actual time for the whole project plus each task within it; (2) relationships between tasks; and (3) 'dependencies', or which task must follow which, and which can run in parallel. Other Gantt chart elements are key deliverables from each task with deadlines and 'milestones', often tied to payments and marked by high-level project meetings.

The Gantt chart was devised in 1910-15 by Henry Gantt, an American mechanical engineer, following the *harmonogram*, invented in 1896 by Karol Adamiecki, a Polish economist, engineer, and early management theorist (Marsh 1975). These revolutionary ways of bringing together different elements of large, complex processes were contemporary with Taylor's *Principles of scientific management* (1911); indeed, Taylor and Gantt worked together in 1887 for two large steel producers (the Midvale and Bethlehem Steel corporations), applying those very scientific management principles. Gantt (1910) emphasized that management's role was to remove interferences from smoothly running processes; as with PRINCE2, the emphasis is on a controlled environment. Taylor, Gantt, and Adamiecki were engineers who sought methods of disembedding and transferring systems-control technology from mechanical production to any environment.[7] One example is the schedule that is reported against at progress and milestone meetings.

Data-gathering meetings with Treasury officials were also plotted out in the Gantt chart, according to a list of interviewees agreed with our client, Emine, who was, in turn, accountable to the World Bank. Each meeting, according to our conventional practice, had a previously circulated and agreed agenda identifying what was to be discussed. Later, we would turn extensive notes into an abstract map of Treasury data and processes. But repeatedly, to our consternation, we found that familiar methods implicitly based on assumptions of a particular kind of community and shared intentionality within a bounded project world just didn't work.

For example, the idea of an organization performing collectively towards a common goal stood little scrutiny.[8] Publishing given datasets gave considerable prestige to a DG. Several Directorates might publish the same variables but with different values and analyses – precisely what a rationalized database will not allow. But no one would relinquish their perceived ownership of the data. Bringing different DGs together in a meeting generated silence or agreement that (we were told later) was given in such a form as to indicate profound disagreement. It took us a long time to be able to read the 'no' in smiling agreement, usually indicated by a qualifier: 'Yes, of course. Although you must be aware that . . .'. Competition within institutions is *not* a Turkish peculiarity (Alexander 2001), it should be noted, and NPM 'internal markets' can add a further mode of division between departments. Resolution was achieved off-stage through Emine's cajoling or threats.

By the same token, our meetings to confirm common understandings after separate interviews often failed. We had yet to learn that it was outrageously impolite for junior staff to speak in front of their peers or bosses. As a result, DGs were the most voluble, but not always the most knowledgeable. Unequal statuses outside meeting spaces persisted within them. It was therefore only possible to refine our understanding of data and processes outside formal gatherings, which generated very different kinds of meetings from those where different voices and opinions are sought *en route* to devising appropriate actions.

The familiar to and fro of question, answer, and discussion was disrupted not only by hierarchies and rivalry enacted within the meeting space but also by an explicit delight in game-playing and performance. Thus, needing confirmation or otherwise that we had understood something correctly, we contacted Adem, the Research Officer who had originally given us the information. He prevaricated. He was busy. He could meet us but was unlikely to be able to help us. We set up a meeting. He took us to the corner of an open-plan office, testily repeating that we could ask him what we wanted but he wouldn't know the answers. People gathered round, grinning. We all knew that he did know the answers but just didn't feel inclined to help – something he demonstrated by folding his arms and leaning his chair back. The others watched as we went to and fro. Some at the back, slightly bored, began to play cards, looking up and listening occasionally. We tried again.

'We'd like to ask you something quite important'.

'Go on then', he said, smiling.

'But we can't, the question is too complex, too big'.

'Try'.

'We can't because it won't make sense on its own without context . . . We need other questions for that'.

'Then try'.

We rattled off questions. He answered quickly.

'And the big question?' he asked.

We looked at each other. The silence elongated and spread through the assembled listeners.

'There is no question is there?' he said. And he laughed. 'Now', he beamed, 'you're thinking like a Turk!'

The audience clapped and after this there were only cordial discussions with this Department. Here the finesse with which the game was played was foregrounded. This was trial by performance, evoking perhaps the improvisational competitions (*aitys*) between Kazakh bards (*akyn*) (Dubuisson 2014) or Sumatran poetic duels that perform political tensions through public dialogic exchange (Bowen 1989). Here, to quote Appadurai on tournaments of value, 'strategic skill is culturally measured by the success with which actors attempt diversions or subversions of culturally conventionalized paths for the flow of things' (1986: 21). While Adem's subversion had more to do with disrupting expected norms and forms than material objects, the explicit recognition of ingenuity still made this a contest. The 'special arena' Appadurai (1986) deems necessary for such tournaments was constituted by the audience. Again, dextrous manipulation of meeting forms is scarcely a Turkish phenomenon, but rarely is this so evident.

The notes from this meeting, in the form of minutes, simply recorded information given, by whom and when. Other meetings' minutes were similarly sparse. It was as if the various diversions, longueurs, and confusions had never happened; they were simply evacuated from the record. Minutes are notes and actions typically for attendees, often also taken to higher-level meetings to evidence progress. As such, they may be classed as a kind of literary technology of proliferation bearing virtual witness, and allowing witness to be borne to the acts of a given meeting. The reductiveness of these minutes indexed an ideal form where people come together simply to propel something forward through discussion.

Meetings also took place with external government agencies with whom the Treasury shared data. These were tricky connections to bring within the confines of a project schedule that crisply itemized and allocated duration to a sequence of phases, as though the environment it referenced were indeed controlled. It was at these meetings with senior colleagues in and outside the Treasury that the dexterity of Emine and her Deputy, Ercan, became apparent. Both had spent many years seconded to the World Bank in Washington, and while they privately complained how hard it was to get things done in Turkey, both were skilled operators with Turkish and foreign colleagues alike, constantly comparing and commenting on how things were done in Turkey, the States, and Europe.

Indeed, as Ercan and I were travelling one evening to a meeting with the Central Bank's Deputy Director to agree data formats, he wryly (and entirely accurately) predicted what would happen:

> He'll welcome us, offer coffee, cigarettes, and chocolate. We'll be taken to admire their mainframe computer, then we'll chat about nothing. After which, he will regretfully say he wished he could help us but it is out of his hands. And then we'll leave. And we'll go through this because we are oriental.

This was neither the first nor the last time Ercan would deploy the trope of Orientalism, placing himself simultaneously within the category – with his mocking 'we are oriental', which was delivered with a knowing grin – and outside it as a commentator who would use such a word. He invited ironic comparison between how such meetings might be seen by an outsider as a pointless exercise, and how things actually operated. And by his grin he acknowledged that he alone could occupy the double position of distance and partiality. This meeting failed as a transparent outcome-generating procedure; it worked, however, to maintain relatively harmonious operational alliances while relations between the Ministers of each institution were less than cordial. Data protocols were quietly agreed the following month.

Meetings with the World Bank and senior Treasury officials to assess progress at key junctures or make significant decisions brought together multiple understandings of what the meeting form was for, and how to achieve the 'outcome' that the Gantt chart and agenda indicated was the reason for gathering. Their significance was marked by holding them in Emine's vast room, which signalled her status and closeness to the Minister of the Economy, and by the retinue of junior staff brought by each senior official. One such meeting was to discuss the British analysts' interim report on hardware and software options with Treasury and World Bank representatives. The agenda set out the order of items. We sat, surrounded by junior staff, at Emine's table alongside her Deputies, senior Treasury DGs, and the World Bank project management team.

Ercan had met us in our hotel the night before to discuss how to play the meeting. We later learned he had also talked to the World Bank funders the same evening; we promptly set up another bilateral get-together with the World Bank. The day's meeting was punctuated by knowing looks between each party referencing their particular extra-camera conversation yet acting, at least in the case of the British and North American participants, as though it had no place in the present discussion.

About forty people were watching the meeting, some catching up with each other in hissed whispers that became louder as they lost interest in the proceedings.

Journal of the Royal Anthropological Institute (N.S.), 80-94
© Royal Anthropological Institute 2017

Mini-meetings sprouted around the room. Some people came and went. Some conferred with their bosses at the table in stage whispers. Coffee boys delivered orders. Occasionally, Emine would theatrically clutch at her heart, exclaiming that her blood pressure was rising to dangerous levels. This was usually a prelude to instructing the audience to be quiet or to announcing a break to restore a propriety more familiar to the World Bank. Such unminuted black holes were familiar from British meetings when angry exchanges, heated discussions, or helpless laughter would surge above the order of the meeting but be lost to the formal record.

The project's internal and external worlds were brought together in other ways. Emphasizing an option that met the Treasury's processing requirements, an analyst observed that a car should not be bought if only a bicycle were needed. The Banking DG's response was that a car was necessary as Ankara was hilly. While apparently a literal response to a metaphor, the comment also had metaphorical intent. While financial prudence indicated less hardware capacity, the Treasury's status among senior government ministries would be enhanced by extensive processing power. A willing funder only needed convincing.

Thus, despite, or because of, the many pre-meets, the meeting had no unified aim. Emine announced the final decision via telephone calls, after further informal, bilateral meetings. None of the documents provided for, or produced after, these Treasury meetings indicated the shifting relationships between the British company, the World Bank, and the Treasury, nor those between Emine, her colleagues, and her subordinates, nor, indeed, those between the Minister of Economy and the heads of other government organizations, all of which had a profound bearing on whether the project would work at all. This was far from being a controlled environment.

Where a NPM frame might applaud the entrepreneurial individual for getting things done (the 'can do, will do' attitude) without recourse to formal meetings, in the Treasury the formal and the informal went hand-in-hand: spectacle was a necessary corollary. Far from being a fiasco, the meeting had been part of the process, providing internal exhibitions of status and relations and external demonstrations of well-run meetings – when matters were hauled back to more recognizable forms. Further, by making explicit relations beyond roles in the meeting, it emphasized the common confusion in British meetings, which are enacted as if only formal, professional roles matter within a set-aside space but also acknowledge, implicitly, that external and internal relations *do* inform meetings.

In the Treasury the rational, ordering form of a meeting did not hold, nor was much store set by the performative technologies of a formal meeting. If a DG wanted to find out what had happened in a meeting, he or she spoke directly to someone who had been present, rather than referring to the minutes. Facts and knowledge did not have to be ritually witnessed in such a forum and formally inscribed. Far from acting as though the meeting were a set-aside space, the formal and the informal were integrated in a form that acknowledged hierarchies, external events, and politics.

There are echoes here with Simpson's account of NGOs' attempts to bring people together after a disaster in Gujarat into non-hierarchical meetings to discuss what to do. Meetings were renamed 'groups' and were rapidly mocked by participants precisely because they ignored social hierarchies that shaped the 'groups'. Simpson (2013: 33) describes how 'groups' became a farcical pastime and source of entertainment: 'we're going to do groups'. The comedy or 'surreal befuddlement' arose from the pretence that actual social organization, prior relationships, and histories were ignored.

Journal of the Royal Anthropological Institute (N.S.), 80-94
© Royal Anthropological Institute 2017

Our initial bewilderment lay in the difficulty in recognizing how decisions were being reached or what was being communicated. Treasury meetings seemed to fly in the face of a common-sense way of doing business efficiently and effectively.

And yet that shared unity of purpose does not always have purchase in a British setting.

PRINCE at home

Dewey (1998: 381) notes two distinct though related meanings for common sense. The first, drawing on the *Oxford English Dictionary*'s definition, suggests 'good, sound practical sense ... readiness in dealing with the ordinary affairs of life'. The second meaning refers to both the general feeling of community and accepted (regulative and normative) meanings within a community. Both traditions speak so closely to anthropology that it seems they have often simply disappeared. Common sense has become nothing but common sense, so obvious it is not extraordinary (see also Crehan 2011); indeed, in Herzfeld's much-quoted phrase, 'cultural anthropology is the comparative study of common sense ... unstated assumptions we share with others in our community' (2001: 1). Thus the typical anthropological take is that while common sense appears to be somehow universal to humanity, or at any rate apparently 'natural' as 'its tenets are immediate deliverances of experience' (Geertz 1983: 85, 83), it is in fact culturally specific. Strathern (1992) takes this a step further, discussing how, in contemporary Britain, the 'normal' is naturalized and a version of nature is normalized into common sense; 'nature' becomes the unquestioned cultural system, in other words.

Dewey's distinctions are useful in the context of meetings: they links their former meaning to 'judging the significance of things and events with reference to what should be done; the other in the ideas that are used to direct and justify activities and judgments' (1998: 381). Meetings that assess actions and events on the basis of reports and devise actions in response draw on both these kinds of common sense. But the second meaning contains more shades still. The notion of commonly held beliefs and meanings appears, somewhat reified, in Thomas Reid and Dugald Stewart's Scottish common-sense philosophy, as the highest authority, and again, with less reverence, in Gramsci's take on common sense. For Gramsci, the Italian *senso comune*, 'the traditional popular conception of the world' (1971: 199), is a heterogeneous jumble (Crehan 2011: 281) that is at once conservative, carries seeds of its transformation, and is profoundly unsystematic (2011: 282).

I suggest that the legacies of eighteenth-century common-sense philosophy continue to shape the meeting form. The *sensus communis* was celebrated by Reid, Stewart, and the Earl of Shaftesbury (Cooper 2001 [1732]) in a clear political stand against absolutist tradition that linked freedom and the voice of citizens; here it was the empathetic link between person and community, or public spirit. This was about the human ability to 'develop civic virtue through ... discovering shared understanding' (Agnew 2008: 55). Thomas Paine's pamphlet *Common sense* (1986 [1776]) emphasized the virtues of simple language and reasoning in discussing the relationship between individuals and large, complex societies: where to find 'the common' in societies that had ceased to be face-to-face.[9] Common-sense realism is thus 'the epistemological frame of modern democratic politics ... the capacity of the public to distinguish facts from fictions constituted the epistemological rationale for empowering democratic citizens and the decentralization of political power' (Ezrahi 2008: 49). This is the language of the French and American Revolutions; it is also the rhetoric of neoliberalism, coterminous with

PRINCE2.[10] Meetings in this frame are egalitarian, comprising plain-speaking, ordinary people. As the Turkish example indicates, this epistemological scaffold does not travel easily. The rhetoric also often fails to persuade closer to home, but still the idea holds that this is how meetings *ought* to be conducted.

Another meaning shadows 'sense'; its roots in old High German and Old English indicate direction, purpose, journeying. The Proto-Indo-European root *sent-* means 'to go'. The French *bon sens*, for common sense, also signifies 'direction'. This kind of gathering of people with a shared direction is something very different from a research symposium or seminar; the forward, purposeful focus translates easily into NPM-style meetings. It certainly allows for a rational, staged, goal-driven trajectory quite in line with both Enlightenment ideas of ordered progress and the phased structure of PRINCE2 punctuated by progress meetings; indeed, van Vree defines the modern meeting as 'gathering together ... to talk and come to a decision about a common future' (2011: 241). But where meetings are the site of performance, they may be concerned less with progress towards an agreed goal than with the affirmation and reconstitution of community – as Myers (1991) suggests was demonstrated in the meeting with the Pintupi and the Central Bank – with spectacle, or with the display of skill and status.

It might be expected that British meetings would show closer alignment with this model of common sense, remembering the genealogy of NPM and the technologies it spawned. However, while PFI meetings presupposed a shared goal, rather hopefully expressed as 'partnership', the project was riven by incommensurate aims: maximizing profit for the developer but long-term utility and staff 'buy-in' for the agency CEO. The freelance project managers working on behalf of the agency wanted work done well, fast, and cheaply: their reputation and future jobs were at stake. Performances might therefore also be used to halt progress in the perceived wrong direction, disturbing the meeting to dramatic effect: an effect only achieved if the participants first shared a sense of the proper form.

Thus, although meetings followed a previously agreed agenda, with the chair orchestrating formal discussion, most participants knew that formal meetings could be a gladiatorial arena where bluster and mockery could trip up 'opponents', making them reveal poor work in public before senior government officials. These subversionary devices worked through the form, rather than round it, as in the Treasury. Providing the technologies of fact creation were in place (the meeting had been 'called': i.e. it was named as such, there was an agenda, and there was quoracy to guarantee representation from all sides and witnesses), the PFI meeting space carried more revelatory heft and drama than in the Treasury. This, despite the occasional overt theatricality in Treasury meetings, and the apparently punctilious politesse of agency proceedings. The agency had its own meticulous Writing Guide, including agendas and minutes, both circulated via what is known as a 'Loose Minute', a precisely structured note short of a formal letter. The Guide emphasizes courtesy.

There were certain points in the life-cycle of this project when the parties' different aims were vividly foregrounded. Thus, in early meetings to define complex contracts, against which progress would subsequently be assessed, there were tensions between potential developers and project managers. In the potent semi-public space of the meeting, the trick was to lure the other side into saying something that would then constitute an agreement, or into revealing knowledge that could only then be used in shaping respective obligations, even if known informally before. Each negotiation meeting was preceded by briefings within each group determining how to 'play' the meeting, followed by debriefings to analyse the meeting and, on occasion, interruptions to the meetings themselves when one group needed to restore its own sense of purpose.

Paul, a former civil servant, now a consultant and lead negotiator, used to explain to his team the necessity of 'holding the line' or 'keeping the ball in the air' during meetings, supporting colleagues in public, whatever confusions might emerge. As one meeting dragged on with a potential American developer, Paul began to draw them into a deal that would tie them to a clear costing mechanism for future work. The American lawyer suddenly shouted, 'Whoa guys! We're entering a low-pressure area!' Confusion then ensued (including on the part of the supplier). The lawyer explained, 'It sucks!' Paul called 'Time!' making a T shape with his hands. We ran into the corridor, Paul hissing, 'What on *earth* is going on?' The other team emerged to have their own huddle clarifying their position before the meeting resumed. Time out was literally an unminuted interval.

As the project moved through PRINCE2 stages, relationships of antipathy or warmth developed within and between teams. But these biographies of meetings had no lasting trace in the escalating pile of documents that went into meetings or minutes that emerged from them, even though, as participants knew, an angry exchange at one meeting, or in external encounters, could result in a highly charged atmosphere the next time. Just as Treasury minutes were emptied of interactions beyond decisions and noted information, so these PFI minutes extracted humour and anger from events, producing only a laconic record that bore witness to due process – often teleologically referencing a possible future audit. Indeed, just as written actions were often ascribed not to people but to the organizations they represented, so, on occasion, would the formality be heightened by individuals being addressed in meetings explicitly as their organization's voice: 'What does the agency consider to be the best way forward?'

Skilled in the arts of formal meetings, Paul was also adept at puncturing the form to foreground or provoke what might otherwise be obscured by careful choreography. Having heard informally that Charles and Simon, two developers, were ignoring agency staff's concerns, Paul would nettle them in the hope they might inadvertently reveal something that could be captured in the formal progress meeting, hoping to draw attention to where observance of the form betrayed the project's nominal purpose. In response to their misleading summaries of staff consultations, Paul would mildly reply, 'Well, of course, you're right, Charlie', or 'It's very simple, Simon'. Irritated responses were followed by a lengthy discussion of what could or could not be recorded: 'Minute that, would you, please?', or 'Strike! strike!' As much time could be spent deciding what would be minuted or not as on substantive discussion. As in the Turkish Treasury, high-level meetings were frequently attended by large numbers on both sides, but this was typically deployed as an intimidatory tactic.

Great care was taken to appear to follow due form, partly because of the power it held to ratify and reveal, partly to avoid challenge from the 'other side'. Thus, in order to maintain outer propriety, coded language arose within the world of the project, a common phenomenon in any institution. Thus 'I was rather surprised to note x or y' was a furious request to explain an event. Paul laughingly detailed the gradations implicit when declaring 'concern', 'serious concern', or, finally, 'grave concern' over inadequate progress. This last indicated that the agency head was likely to be warned of poor work. Such codes within the project's world, and again within each group, were arguably at odds with the idea of a transparent language for the common person.

Again, echoing Ercan's distancing move, Paul would occasionally try to halt particular decisions by saying to either the agency (his employer) or the developer, 'As a *tax-payer*, I am seriously concerned ... ', deftly rearranging relations of accountability, restoring the multiple contradictory relations and roles each person held, and recalibrating the direction. Such interventions deliberately ruptured formality, highlighting dissonances between external complexity and internal assumptions around singular roles and the set-apart space of meetings.

Two traditions are at play in granting legitimacy to who is entitled to speak, make representation, and assent to facts. Van Vree (2011) describes the 'meeting class' of the Dutch Republic, an elite defined by its ability to participate correctly in such gatherings. This league of gentlemen is quite different from the community of plain-speaking people to whom Paine addressed himself in plain tongue: one is bound together by markers of distinction, the other by empathy. These contradictory legacies of the right of members of a gathering to speak, note, and contribute indicate the multiplicity of persons, or, one might say, hats, coexisting in a meeting: persons there by right of a role (who may well have other roles); persons there by right of membership of a given project or community, represented by that meeting, who speak as persons with a life beyond the role; and persons speaking as their role(s) (the hats). This plethora of personae being simultaneously inhabited may partly account for confusions around the meeting table ('Which hat are you speaking with now?') and tensions over whether all members' speech is equally valid.[11] Summoning the notion that everyone present was accountable to tax-paying citizens, brought in quite a different public, a different logic of representation and legitimacy, and gave Paul a different voice and relation to those present and those beyond the room.

Paul's manoeuvres also challenged the formal space/time of the meeting. Almost like a laboratory, meetings are set up as a defined, separate space (identified on both the agenda and the minutes), selecting phenomena from the project's world, but standing outside it in order to contemplate and act on selected elements. But as countless studies of laboratory science have shown (e.g. Latour & Woolgar 1979; Traweek 1992), far from being a white-coated retreat in contemplation of the natural world, labs are as overflowing with complex human relationships and politics as anywhere else, both within a given laboratory community and in the external political forces that shape it. And this is my point with project meetings. Seligman, Weller, Puett, and Simon argue that ritualized frames for actions create a shared 'subjunctive ... "as if" or "could be" universe' (2008: 7-8, 17-42). The potency of ritual is shared by that form of the meeting that is 'called' into being. Thus meetings are taken *as if* they were set-aside places outside time for the purposes of ordering and making time; members are supposed to act *as if* they were one part of an equal meeting membership, *as if* they were representative roles, with no other connection; material and literary technologies, to kidnap a phrase, display meetings *as if* they were abstract, logically ordered, dispassionate events. This is a subjunctive aesthetic; the meeting is a subjunctive form.

The fact of sociality within and beyond the meeting room, of ruptures to orderliness, of uncontained inflowing external relations, of rancour and humour, always seems to come as a surprise to those less adept at playing through the form.

British meetings that rigidly exclude the informal are more likely to provoke exasperation among participants attempting to enact the selective relationality demanded by the subjunctive form: as if prior relationships between participants do not exist; as if the meeting space is framed and held by its technologies of knowledge production; as if times, spaces, events, and relations external to the meeting technologies affect neither discussion nor decision; as if singularity and coherence of purpose unite people and practice.

A comparative coda

This has also been an exercise in comparison. The very notion of a special issue suggests that meetings are a sufficiently common ethnographic category to allow instances to be examined side by side, in what Candea (2016) calls 'lateral comparison'. The form of the two case studies presented here invites comparison, although more of the implied 'West'/home versus 'Rest' variety. But that is not my intention. I have instead considered how each instance compares against an abstract model, the very existence of which assumes comparison is possible, that there is a common essence to these events, which allows discrete instances to be marshalled into a single frame. The possibility of comparison is embedded in the globalization of certain methods of 'doing meetings', the idea that they can be enacted in the same way, to the same effect each time.

I have suggested, however, that the formal meeting has been shaped by assumptions now partly out of time and often out of place. Nevertheless, in some contexts, it can endow what is said and done with a certain legitimizing ritual power. Skilful players can subvert the form in different ways using the public setting and formal legitimacy to give informal knowledge the weight and potency of revelation, juxtaposing and comparing formally presented documents with alternative or fuller accounts from which they were extracted. Notable in both cases was the strategic use of self-reflection and assertion of different, sometimes contradictory, roles and affiliations in order to provide an external point from which comparative critique could be made – and the disjuncture foregrounded between inflowing externalities and complexity and the subjunctive form of the set-aside space where unity, democractic deliberation, and orderly progression are enacted. Even if I have not intended a West/Rest comparison, Ercan, mockingly, placed it centre-stage.

The implied abstraction of the meeting form obscures its genealogy: the content of the form is specific. Where a West/Rest comparison mediated by common characteristics might be expected, a form appears instead that is a necessarily incomplete rendering down of external complexity, and often deployed to ends quite different from those on the nominal agenda. Informants move in and out of subjunctive meeting frames to ensure progress happens, either by physically walking outside a room or by indicating what is and is not to be recorded, or by switching roles, joking, using subtexts, and drawing the outside in. Thus the trust in the form and in the apparent transparency that it brings, as legacies from a particular kind of emergent public, is variously traduced and bolstered by the amplitude of relations, activities, and documents that surround and invade the leaky worlds of project meetings.

NOTES

My thanks to the editors for inviting me to take part in the initial ASA panel and this special issue and for their comments, particularly those of Adam Reed and Tom Yarrow. I am grateful both to Michael Carrithers for his close reading and all-round kindness and to the *JRAI* reviewers for their extremely helpful comments.

[1] These partnerships have been criticized for merely delaying or hiding public sector debt, increasing infrastructural cost (Gaffney & Pollock 1999), and creating a contractual lock-in to a single supplier (e.g. Lonsdale 2005).

[2] I worked on these projects as a consultant before, during, and after training as an anthropologist, continuing to reflect on these Treasury experiences with informants the following year during fieldwork in

other Turkish institutions. All such projects included long reflections with colleagues on meetings and the broader success or not of these abstract forms that inhibited some actions and demanded others. I kept copious notes as the Office of Government Commerce (OGC) representative on this PFI project and was interested in a research project, once I returned to academia, into why so many IT projects fail. The OGC used to sponsor best practice in procurement. It was closed in 2011.

³ The thought, as with so many, was sparked by a comment made by Keith Hart.

⁴ Junior civil service staff usually prepare briefing notes for senior meeting discussions or indicate to their bosses, through red tabs inserted into large documents, where the key items are to be found. The power to determine what is and is not made formally visible thus often rests with junior staff.

⁵ Although this macroeconomic database project took place in 1993, the same projects continue to be funded by the World Bank.

⁶ All names have been anonymized.

⁷ Akin notes that Gantt sought to take rational managerialism far further than Taylor, setting up a political organization in 1916, the New Machine, which aimed to bring harmonious efficiency to social and political life as much as industry in the interests of 'true democracy' (1977: 52).

⁸ This was exacerbated occasionally by different economics professors having different views on how best to approach economic definitions and management. Thus, the State Planning Organization and the State Institute of Statistics favoured different baskets of items for calculating the Consumer Price Index (CPI). In turn, depending on affiliations, loyalties, and networks often forged at university, different Treasury officials would use different CPIs for calculations.

⁹ Paine does not, of course, base his reasoning on common sense as common usage or universal consent.

¹⁰ While Arendt (1990: 236) thought the failure to cultivate common sense as found in New England town meetings might explain why democracy had not prevented twentieth-century totalitarianism, Rosenfeld (2011) notes that, in contemporary politics, appeals to common sense are mainly made by right-wing politicians.

¹¹ Specialist knowledge might be via additional invited members of a meeting, noted as being 'in attendance', and who typically have fewer rights to engage in meetings through discussion and decision.

REFERENCES

AGNEW, L.P. 2008. *Outward, visible propriety: Stoic philosophy and eighteenth-century British rhetorics.* Columbia: University of South Carolina Press.

AKIN, W. 1977. *Technocracy and the American Dream: the technocrat movement, 1900-1941.* Berkeley: University of California Press.

ALEXANDER, C. 2001. Legal and binding: time change and long-term transactions. *Journal of the Royal Anthropological Institute (N.S.)* **7**, 467-85.

——— 2002. *Personal states: people and bureaucracy in Turkey.* Oxford: University Press.

——— 2009. Illusions of freedom: Polanyi and the third sector. In *Market and society: The great transformation today* (eds) C. Hann & K. Hart, 221-39. Cambridge: University Press.

APPADURAI, A. 1986. Introduction: commodities and the politics of value. In *The social life of things: commodities in cultural perspective* (ed.) A. Appadurai, 3-63. Cambridge: University Press.

ARENDT, H. 1990. *On revolution.* Harmondsworth: Penguin.

BARRY, A. 2013. *Material politics: disputes along the pipeline.* Oxford: Wiley-Blackwell.

BOWEN, J. 1989. Poetic duels and political change in the Gayo Highlands of Sumatra. *American Anthropologist* **91**, 25-40.

CANDEA, M. 2016. De deux modalités de comparaison en anthropologie sociale (trans. F. Lemonde). *L'Homme* **218**, 183-218.

COOPER, A.A. (Earl of Shaftesbury) 2001 [1732]. *Sensus communis, an essay on the freedom of wit and humour.* In *Characteristicks of men, manners, opinions, times* (ed. D. Den Uyl), vol. **1**, 57-94. Indianapolis: Liberty Fund.

CREHAN, K. 2011. Gramsci's concept of common sense: a useful concept for anthropologists? *Journal of Modern Italian Studies* **16**, 273-87.

DEWEY, J. 1998. Common sense and scientific inquiry. In *The essential Dewey*, vol. 1: *Pragmatism, education, democracy* (eds L.A. Hickman & T.M. Alexander), 380-90. Bloomington: Indiana University Press.

DUBUISSON, E.-M. 2014. Dialogic authority: Kazakh *aitys* poets and their patrons. In *Ethnographies of the state in Central Asia: performing politics* (eds) M. Reeves, J. Rasanayagam, & J. Beyer, 55-77. Bloomington: Indiana University Press.

EZRAHI, Y. 2008. Einstein's unintended legacy: the critique of common-sense realism and post-modern politics. In *Einstein for the 21st Century: his legacy in science, art and modern culture* (eds) P. Galison, G. Holton & S. Schwever, 48-58. Princeton: University Press.

GAFFNEY, D. & A. POLLOCK 1999. Pump-priming the PFI: why are privately financed hospital schemes being subsidized? *Public Money and Management* **19**, 55-62.

GANTT, H. 1910. *Work, wages and profits: their influence on the cost of living*. New York: Engineering Magazine Company.

GEERTZ, C. 1975. Common sense as a cultural system. *The Antioch Review* **33**: 1, 5-26.

——— 1983. *Local knowledge: further essays in interpretive anthropology*. New York: Basic Books.

GRAMSCI, A. 1971. *Selections from the prison notebooks* (trans. Q. Hoare & G. Nowell-Smith). London: Lawrence & Wishart.

HERZFELD, M. 2001. *Theoretical practice in culture and society*. Oxford: Wiley-Blackwell.

HOOD, C. 1991. A public management for all seasons. *Public Administration* **69**, 3-19.

KAVALSKY, B. 2006. *The World Bank in Turkey, 1993-2005: an IEG Country Assistance Evaluation*. Washington, DC: IBRD/World Bank.

KUZMANOVIC, D. 2012. *Refractions of civil society in Turkey*. Basingstoke: Palgrave Macmillan.

LATOUR, B. & S. WOOLGAR 1979. *Laboratory life: the construction of scientific facts*. Beverly Hills, Calif.: Sage.

LONSDALE, C. 2005. Post-contractual lock-in and the UK Private Finance Initiative (PFI): the cases of National Savings and Investments and the Lord Chancellor's Department. *Public Administration* **85**, 67-88.

MARCUS, G. & M.J. FISCHER 1986. *Anthropology as cultural critique: an experimental moment in the human sciences*. Chicago: University Press.

MARSH, E. 1975. The harmonogram of Karol Adamiecki. *The Academy of Management Journal* **18**, 358-64.

MYERS, F. 1991. *Pintupi country, Pintupi self: sentiment, place, and politics among Western Desert Aborigines*. Berkeley: University of California Press.

PAINE, T. 1986 [1776]. *Common sense* (ed. I. Kramnick). London: Penguin.

RILES, A. (ed.) 2006. *Documents: artifacts of modern knowledge*. Ann Arbor: University of Michigan Press.

ROSENFELD, S. 2011. *Common sense: a political history*. Cambridge, Mass.: Harvard University Press.

SCHWARTZMAN, H.B. 1989. *The meeting: gatherings in organizations and communities*. New York: Springer.

SELIGMAN, A., R. WELLER, M. PUETT & B. SIMON 2008. *Ritual and its consequences: an essay on the limits of sincerity*. Oxford: University Press.

SIMPSON, E. 2013. *The political biography of an earthquake: aftermath and amnesia in Gujarat, India*. London: Hurst.

STRATHERN, M. 1992. *After nature: English kinship in the late twentieth century*. Cambridge: University Press.

TAYLOR, F. 1911. *The principles of scientific management*. New York: Harper & Brothers.

TRAWEEK, S. 1992. *Beamtimes and lifetimes: the world of high-energy physicists*. Cambridge, Mass.: Harvard University Press.

VAN VREE, W. 2011. Meetings: the frontline of civilization. *The Sociological Review* **59**: S1, 241-62.

De la réunion comme forme subjonctive : projets informatiques publics-privés dans les bureaucraties nationales britannique et turque

Résumé

Sur la base de réunions dans des environnements de projet structurés, en Turquie et en Grande-Bretagne, cet essai cherche à savoir si ce type de réunion très rationnelle et instrumentale voyage bien, et si oui, comment, et pourquoi elles paraissent si frustrantes à la plupart des participants britanniques. Les réunions qui ont lieu au sein de la direction administrative turque n'ont pas répondu aux attentes : elles incluaient des relations tant formelles qu'informelles et tournaient au spectacle et au concours de compétences. L'auteure suggère que les critères définissant une réunion en bonne et due forme découlent d'une généalogie britannique de bon sens et de technologies de création de faits qui n'ont pas forcément cours ailleurs. Leur application ne va d'ailleurs pas de soi « chez nous », bien que le « bon sens » soit souvent considéré comme le simple équivalent de l'action pratique dans les systèmes culturels, c'est-à-dire la façon dont on fait les choses. Au lieu de cela, la réunion type modelée par la tradition s'avère une forme subjonctive, une fiction de relationnalité sélective dans laquelle la réunion et le projet sont traités comme s'ils étaient des espaces à part, où les participants agiraient comme s'ils n'avaient qu'un seul rôle formel, isolé de leur tissu de relations formelles et informelles, et où des informations hautement synthétisées permettraient que la discussion progresse vers un but commun.

Journal of the Royal Anthropological Institute (N.S.), 80-94
© Royal Anthropological Institute 2017

5

Where knowledge meets: heritage expertise at the intersection of people, perspective, and place

THOMAS YARROW *Durham University*

Drawing on ethnographic research with heritage professionals in Scotland, the essay explores meetings as organizational devices for differentiating and relating various forms of epistemic, social, and material context. The account describes how the bureaucratic ideal of institutional consistency is achieved through staged encounters between the perspectives of the various people who meet, and the buildings that are the objects of their meeting. These ethnographic examples are used to develop two linked points. Firstly, it is suggested that the lens of 'meeting' complicates the relatively monolithic characterizations of heritage expertise evident in widely influential deconstructive critiques of heritage practice. Secondly, it is argued that heritage practitioners' own accounts of these negotiations highlight material and spatial dimensions of bureaucratic conduct that have that have received relatively little ethnographic attention in prevalent textually orientated accounts.

Recent work on heritage has given relatively little attention to the practices through which the past is produced by heritage experts and the institutions for which they work. Brumann notes that '[i]n comparison to what we know about the carriers and consumers of heritage, we are much less informed about heritage institutions and their personnel' (2014: 182). He suggests various reasons for this: methodological issues of institutional access mean that texts are often taken as a proxy for the institutional practices they supposedly represent; theoretically, recent critical scholarship has led to insightful descriptions of the politics of heritage knowledge, but often at the expense of a more ethnographically grounded understanding of practices and concepts in which heritage professionals engage (cf. Jones & Yarrow 2013). Since the 1980s, poststructurally inspired, critically deconstructive approaches have developed from a once radical critique to an orientation that now has a near hegemonic hold on interdisciplinary accounts of heritage practice. While anthropologists have contributed insightfully to these debates, ethnographic engagements have often been circumscribed by analytical and methodological assumptions that pertain more generally in accounts of bureaucratic practice. As Brown recently highlights: '[A]nthropologists are less inclined to treat bureaucracy as an object of study in its own right than as a backdrop for meditations on the "injustices of social stratification"' (2010: 741). Anthropologists of organizational practice (as discussed by Mosse 2005 and Yarrow, 2011), like interdisciplinary accounts of heritage studies (see Brumann 2014; Jones & Yarrow 2013), have more prevalently engaged in morally inflected critiques of bureaucratic conduct than in situated ethnographic accounts of the ethical and ideological commitments of those involved.

Extending recent efforts to move beyond these analytical frameworks (Brumann 2012; 2014; Jones & Yarrow 2013; Macdonald 2009; Yarrow & Jones 2014), and building on conceptual frameworks outlined in the introduction to this volume, I aim to develop an ethnographic description of the forms and effects of meetings as central elements of heritage practice. The account draws on ethnographic research based at Historic Scotland,[1] the national government agency with responsibility for conserving, investigating, and promoting the historic environment. Focusing on two forms of meeting, I highlight how these gatherings are constituted as a situated interplay between difference and similarity, in which epistemic, personal, and institutional issues are simultaneously and complexly at play. My account builds on earlier accounts of meetings, in particular Schwartzman's (1989) theorization of these as organizational devices, involving staged relationships between those negotiations framed as 'internal' to the meeting, and the various 'external' objects that frame and are framed by these interactions. However, her focus on these as 'communicative events' elides key dimensions of the meetings at the heart of this essay. Seeking to highlight the material and spatial dimensions of these meetings as integrally constitutive of social relations and epistemic forms, I take inspiration from recent accounts which have variously questioned a material/social distinction as an adequate analytical basis for understanding organizational knowledge (Boyer 2008; Bruun-Jensen & Winthereik 2013; Hull 2012; Mol 2002; Yarrow 2011). Rather than understand expertise to inhere in abstract propositional claims or universalizing discourses, I examine institutional knowledge as this unfolds through meetings as a series of situated relationships between people, places, tools, and documents (Latour 1993; Law 1994; Mol 2002). While, analytically, I start from an essentially Latourian understanding of action as a distributed property of these relationships, I aim to describe concepts and practices animated by heritage professionals' own more binary conception of the subjects and objects of meeting.[2] Specifically, the essay highlights heritage experts' understandings of historic buildings as active participants in the process of negotiating and aligning perspective.

Central to the account is the issue of how the aim of institutional consistency is achieved in the face of multiple, often contradictory, expert perspectives, in indeterminate relationship to the specific qualities of buildings that are the objects of their attention. I trace how meetings 'conjure' (Abrams, this volume) buildings as objects through which institutional (epistemic and personal) relationships are staged and manged. By the same token, the account explores how buildings are attributed a range of qualities, including 'character', 'personality', 'authenticity', and 'integrity', that are imagined to facilitate the institutional meeting of people and expertise.

Conservation and consistency

Employees of Historic Scotland see conservation as a complex endeavour in which the broad aim of preserving nationally significant elements of the historic environment involves co-ordination of diverse forms of expertise, including from architects, archaeologists, scientists, historians, and career civil servants. These various experts share an understanding of their knowledge as 'complementary', an idea often concretized in the image of their different approaches as 'pieces in a jigsaw'. Heritage experts also recognize the problems that result from epistemic plurality, specifically describing how this can be inimical to the aim of achieving an 'institutional view' characterized by a consistency of approach across time and space.

At Historic Scotland, the importance and ubiquity of 'meeting' relate to the central importance placed on the consistent realization of an 'institutional approach'. James expresses the importance of collective decision-making as part of a broader civil service orientation:

> When we speak, when I speak, [if] I'm responding to people regarding a planning case, it's not just me. It's my face, my words, but it's Historic Scotland that's speaking . . . So you've got however many people's knowledge that you can tap into and discuss things with . . . We've all got to deal with the same environment that we work with, so we'd all sit to discuss it.

Brian, a Heritage Manager with a degree in archaeology and architecture, is responsible for the protection of buildings of designated historic significance via various forms of 'listing'. During an interview, he acknowledges his own 'personal' interest in buildings even as he highlights the need to suspend this:

> There is a conservation value in itself in doing something consistently and impartially because there's that idea that you need a system that is trusted and is considered to be a good system for decision-making about the historic environment and so the consistency feeds into that. Consistency and impartiality is pretty important to the protection of buildings.

As has been described in other civil service contexts, the ethical attributes of the 'good' bureaucrat are articulated in Weberian terms as a commitment to a form of objective conduct (du Gay 2000). Shared institutional procedures, aims, and professional dispositions are utilized as ways of detaching 'what' is known from the 'personal' perspectives, interests, and subjectivities of the specific people who know it. In this context, bureaucratic detachment is valued as a way of maintaining the historic environment 'as it is', isolating it from the various current interests that can threaten it.

As civil servants, employees' commitments to the institutional ideal of consistency are grounded by national policy and legislation, reflecting conservation approaches set out in a series of international charters. From the Burra Charter (ICOMOS 1999 [1979]) onwards, there has been increasing recognition of the 'intangible values' of heritage and of the need to conserve the past with an understanding of the 'social values' attributed to it by various people in the present (see Pendlebury 2009 for a detailed discussion). Even so, much of the focus of conservation at Historic Scotland, as more generally in conservation organizations, continues to be on the maintenance of the 'authenticity' of buildings, monuments, and objects, defined in more materialist terms. These explicitly draw on the nineteenth-century conservation movement, notably the ideas of William Morris and John Ruskin, and on earlier international charters (e.g. ICOMOS 1964). Where history is regarded as process of temporal progression, the unfolding of unique sequentially ordered events, buildings, monuments, and artefacts acquire a value as uniquely authentic embodiments of these times. Throughout the organization, employees describe the existence of a common 'conservation philosophy' reflecting these ideals: the authenticity of historic fabric is protected through the key principle of 'minimal intervention', an acknowledgement of the damage entailed in any form of modification; the principle of conservation 'as found' likewise relates to an axiomatic understanding of the impossibility of reconstructing what has been lost;

Journal of the Royal Anthropological Institute (N.S.), 95-109
© Royal Anthropological Institute 2017

finally, where intervention is judged to be necessary, an 'evidence-based' approach is used to ensure that damage is minimized. As set out in national policy and guidance (much of which Historic Scotland has helped to formulate), these provide the framing criteria for a consistent approach.

Policies necessarily exist at a level of abstraction that is consistent with the policy imperative of universal applicability, but complexities, ambiguities, and differences of opinion inevitably arise as these are related to specific contexts and cases. Across different parts of the agency, particularly in relation to the Conservation and Heritage Management division, much of the work of conservation inheres in the tensions that become evident in this shift from the general to the particular. Joe, a Heritage Manager with an archaeological training, articulates this broader point in relation to his own experience dealing with applications to undertake work with the potential to impact the buildings or monuments of designated historic significance: 'It's about mediating between legislation and policy and the needs of any given applicant'. Various forms of indeterminacy arise from these shifts between clearly but abstractly defined 'policy' and the complex and specific details of cases in 'practice'.

The distinct interests, approaches, and epistemic commitments of these various heritage experts likewise relate to differences that are seen to require negotiation and reconciliation. Heritage Managers, for example, have training in architectural and archaeological backgrounds that are associated with distinct, sometimes conflicting, orientations to the importance of form and fabric as respective arbiters of authenticity (Jones & Yarrow 2013). In simplistic terms, architects tend to privilege originality of appearance, seeing buildings as embodiments of the creative visions of specific individuals, by contrast to archaeologists, whose concerns to protect fabric are underpinned by understandings of this as a record of historic process. These differences are reflected in, and reproduced through, distinct legislative instruments for protecting the historic environment: 'scheduling' is used to protect archaeological monuments, placing greater emphasis on the protection of 'original fabric' than is the case for 'listed' buildings, a designation normally applied to structures that are roofed and in use. Even amongst colleagues with similar training, different specialisms and personal perspectives lead to more or less divergent assessments, not only about how this legislation should be interpreted, but even, more rarely, about which of these legislative instruments is most appropriate to use. Heritage Managers acknowledge the necessarily interpretative nature of what they do in the often-recounted joke that in a meeting of ten, there will be eleven opinions on any given issue.

At the intersection between a regulatory ideal of consistency and one that celebrates interdisciplinary collaboration, meetings are regarded as key institutional contexts in which epistemic differences are expressed, negotiated, and aligned. Where, to paraphrase Mol (2002), there is always 'more than one' perspective on what should happen, the imperative of consistency requires that these must always be resolved as outcomes and agreements through which difference is aligned as 'less than many'.

The subsequent ethnographic sections of this essay demonstrate how meetings accomplish this in a range of ways. In order to highlight the emergent qualities of these interactions, my account unfolds via two extended ethnographic vignettes. Through these, I aim to demonstrate how, from the perspective of those involved, the achievement of consistency emerges by means of meetings that involve the simultaneous negotiation of various forms of epistemic, social, and material context.

Journal of the Royal Anthropological Institute (N.S.), 95-109
© Royal Anthropological Institute 2017

Site meeting

Graham, a District Architect, echoes others at Historic Scotland when he stresses the importance of site meetings: 'No matter how much documentation you put in front of someone, it's a bit like reading a book about Venice without actually experiencing the place ... it's a different thing. But when you're all looking at the problem right then, you with me, that's it!' Resonating with broader institutional discourses, he stresses the 'practical' nature of these interactions as key to the resolution that results: 'We all have postgraduate degrees ... [but] at the end of the day it all comes down to pragmatic decisions on site'. From the perspective of those involved, the epistemic meeting of disciplinary and institutional difference emerges through a physical meeting with specific buildings and sites. As Graham makes explicit, perspectives are changed when experts are moved from office to site.

Some of these dynamics are evident during a site visit to Dunkeld Abbey, undertaken as part of the Annual Monument Audit (AMA), a yearly assessment of the condition of the properties in Historic Scotland's care, and a chance to plan future conservation strategies and interventions. The Abbey, which is mostly Norman and Gothic, is set amongst trees, with manicured lawns sloping down to the nearby River Tay. The front part is roofed and is still in use. The back is un-roofed with the stone severely eroding. Although the building is conserved to appear as a timeless relic of the past, its materially and structurally precarious state raises a series of conservation issues that are a central focus of the meeting. The question of what to do is complex and unresolved, for two main reasons: not only are a range of possible actions consistent with the conservation principles and philosophies that frame their engagements, but also differences of role and training situate these issues in specific ways.

As at other AMAs, the meeting is overseen by the District Architect, the person with responsibility for planning and overseeing conservation work. Originally from the West of Scotland, Clare has a background in commercial architecture, and while she stresses the importance of conservation principles, she characterizes her own approach as that of a 'pragmatist'. Clare's counterpart in the Heritage Management team is Peter. An archaeologist by training, his role is to ensure that conservation interventions are consistent with the agency's regulations and approach, both through informal guidance and through overseeing a formal consent process. Also present at the site visit are Gordon, whose role as the regional head of the Works team is to oversee and direct the squads who undertake the practical work of conservation, and Vicki, the cultural resource expert, who has a degree in history, and brings to the meeting a detailed knowledge of the cultural and historic significance of the site. Reflecting international guidance laid out in the Burra Charter, considerations of 'significance' are formally central to conservation decision-making in Historic Scotland, but the 'pragmatic' tenor of the meeting seems often to leave Vicki with little to say about these ostensibly less tangible considerations. Authority is negotiated through interactions in relation to institutional and material contexts that give some claims more traction than others.

Dressed in hard hats, we climb to the top of the scaffolding. The meeting takes the form of a walking tour, following the sequence of illustrated issues laid out in the document produced by Clare: a series of plans, highlighting key problems and issues. The point, as both Clare and Peter make explicit, is to establish 'principles' and a 'methodology' as the basis for an approach that will inform a later, formally documented application for the work to be undertaken. Clare has planned the meeting as a tour of the building, with particular elements selected to highlight broader issues and to enable

Journal of the Royal Anthropological Institute (N.S.), 95-109
© Royal Anthropological Institute 2017

agreement on an approach that is acceptable to all. Peter explains the consent process she will need to follow: 'So you need an example photograph: what's going to happen and why'. Conversation is orientated towards the agreement of decisions and 'actions', prefigured in the site pro-forma filled out by Clare.

The first element selected is the wallhead, 'rough racked' stone, where Clare indicates how the existing asphalt covering has eroded to reveal the stones beneath. Her preferred approach is replacement of the original. Peter wonders whether it might be possible to use Sarnafil, a product that is cheaper and can be less damaging to the existing fabric. There is discussion between Clare and Peter about the potential of using this. No consensus is reached, beyond the conclusion that more research needs to be done. Clare notes this as a future 'action' she will need to initiate. We walk along the scaffolding to the next example. Clare holds her annotated diagram up against the stone. Eyes move between the two. Gordon is brought into the discussion by Clare: 'What do you think as a mason, Gordon?' He feels the stone, knocks it, and picks at some loose material: 'I'd just leave that; that's pretty sound'.

Clare's role is to choreograph the perspectives of others, drawing out different views and opinions, and seeking to ascertain where these depart and where they coincide. By training, these experts read the building differently from each other, their visions inculcated through formal education and practical experience, in ways of seeing that are indissoluble from ways of thinking and acting. Even as these dispositions impose constraints on what and how these professionals see, their knowledge is more or less significantly extended through their interactions with one another and with the material conditions of specific sites and the issues these raise (Jones & Yarrow 2013). The meeting constitutes a specific 'ecology of attention' (Grasseni 2007) in which perspectives align and bifurcate through situated encounters with the building. Conversation emerges at the intersection of these perspectives, sometimes in consensus and agreement, sometimes in conflict. The choreography of the meeting is intended to ensure that even where perspectives diverge, they do so in relation to an object that is shared. Experts congregate, eyes focused, drawn together by pointing hands, and by the graphical representations that Clare has made: diagrams, as stripped-back versions of an otherwise unthinkably complex building, focus attention on 'key points' and make the building legible as a series of 'issues'.

Peter makes explicit the bigger problems they are facing at the site: 'Multi layers of conservation history stacked on top of each other – where do we start? One hundred years from now its age is going to be *circa* 1920'. His comment highlights the difficulty of defining 'authenticity' and the paradox that conservation itself leads to change, even as it stresses continuity. Conservation guidelines dictate an approach of 'minimum intervention', but the term entails a contradiction that allows for different possible interpretations. Peter is concerned that measures to stabilize and conserve the building could entail a loss of original fabric: 'All the proper masonry will have gone'. Clare responds, conveying her sense that the difficulty of the situation shouldn't prevent any action from being taken: 'I think what we're doing is maintenance in one big chunk that would have been done over the centuries. We shouldn't use the problems as an excuse not to do anything. *We need to do something!*' she exclaims in a tone of frustrated urgency: 'It's just folly to walk away from it – more pieces are going to fall'. We walk to the next point, looking for the stonework depicted on Clare's diagram. Clare remarks drily, 'We'll be replacing the rotten scaffold before we get to the stone'. She is joking, though her point is serious: aware as she is of the need for a careful and consensual approach, she is cognizant of the dangers and costs of delaying intervention. Later she will explain these to me in the car back to the office. Scaffolding has been in place for several months, tying up resources that could more productively be used for other projects. She acknowledges that the consent process is important but is frustrated at the time it takes when problems are pressing and funds, particularly in light of significant cuts to public funding, are scarce.

We stop and congregate, this time to consider an example of the issues relating to decaying window tracery. Most windows have tracery in two parts but one has three sections: the question is whether this is 'original' or 'replacement', and if the latter, whether this later addition should be copied, or the detail inferred from earlier examples? There is also a question of how much should be replaced. Architects often advocate for a higher degree of intervention than archaeologists are comfortable with, giving more weight to the preservation of visual appearance than to the conservation of original fabric, and being professionally disposed to emphasize considerations of structural integrity (Jones & Yarrow 2013). Differences of expertise are compounded by the distinctive roles they occupy. Because the District Architects oversee budgets, they may be more willing to countenance higher levels of intervention where this reduces longer-term expenditure on maintenance. How these disciplinary approaches play out is a matter of contextual assessment. Peter suggests that technical advice will be needed to ascertain how much is likely to go and how quickly. Indeterminacies and unknowns are factored out and carried forward as a series of 'action points'. Agreement is achieved by displacing unresolved differences beyond the immediate confines of the space and time in which the meeting takes place.

The final point relates to the issue of 'bossing'. Gordon, the Works Manager, explains that in places stone has been hollowed out by water penetration, leaving ashlar (masonry made of large square cut stones) that appears secure but is in reality structurally compromised. Clare describes the process she and Gordon have jointly been through, tapping the individual stones and listening to the sound as a measure of material integrity. They had tried a coin for this purpose but found a bulldog clip to be the most successful, making a 'good resounding noise'. Peter consents to this approach. Agreement is noted by Clare, and the meeting concludes with a walk back to the cars.

Site meetings are the means by which these differences of expertise are staged and resolved. At issue is the need for consistency that responds to and aligns difference along two key planes: intervention must be consistent with broader conservation principles while also responding to the context of the site. Emphasizing the central importance of the context of a site on another occasion, Susan, a Heritage Manager, highlights the limits to institutional abstractions, claiming that 'there's never one answer':

> You can't write a book that says every time you point it will look like this and you'll do this. It depends on the stone, it depends on the location, it depends how much of the building is left, it depends on the skill of the people doing it.

Site meetings occupy and resolve forms of indeterminacy that arise in the disjunction between policy and site, and from the overlapping but distinct forms of expertise that are assembled in relation to it. Through site meetings, perspectives align and bifurcate, not simply as discursively expressed 'opinion', but as artefacts of relationships that unfold between various experts, and the material conditions of the buildings that bring them together. Their emphasis on the 'feel' that can only be ascertained through 'direct engagement' with a building highlights how their various perspectives are materially enacted (Mol 2002) even as they are partly prefigured through documents and forms that are central to these meetings. At times, difference takes the form of complementarity. Clare, unaware of the precise nature of the consent process, asks Peter to clarify, just as her acknowledged ignorance of the practicalities of stone-working are compensated for by the presence of a mason. At other times, the delimitation of role and expertise is itself at issue in divergent assessments of what should happen. Differences of perspective do not always resolve neatly. Heritage Managers with oversight of the consent process are primarily concerned to understand and protect the historic significance of the building or monument. Works squads and District Architects also recognize the importance of such considerations, but for them, trained to see the building primarily as a structural, pragmatic, and financial set of problems, the process of consent can sometimes seem overly time-consuming or unneccesarily 'bureaucratic'.

Through site meetings, historic buildings stage specific differences between the visions of those involved. The meeting 'enacts' (Mol 2002) the building through a journey, simplifying it as a series of 'issues' and 'decisions'; turning it into a series of objects that bring differences of perspective into view. Participants in these AMAs also foreground the more active sense in which meetings are conjured by the presence of the building. Graham, the District Architect responsible for Glasgow Cathedral, argues that 'the building needs to be there with its own voice and views, and that adds to the decision-making process immensely. If too much is formalized and codified, the building's "voice" becomes lost'. Going 'too deep with the paper' negates the 'bit-by-bit process' of conservation: 'Each stone, never mind each part of the building, needs a different thought process because it's literally bit by bit by bit, literally like building up a big painting with lots of dots and so you can't do it all on paper'. Notions of the building as an integrated whole are expressed in a range of ways, including through concepts of 'integrity', 'personality', and 'voice'. The integration of perspectives within the meeting (i.e. of the experts who meet) is understood to be facilitated by the integrating qualities of the place in which they meet.

Site meetings exemplify how meetings stage and resolve internal differences of knowledge and perspective, harnessing the animating qualities of buildings as a way of arriving at 'actions' and 'decisions'. In the second ethnographic section, I explore how buildings constitute and are constituted in relation to a different kind of meeting located away from the sites that are their focus.

Office meeting

In a room in the headquarters of Historic Scotland, the Listings team congregate for their weekly meeting. The team are responsible for the process by which historic buildings are assigned the status of designated historic significance under a process of 'listing' that provides varying levels of statutory protection. Members of the team file in clutching hot drinks and sheaves of paper. A handful of Listings Officers are present. They have different regional and period specialisms, but most share a background in architectural and art history. Pleasantries are exchanged – personal chat and institutional gossip. Without command the talk dies down and a tone of formality gradually settles. Though nothing has been said, it is obvious that we are 'in' the meeting. Faces look suddenly serious, attentive, eyes and words are connecting, orientated by the agenda that all have before them, by the circular composition of chairs around a table, and by unstated conventions of discursive turn-taking. Chaired by the team leader in an affable but business-like manner, there are a series of updates and news items before presentation of the listings cases commences.

As in the case of site meetings, listings meetings constitute the buildings as central and significant elements of the decisions that are made in relation to them. While an understanding of the building is a necessary first step, decisions about listing require that these empirical specificities be linked to a set of formal criteria. In order to determine whether to 'list' buildings and at what level to do so, they are assessed in relation to three key elements, set out in the Planning (Listed Buildings and Conservation Areas) (Scotland) Act of 1997, namely (1) the age and rarity of a building, (2) its architectural and historic interest, and (3) 'close historical association' – for example, through a relationship between a building and an important person or event. Michael, a Listings Officer, echoes others when he explains to me the rationale:

> If you're listing, adding things to that list is an impartial kind of academic thing that's separate to an extent from all the political and economic whirlwind that's going on around it. The fact that it isn't led by that, it's just what it is . . . The interest of the building is recognized purely for its value in some way and recognizing what that value is might help other people to rally around it.

The listings process is regarded as 'objective' in a number of linked senses. These configure understandings of the procedure and conduct appropriate in meetings, and constitute the very rationale for meeting. While listings criteria are formally clear, members of the team recognize that the relation between abstractly specified criteria and particular buildings is necessarily interpretative. Empirical understanding of buildings is always the starting-point for interpretation but cannot of itself determine significance. Since the importance of a building relates to 'character', an ineffable quality that is difficult to define, assessments are never straightforwardly procedural.

For each building, there is a short presentation given by the Listings Officer overseeing the case. Today a range of buildings are being considered, including a Victorian hospital, a 1960s brutalist modernist school, and a series of domestic houses. Some of these are already 'listed' and are being considered for 'de-listing', often in response to requests from owners. In other cases, the question is whether to list an unlisted building, or to upgrade an existing designation. The Listings Officer sits at the head of the long table around which all are congregated and delivers a running commentary on the key points and issues as images of the case are projected on a screen. The tone is informal, descriptions of the buildings mixed with jokes and asides relating to the site visits, but unspoken conventions are implicitly at work. Presentations begin with contextual information on the architect, period of construction, and background to the case. Photographic images of key external façades are presented before moving to internal photographs of significant architectural features. Site visits to buildings are normally undertaken alone and provide Listings Officers with an empirical understanding of buildings, which they bring to their presentations. A sense of the space is conveyed through movement back and forwards between pictures and plans.

The meeting room has a sanitized institutional feel that contrasts strikingly with the qualities of the historic buildings the team have gathered to discuss. As a 'non-place' (Augé 2009), it engenders a globally recognizable office aesthetic that seems deliberately to erase spatial specificity. These qualities of placelessness act to direct attention beyond the immediate locale of the meeting, and to amplify the 'character' – the term is repeatedly used – of the different buildings the team have gathered to consider. The Historic Scotland website notes the central importance of this: 'Listing ensures that

Journal of the Royal Anthropological Institute (N.S.), 95-109
© Royal Anthropological Institute 2017

a building's special *character* and interest is taken into account'. During an interview, the Head of Listings explains that this refers to 'the essence of a building', though what this is can only be understood contextually and interpretatively as the relation between a range of factors. These include, for example, use of materials, condition of fabric, degree of 'intactness', 'aesthetic significance', and 'architectural interest'. Other members of the Listings team explain that it is 'difficult to pin down', 'nebulous', 'hard to define'. For this audience, seeking to understand these buildings at a remove, the spatial and material qualities of meeting rooms are incidental to their gaze, which is directed beyond these to the specific qualities of 'the building itself'. Listings meetings thus conjure a 'thirdspace' (Soja 1996), as a set of imaginative architectural possibilities made available by an intricate interweaving of texts, images, and spoken words that direct attention beyond the immediate locale of the meeting.

In this, as in other listings meetings, a range of building periods and styles are under consideration. A 1960s modernist school quickly produces consensus. Feedback from the Twentieth-Century Society, consulted to provide opinion on significance, has produced a 'not very enthusiastic response'. Amongst those gathered there is general enthusiasm for the building as a piece of design, but acknowledgement that it fails to meet the listings criteria; it is not sufficiently 'architecturally significant'. The term is central to their assessments, referring to architectural quality and importance, as distinct from subjective aesthetic judgement. The meeting chair, Rachel, brings this brief, consensual discussion to a conclusion: 'It's interesting but very difficult to justify'. Another Listings Officer presents the case of a Victorian police box. It is already listed but renovation work is being proposed on some adjacent steps and the council want it moved. The council are proposing de-listing the structure in order to allow this. Rachel, Head of Listings, is keen to keep the police box. In her view, it clearly meets the listings criteria, but the significance of the structure is not a function of where it is currently related. In principle the meeting reaches consensus that the police box can be moved, but there is uncertainty as to how this can be achieved within the legislative framework. The difficulty is that listing relates to the location, not simply the structure. Discussion focuses on whether and how this will be bureaucratically accommodated.

During presentations, a collective understanding of these spaces is evoked through the interplay between images and spoken words. Images elicit qualitative descriptions of the 'experience' and 'feel' of the building, and are the cue for presenters to provide further description. Images of photographs and plans are invoked where verbal descriptions reach their limits: it is held that much of what is important in these buildings can only be appreciated by seeing them. Listings Officers attempt to convey this 'experience' in absentia. Conversation interweaves a technical descriptive language of space and aesthetics with the evaluative concerns of conservation legislation. There is talk of the 'architectonics of spaces', of the 'narrative' of buildings and of their 'visual grammar', of levels of 'intactness' and 'integrity', and of the extent to which structures are of broader 'historic importance' and 'significance'.

While the relationship between building and criteria requires 'judgement', this is predicated upon certain understandings of the kind of person required to make it. 'Personal' responses are irrelevant to these considerations, the only issue being how the buildings measure up to the listings criteria. Subjective assessments emerge in the interstices of the process in irreverent and ironically uninhibited remarks and asides – an interesting Victorian hospital is presented to round approval: 'Ooh, that's really nice!'; 'Wow, what a great building!'; 'I really like that'. The case of a listed building with un-consented work receives a less enthusiastic assessment: 'Oh yes, it's dreadful!' 'Personal' responses are deliberately overplayed in ways that simultaneously acknowledge their existence and mark them as extrinsic to the process. At various points, the team leader makes explicit for our benefit the otherwise unstated but crucially important point: 'It's not about whether we like it or not'. During an interview Jane, a Listings Officer, explains how this engenders the important distinction between personal opinion and an academically grounded appreciation of what is historically important: 'There has to be an intellectual basis . . . Something like a concrete block could actually be incredibly important. It's not necessarily beautiful. Not all listed buildings are beautiful country houses or cute thatched cottages'. While the meeting brings together various relevant people, their participation is predicated on this axiomatic distinction: they participate as embodiments of expert knowledge and engender specific roles, while other, more 'personal' judgements are factored out. These views may be expressed, but go unrecorded and are not recognized as legitimate considerations in the decision-making process.

Unlike 'personal' differences, the expression and reconciliation of 'professional' differences are central. 'Robust' decision-making requires that these are considered and aligned through a process of discussion and debate. Buildings are understood to have an empirical objectivity and hence independence that ultimately mediates and grounds these differences. At various points during the presentations, differences of opinion emerge, for example pertaining to the degree of 'architectural significance' of a specific building, or the essential qualities that define its 'character'. Conversation amplifies these differences of perspective with the ultimate aim of aligning them: additional perspectives are elicited from others in the team until consensus is achieved; further contexts are evoked, for example, by reference to other cases or previously undisclosed details. The meeting is determined by egalitarian and consensual principles of decision-making, but, relative to any given case, there is tacit acknowledgement of a hierarchy of expertise. Management of these perspectives is orchestrated by the team leader, who brings in people where particular forms of expertise seem required. Questions from the team leader are directed at moving the process on through consideration of comparative examples, experience, and various forms of evidence: 'Do you know if there are any other surviving examples from this period?'; 'Have you seen anything of this quality before?' In most cases consensus settles easily as a collectively shared interpretation of how building and listing criteria relate. Where this seems in doubt, the team leader interjects: sometimes to make his or her own judgement, but more often to make explicit where consensus seems to lie.

Daston and Galison propose that we approach objectivity not as a concept but rather as a 'smear of meanings' that can be empirically studied in relation to the range of activities through which these practically emerge:

> Instead of a pre-existing ideal being applied to a workaday world, it is the other way around: the ideal and ethos are gradually built up and bodied out by thousands of concrete actions . . . To study objectivity in shirtsleeves is to watch objectivity in the making (2007: 52).

In this and other listings meetings, objectivity is a regulatory ideal that orientates practice without entirely determining it. Because it is not given, it has to be achieved. While the process presupposes and even requires that differences of perspective will legitimately emerge, it also allows for their negotiation and resolution. In an interview with Rachel, Head of Listings, she makes this explicit:

> We're very much about making a collegiate decision so there's never one person says, 'Oh, that should be listed', and they go off and list it. It's very much the whole team taking part. We've got different knowledge and expertise but also [it's important to] get away from the [public] idea that, 'Oh, it's someone sitting in Edinburgh, it was their whim, that's why it got listed'. So it's absolutely ... every single case will be looked at, and the decision made by the whole team.

Michael, the Listings Officer introduced earlier, explains that meetings are particularly important where a decision is unclear or where there may be initial disagreement:

> If you're not certain, it needs to be re-thought through, and that's why the decision is never made at one meeting unless it's obvious. Sometimes you can have up to ten meetings on the same building, because it's complex. That's why the meetings are important. You end up at a situation where, 'Ah, now we can take this forwards'. Whereas before you weren't [clear]. That kind of galvanizes at the meeting.

A complex building makes for a complex decision. Knowledge required to understand the building expands beyond that of any individual expert. Attributed a singular character of their own, buildings are understood as ultimate arbiters of the perspectives that can proliferate in relation to them. Members of the Listings team frequently make this point explicit: 'It's either listable or its not'. Insofar as the building is objective, empirical understanding draws together what is initially separate: opinions derived from different forms of expertise coalesce as this objectivity is established.

On occasion, individual members of the team can feel aggrieved when their own perspective is overlooked or marginalized. Consistency entails compromise that can feel personally frustrating. However, meetings are also understood in more intellectually expansive terms. Michael makes this idea explicit in the image of the team brought together in meetings as a kind of 'collective brain': 'Individually you may not know, but normally consensus emerges through discussion'. The metaphor of the brain makes evident how the ideas articulated in meetings exceed individually held 'roles' or 'perspectives' in collective understandings that are more than the sum of their parts. Meetings are thus moments of revelation as much as conflict, and are constitutive of knowledge at the interstices of people, perspective, and place.

Conclusion: meeting place

At Historic Scotland, meetings are organizational devices that render differences of perspective present in order to integrate them. In both meetings explored above, buildings are regarded by participants as key actors that simultaneously generate and integrate differences of perspective. Listings meetings, like site meetings, frame historic buildings as specific kinds of objects, external to, but constitutive of, relationships within meetings. In each example, the integration of the perspectives of experts within the meeting is established through the negotiation of the qualities of the historic buildings that are their external referents. One may say that meetings bring about the objective singularity they presuppose through a process of aligning perspectives, but, ethnographically speaking, the reverse is stressed: for those involved, it is the objective integrity of buildings that draws together perspectives on them.

AMAs and listings meetings so position the building that it can act on participants in this singularizing fashion, but the ways in which this happens are qualitatively distinct. In the case of AMAs, the meeting takes place within the building, which acts as an external, encompassing frame. The building facilitates decision-making partly through a shift in scale: otherwise abstractly intractable policies, principles, and perspectives are resolved through their concrete location. Policy contradictions and differences of perspectives are resolved through disaggregation as a series of specific assessments and decisions about particular elements of the building. By contrast, listings meetings make multiple buildings present within the single frame of a meeting. Images, plans, and words are assembled so that each building is seen and understood 'as a whole'. Unlike site meetings, where the building is a physically encompassing presence, these office-based gatherings constitute buildings as an external presence that is brought within the meeting through the performance of words, images, and office infrastructures that are incidental to the character they seek to convey. Site meetings achieve a series of 'decisions' and 'actions' by drawing experts into the specific material contexts of historic buildings that disaggregate decisions and situate knowledge. By contrast, participants in listings meetings establish a distance from these buildings, seeking to detach their own knowledge from the objects to which they pertain.

These meetings highlight a series of dynamics that have received relatively little attention in interdisciplinary accounts of heritage practice. The recent burgeoning of the field of critical heritage studies has done much to illuminate the 'consumption' of heritage via various practices of reinterpretation, appropriation, and resistance to professional presentations of the past, but has had much less to say about the practices through which these understandings are produced by various heritage experts (Brumann 2014; Jones & Yarrow 2013). While this essay's focus on heritage experts helps to redress this imbalance, the lens of 'meeting' highlights a specific set of negotiations that complicate and refine understanding of the work of these professionals. In a range of heritage contexts, objectivity has been seen as central to an 'authorized heritage discourse' (Smith 2006) that supports elite interests and excludes subaltern perspectives. Such approaches usefully foreground the political dimensions to heritage expertise, but the discursive focus of these accounts, allied to methodological reliance on institutionally authored texts, leads to an overly monolithic portrayal that does little to illuminate the specific contexts in which these ideals emerge. A focus on meetings therefore sheds new light on the dynamics through which historic built environments are created and reproduced at the intersection of various forms of knowledge and practice.

Focusing on meetings, I have shown how linked ideas about the need for consistency and objectivity frame a series of situated negotiations (Daston & Galison 2007). For heritage professionals, meetings are organizational devices that help to deal with various forms of contingency, uncertainty, and irresolution. Meetings, in other words, involve a series of situated practices that are not organiz*ed*, but organiz*ing* (Mol 2002; Mosse 2005). As spaces for the resolution of various forms of indeterminacy, they produce outcomes which, while in one sense never entirely surprising, are neither predetermined nor wholly predictable. From the perspective of those involved, this is not only because heritage conservation requires situated accommodations between different, more or less contradictory, forms of expertise, but also because the question of how these come together is always also in relation to the contextually specific material circumstances of particular monuments and buildings.

This ethnographic lens highlights a range of dynamics that have received relatively little ethnographic attention in wider discussions of bureaucracy, where discursive analyses have often acted to reproduce assumptions about bureaucratic and institutional conduct as immaterial and placeless (Hull 2012). Even where place has figured, it is more often as a context to organizational interaction than as an artefact of these practices. At Historic Scotland, conservation professionals highlight the importance of meeting

Journal of the Royal Anthropological Institute (N.S.), 95-109
© Royal Anthropological Institute 2017

as a way of producing specific relationships between the 'what' and the 'where' of knowing. Through their interactions in meetings, different experts objectify place in different ways that render explicit and visible the distinct qualities of the buildings they seek to understand. Ideas about 'character', 'personality', 'authenticity', and 'integrity' of buildings can be seen as elements of this objectifying gaze, but are also ways of acknowledging the irreducibility of place to their institutional efforts to know it. From this perspective, institutional knowledge can never simply be 'applied', being more or less subtly transformed as it is bent to materially specific circumstances.

NOTES

[1] The institutional terminologies and structures I refer to are consistent with the 'ethnographic present' of fieldwork, undertaken between 2010 and 2014. Since then various institutional reforms have taken place, partly catalysed by a merger with the Royal Commission. The merged organization is now known as Historic Environment Scotland. Many of the roles and institutional structures to which I refer now bear different names. The account builds on collaborative research undertaken with Sian Jones (University of Stirling), drawing on participant observation and interviews undertaken through three phases between 2010 and 2014. Research was supported by a British Academy grant (SG100577) and by a British Academy/Leverhulme grant (SG122587). I am grateful to Sian, not only for allowing me to draw on that material here, but more generally for the inspiration her friendship has provided. The essay is informed, less directly, by an AHRC/EPSRC project funded under the Science and Heritage programme (AH/K006002/1), led by John Hughes. I gratefully acknowledge Historic Scotland for allowing me to undertake the research. In keeping with their wishes, all names have been anonymized.

[2] Indeed, this conception could be argued to be more Gellian (cf. Gell 1997).

REFERENCES

Augé, M. 2009. *Non-places: introduction to an anthropology of supermodernity* (trans. J. Howe). London: Verso.
Boyer, D. 2008. Thinking through the anthropology of experts. *Anthropology in Action* **15**, 38-46.
Brown, M.F. 2010. A tale of three buildings: certifying virtue in the new moral economy. *American Ethnologist* **37**, 741-52.
Brumann, C. 2012. *Tradition, democracy and the townscape of Kyoto: claiming a right to the past.* Abingdon, Oxon: Routledge.
——— 2014. Heritage agnosticism: a third path for the study of cultural heritage. *Social Anthropology* **22**, 173-88.
Bruun-Jensen, C. & B.-R. Winthereik 2013. *Monitoring movements in development aid: recursive partnerships and infrastructures.* Cambridge, Mass.: MIT Press.
Daston, L. & P. Galison 2007. *Objectivity.* Brooklyn, N.Y.: Zone Books.
Du Gay, P. 2000. *In praise of bureaucracy: Weber, organization, ethics.* London: Sage.
Gell, A. 1997. *Art and agency: an anthropological theory.* Oxford: University Press.
Grasseni, C. 2007. Introduction: skilled visions: between apprenticeship and standards. In *Skilled visions: between apprenticeship and standards* (ed.) C. Grasseni, 1-20. New York: Berghahn Books.
Hull, M. 2012. *Government of paper: the materiality of bureaucracy in urban Pakistan.* Berkeley: University of California Press.
ICOMOS 1964. International Charter for the Conservation and Restoration of Monuments and Sites (The Venice Charter, 1964) (available on-line: *https://www.icomos.org/charters/venice_e.pdf*, accessed 19 January 2017).
——— 1999 [1979]. The Burra Charter: the Australia ICOMOS Charter for Places of Cultural Significance (available on-line: *http://australia.icomos.org/publications/burra-charter-practice-notes/burra-charter-archival-documents/#BC1999*, accessed 23 January 2017).
Jones, S. & T. Yarrow 2013. Crafting authenticity: an ethnography of hertiage conservation. *Journal of Material Culture* **18**, 3-26.
Latour, B. 1993. *We have never been modern* (trans. C. Porter). Cambridge, Mass.: Harvard University Press.
Law, J. 1994. *Organizing modernity.* Oxford: Blackwell.
Macdonald, S. 2009. *Difficult heritage: negotiating the Nazi past in Nuremberg and beyond.* London: Routledge.

Mol, A. 2002. *The body multiple: ontology in medical practice*. Durham, N.C.: Duke University Press.

Mosse, D. 2005. *Cultivating development: an ethnography of aid policy and practice*. London: Pluto Press.

Pendlebury, J. 2009. *Conservation in the age of consensus*. Abingdon, Oxon: Routledge.

Schwartzman, H. 1989. *The meeting: gatherings in organizations and communities*. New York: Springer.

Smith, L. 2006. *The uses of heritage*. London: Routledge.

Soja, E. 1996. *Thirdspace: journeys to Los Angeles and other real-and-imagined places*. Oxford: Blackwell.

Yarrow, T. 2011. *Development beyond politics: aid, activism and NGOs in Ghana*. Basingstoke: Palgrave Macmillan.

——— & S. Jones 2014. 'Stone is stone': engagement and detachment in the craft of conservation masonry. *Journal of the Royal Anthropological Institute (N.S.)* **20**, 256-75.

Là où les savoirs se rencontrent : l'expertise du patrimoine, au croisement des gens, des points de vue et des lieux

Résumé

À partir d'une recherche ethnographique auprès de professionnels du patrimoine en Écosse, l'auteur examine les réunions en tant que dispositifs organisationnels permettant de différencier et de mettre en relation différentes formes de contexte épistémique, social et matériel. Son récit décrit la manière dont l'idéal bureaucratique de cohérence institutionnelle est atteint par des rencontres graduées entre les points de vue des différentes personnes en présence et les bâtiments qui sont l'objet de leur réunion. Ces exemples ethnographiques permettent de développer deux points qui sont liés : d'une part, l'auteur suggère que le prisme de la « réunion » complique les caractérisations relativement monolithiques de l'expertise du patrimoine, telles qu'elles transparaissent dans les très influentes critiques déconstructives de la pratique de la conservation du patrimoine. D'autre part, les récits de ces négociations faits par les professionnels du patrimoine eux-mêmes mettent en évidence des dimensions matérielles et spatiales du comportement bureaucratique qui, contrairement aux comptes-rendus principalement textuels des pratiques institutionnelles, n'ont pas reçu beaucoup d'attention ethnographique.

6

Political exhaustion and the experiment of street: Boyle meets Hobbes in Occupy Madrid

ALBERTO CORSÍN JIMÉNEZ & ADOLFO ESTALELLA *Spanish National Research Council (CSIC)*

This essay describes the complex negotiations around stranger sociability, public space, and democratic knowledge that shaped the meetings of popular assemblies in the wake of the Spanish 15M/Occupy movement. The work of assembling was 'exhausting', by which participants would mean two things. In one sense, meetings would often turn into tiresome affairs, trying the patience and resilience of participants. In another sense, attendants would describe assemblies as spaces of political 'exhaustion', where politics as usual was emptied out and replaced by new democratic possibilities. We offer here an account of exhaustion as an ethnographic category. We are particularly interested in the role accorded to exhaustion as a vacuum enabling the appearance of novel social and political roles. We develop our argument by drawing a provocative analogy with the early history of scientific experimentation, where the nature of an 'assembly' of trusted peers and its location in genteel space became constitutive of a new type of experimental knowledge. What social and epistemic figures are popular assemblies bodying forth today?

And now let us rise and go out into the streets, among people, to see whether a little shared tiredness may not be waiting for us and what it may have to tell us
                                    Peter Handke, 'Essay on tiredness' (1994: 43)

The man sitting next to me mumbles unintelligibly. He always does. Over the weeks I [Alberto] have come to realize he is just repeating the words of the speaker to himself. It is an innocent gesture, but it is unsettling and distracting. Clara, who used to sit next to me at every assembly, now deliberately avoids him every Saturday. 'It's the last thing I need', she says; 'it's exhausting enough having to make it through three hours of meeting without having to put up with all this hissing and mumbling'. I was put off myself at the beginning. But then, some three Saturdays ago, he asked for the microphone. He stood up and started talking about the history of state schools in our neighbourhood. It turns out he is a retired schoolteacher. His name is Jacinto. He was eloquent and engaging and lucid. He has made three or four interventions since, always concise, yet enriched with the candour of hindsight and experience, and very often bringing a historical angle too, about the *barrio*'s (neighbourhood) shifting demographics and the contradictory pushes of immigration, working-class impoverishment, and gentrification. I have tried to engage him a couple of times at the end of the assembly, or during some of the assembly breaks, but it seems we are both a bit shy and I always feel lost for words. I despair at our mutual timorousness, which feels childish. Though perhaps it is not timidity that it is at stake. Our gathering in the open air makes for a strange social form. Whatever reasons bring people

Journal of the Royal Anthropological Institute (N.S.), 110-123
© Royal Anthropological Institute 2017

to the assembly, there is a sense in which they *have* to collapse the moment the assembly is disbanded. Over time we have come to witness each other with wonder and trepidation as we pulsate and sound out the limits and thresholds of a nascent social body. We sit, and we listen, and we witness, and sometimes we touch something, we find something, someone. In honesty, it is not always clear what remains at the end of the assembly.

In the wake of the Spanish Occupy movement, which took to the streets on 15 May 2011, thousands of people gathered in the open air in plazas and public spaces all over the country to deliberate on and bring about a 'real democracy' at a municipal level. Over a hundred such local popular assemblies blossomed in Madrid alone. The meeting of the assemblies on a weekly basis suddenly transformed the public qualities of neighbourhood spaces. Attended by professionals and the unemployed, the elderly and the young, people who introduced themselves as 'feminists' or 'long-term political strategists' or 'hackers', the gatherings reproduced the conventional sociological dictums on urban cosmopolitanism (Vertovec & Cohen 2002).[1] Yet they did so in a format rarely seen before in public space. Assemblies took place in the open air, and in doing so blurred the lines separating formal and informal sociability. They shaped themselves into a public body that was at once a permeable yet robust structure, a space of engagement and invitation as well as a device for programmatic decision-making and action. As a specific type of get-together, the gatherings drew on the protocols and routines of conventional meetings, yet their public orientation and openness tested these in fascinating ways. Assemblies challenged not a few of the spatial, temporal, and social qualities that uphold the *form* of meetings as organizational projects.

For example, strangers and passers-by were always invited to join ongoing conversations, at the risk of having to suspend or interrupt the passing of important judgements or decisions. Occasionally, speakers would go on a rant, deviating abruptly from the topic under discussion. At other times, assemblies would be interrupted by nearby noises, such as the marching-by of a local school's music band, the alarming siren of a racing ambulance, or simply the dissonant falsettos of a high-spirited drunkard. Thus, the form of collective thinking and speaking that assemblies aimed for proceeded slowly, sometimes desperately so. As Clara put it somewhat harshly in the vignette above, assembly-goers conceded that assembling was exasperatingly tedious; at the *agora* of the assembly, politics was sometimes antagonistic, sometimes agonistic, but always '*agotador*' (Spanish: exhausting, tiring, tedious).[2]

This article reports on ethnographic work carried out at three popular assemblies in Madrid (Lavapiés, Prosperidad, and the General Assembly in Puerta del Sol) from June 2011 to June 2012. In this period we attended the weekly meetings of two *barrio* assemblies (Lavapiés and Prosperidad), and one of us (Adolfo Estalella) joined the 'facilitating taskforce' in charge of organizing the weekly gatherings of the Lavapiés crowd. Jointly or individually, we attended hundreds of assemblies, preparatory meetings, working groups, demonstrations, or direct actions. Our account builds on participant observation in all of these sites, as well as on formal and informal conversations, discussions, and interviews with assembly-goers across Madrid. We focus here on assembling as a social, material, and political process, and in particular on the significance of its taking residence as a form of meeting in the open air.

Central to this open-air location was the assembly's capacity to negotiate and measure up to the challenges of 'exhaustion'. The fieldwork extract with which we opened the essay, which rehearses elements of a conversation that Alberto had with some fellow

Journal of the Royal Anthropological Institute (N.S.), 110-123
© Royal Anthropological Institute 2017

assembly-goers over the purpose and nature of assembling, captures nicely the thrust of our argument. Exhaustion, we want to suggest, is a complex social form, where tiredness, hopefulness, and indeterminacy coalesce in the sustenance of a social and political project. As we will see shortly, the assemblies delineated and carved out a cultural space that people described expressly as being 'evacuated' (*vaciado, agotado*) of its formal properties and wherein, it was said, a new democratic and political culture could be essayed and forged. However, negotiating the boundaries of such an emptied space 'in public' was far from straightforward. It called for an exploration of the limits of stranger-sociability, an exercise that, as the vignette illustrates, often taxed the patience of attendants. The body politic of the assembly became palpable, quite literally, in the exhaustion endured by participants.

This essay offers the concept of 'exhaustion' as a placeholder for understanding the peculiar and innovative type of meetings that assemblies brought forward in public space. Whilst it is true that in searching for 'freedom' or 'democracy' participants at the assemblies would generally encounter 'endless meetings' (Polletta 2002), there is also a sense in which the work of exhaustion reached beyond physical or emotional distress or tiredness. As we shall see, the thresholds of exhaustion marked also the material borderlands of the assembly as an urban object, its ambivalent and shifting status as a 'public' body, a gathering of people and things that suddenly destabilizes what public space is and how it gets invoked. Exhaustion also marks the umbra of hospitality, insofar as the assembly aspires to negotiate its way in and out of social relations of neighbourliness and passer-by witnessing (Spanish: *mirones*[3]), and, more amply, holds in suspension what stranger-sociability might mean (Sennett 1977; Simmel 1972). Finally, exhaustion affects the symbolism and imagination of the assembly. It summons a poetics of ruination and fatigue that has, notwithstanding, become constitutive of a new political awakening.

The centrality we accord to the notion of exhaustion makes for a slight departure from the existing literature on the global Occupy movement, which has either broadly focused on the epidemiology of protest (Postill 2014), where, as the argument goes, 'tweets' and 'streets' have played an equal and increasingly important part in the formation of a novel political ecology of direct action (Gerbaudo 2012); or it has argued for its entanglement within broader historical genealogies of radical political praxis, harking back to local traditions of anarchism (Graeber 2011), national traditions of minority rights advocacy (Martínez 2012; Moreno-Caballud 2014; Razsa & Kurnik 2012), or even larger agendas for urban transformation such as the 'right to the city' movement (Harvey 2012) or the Mediterranean tradition of urban political spontaneity (Leontidou 2012).

In this essay we break from from these traditions of political analysis and rehearse an alternative argument about the role of 'exhaustion' in the shaping of an emerging culture of political experimentation. We use the word 'experimentation' purposely, for it is in conversation with recent works in the history and sociology of science that we wish to explore the kind of epistemic work that exhaustion brings to the fore. In particular, we shall draw a provocative analogy between the 'assemblies' of seventeenth-century genteel experimentalists and Madrid's open-air assemblies in order to highlight the role that exhaustion played as an engine of political ontology in both cases. If the assemblies of natural philosophers are known today for having entangled anew the 'relations' of knowledge and/with the relations between people (Strathern 2014), we wish to explore here what novel epistemic and social bodies (if any) the Madrid assemblies might have brought forth into existence.

Journal of the Royal Anthropological Institute (N.S.), 110-123
© Royal Anthropological Institute 2017

Assembling

When a call to organize popular neighbourhood assemblies was launched following the occupation of Madrid's Puerta del Sol on 15 May 2011, over a hundred initiatives responded across the city's *barrios*. Organizing the assemblies proved a relatively straightforward affair, insofar as they were all modelled after the 'assembly format' that had by then become a standard within the main Occupy encampment at Puerta del Sol (Corsín Jiménez & Estalella 2014). For instance, a week into Sol's occupation, a 'Neighbourhoods Commission' drafted a document known as the 'Quick Guide for Facilitating Assemblies' that thereafter functioned as a manual for organizing assembly work everywhere (AcampadaSol 2011). The guide was compiled using a variety of sources and expertise, including similar texts in use in the squatting movement (Lorenzo Vila & Martínez López 2005), field guides for community empowerment in developing contexts, or insights from the autonomous governance of ecovillages. This hybrid of expertise became a common feature throughout the assembly movement, for it was not unusual for assemblies to be attended by university professors, school teachers, architects, engineers, or development consultants in a variety of specialized fields.

The Quick Guide identified three areas of intervention: first, a series of protocols and procedures facilitating the installation of assemblies in public space; second, an inventory of tools and materials necessary for lending the assembly infrastructural continuity and coherence over time; and, third, a list of social techniques to help make the encounter between strangers in public space more congenial and hospitable. With regard to the protocol and method of assembling, the document recommended that all assemblies be facilitated by a 'moderator, a secretary in charge of taking minutes, someone responsible for taking turns for questions, and a group facilitating the production of consensus'. The document also offered some recommendations regarding the physical installation of the assembly in public space. Thus, it was suggested that the plaza or street be demarcated into two zones: a 'moderating space' and the assembly space proper. The former could be simulated into a theatrical stage of sorts, by having a 'rectangular perimeter mark out [the moderating space] with chalk or coloured tape on the floor'. The moderating space should be occupied by the person whose turn it was to speak. A team of people in charge of taking questions from the assembly would stand next to the speaker. They ought to be located 'as far away as possible from the team of secretaries, who are in charge of taking minutes, and who shall be close enough to the moderating space to request a repetition, a synthesis, or a copy of a document presented to the assembly'. The Guide also made specific recommendations on how to take minutes, which should include the day's agenda, a record of the various reports received (from specific taskforces or commissions), proposals made, discussions had, and any consensus reached.

Notwithstanding the recommendations made by the Guide, the practical management of assemblies was often a casual affair in which organizational formats had to be improvised for unplanned on-the-spot interventions. Adolfo joined Lavapiés Assembly's Facilitating Taskforce (*Grupo de Dinamización*) in September 2011 and remained a core member of the team for over ten months. The taskforce met one or two days ahead of the assembly to prepare the agenda and assign a rota of turns for each role (moderator, minute-taker, etc.). The following extract from Adolfo's fieldwork diary provides an insight into the tension between formality and informality that traversed assembly work:

Journal of the Royal Anthropological Institute (N.S.), 110-123
© Royal Anthropological Institute 2017

March 24, 2012

We are having today's assembly at Plaza de Lavapiés, by the stairways to the National Centre for Drama. I arrive twenty minutes late. There's some people there already, included Emilio, who's been away for the past four weeks ...

I speak to Emilio and see no agenda has been prepared. We were going to have a 'thematic assembly' to speak about police repression but it looks like the people who volunteered to organize it haven't showed up either ...

Emilio and I talk about how to improvise an agenda for today's meeting. Amparo joins us and notes that someone from Tetuán's Assembly has offered to drop by to give us a talk on the new Employment Law and labour reform ... We decide to draft an agenda on the spot, asking people for items to be included ...

I get an SMS from Alicia saying that two police vans have parked next to Austria's Assembly. We wonder whether we should report it out loud in the assembly, but in the end decide not to, for fear that people will leave.

Since there's no agenda proper, the whole assembly is dedicated to 'other business'. There are a couple of issues raised: about last week's police raids against the protests organized in opposition to immigration policy, and about the protests against foreclosures. There are a couple of announcements too: two fundraising parties to help support work in support of illegal immigrants and against housing evictions ... I take minutes and read them out loud. Emilio asks if there's consensus on the points raised. There is no dissent so we take that for a yes.

The person from Tetuán's Assembly is ready to talk about the labour reform. He talks for about twenty minutes. He is very clear and didactic. Quite a number of people stop by to hear what he has to say. By the time he finishes there are about fifty seated people listening ...

We bring the assembly to an end with an anti-repression performance. A young man from an anti-repression group invites us to stand up. We're about thirty people now. A young woman holding a ball of wool calls her name out loud and throws the ball to another person whilst holding one end of the string. We're each meant to mimic her gesture. As the ball flies from one person to the next it weaves a web that connects us together. The performance draws the attention of numerous passers-by who stop to watch. We're then handed a balloon each, which we have to inflate. When we're ready, we start walking and moving around the plaza. At that point, a couple of young men start to chase us, bursting the balloons with needles. We are told to protect and care for the few people left with balloons. We run around trying to navigate the complex web and organize ourselves into some sort of caring structure. It has been lots of fun and we have pulled in quite a bit of an audience.

The assembly is over. Some of us decide to go for lunch at a nearby bar. We talk about the performance. It was a nice image: weaving a network of caretakers in public ...

As the above example shows, over time, vulnerability and fragility became central markers of the assembly's 'public' identity. However, placing care at the heart of the assembly's residence in public space came at no small price. It demanded developing a concomitant 'methodology of care' (*metodología del cuidado*), as participants would put it. Such a methodology had both a social and a political dimension. We might think of it as a trap of sorts, a complex and ambiguous interface that had to mediate and care for the relationships within the group at the same time as it attempted to 'capture' the attention of *mirones* (passers-by) and strangers. As a meeting in public space, then, the assembly performed a complex double movement: on the one hand, a continuous eversion outwards, diluting its boundaries so as to become inviting and hospitable; on the other hand, and simultaneously, an attentive tending for and nurturing its insiders, lubricating and taking care of any frictions and hostilities.

Journal of the Royal Anthropological Institute (N.S.), 110-123
© Royal Anthropological Institute 2017

For example, the emphasis on reaching 'consensus' noted in the vignette above was part and parcel of the methodology of care. From the earliest days of direct action at Sol's encampment, the notion of 'consensus' played a fundamental part in the work of assembling. In many respects, assembling was conceived as both a political philosophy and a sociological theory of consensus. The first draft of the Quick Guide, published fifteen days after the occupation, already defined a 'Popular Assembly' as a 'participatory decision-making tool (*órgano*) that aims for consensus'. Consensus became the *raison d'être* of assembling, the mechanism for its perpetual motion. The various roles assigned to the team of facilitators (moderator, minute-takers, question-takers, etc.) aimed to work as the assembly's sensorium, making sure that the method of consensus would do double duty as a device for political reasoning and bargaining, at the same time as it assured the assembly's singular expression as a knowing and caring body.

In this latter sense, the production of consensus was also understood to require a particular modality of sociability, a social 'climate of relaxation, listening, respect, and complicity among attendants', as the Quick Guide put it. Crucial in this regard was the construction of the assembly as a hospitable environment. The Guide spoke of the importance of keeping a 'relaxing and respectful atmosphere' throughout the assembly, and supplementary texts provide specific advice and techniques on how to accomplish this. The general tenor of these texts presents the assembly as an all-in-one therapeutic, ludic, and political installation. For example, 'When someone who is known to be sensitive and positive finds herself constrained and incapable of reason, we embrace her and tell her: "Dear friend, we know what you are capable of"'. Similarly, facilitators were encouraged to greet newcomers so they would not feel like strangers, and in a related, if somewhat different, vein, it also became common for assemblies to organize parallel activities to the forum itself, in the hope that the presence of the assembly in the open air would become welcoming and inviting to bystanders or neighbouring families. In the neighbourhood of Coslada, for example, one of the attendees, a professional clown, regularly performed in the assembly space to break up the long hours of meetings. In Lavapiés and Dos de Mayo, children's assemblies (*chiqui-asambleas*) were hosted for the young to discuss matters of interest to them, while their parents attended their own assembly. Assemblies have also been known to organize barter markets, workshops, and walks, or to open or close their meetings with collective and public meals.

Exhaustion

Assemblies have sustained themselves in public space as amphibious formations, at once political gatherings, theatrical productions, co-operative markets, open-air festivals, public spectacles, and children's playgrounds. Right from the outset, assembly-goers were conscious of the importance of keeping control over the temporal and spatial forms of the assembly and their hold over attendees. It was widely understood that the form of the assembly as an open meeting in public space had a fragility that had to be cared for. 'Haste and tiredness', the Quick Guide alerted on its first page, 'are the enemies of consensus' (*la prisa y el cansancio son los enemigos del consenso*). The question of tiredness or exhaustion (*cansancio, agotamiento, desgaste*, in three of the most usual formulations) quickly became one of the central tenets of the management of expectations within assemblies. Perhaps the most famous slogan of the assembly movement, '*vamos despacio porque vamos lejos*' (we move slowly because we aim high), already identifies the temporality of exhaustion as an inevitable political horizon, at once its condition of possibility and a potential source of strain and destruction.

Journal of the Royal Anthropological Institute (N.S.), 110-123
© Royal Anthropological Institute 2017

The idiom of exhaustion popped up everywhere in people's accounts of assembly work. At times it figured as an image of fear, a menacing place that threatened to paralyse and trample everything that had been accomplished to date. Exhaustion triggered a particular type of self-consciousness about the productivity of political work. For example, some people explicitly described Sol's General Assembly as 'an assembly that works by and through exhaustion (*cansancio*), where decisions are always reached in the eleventh hour'. Exhaustion would regularly be invoked in this sense as a limit-holder, an ambiguous threshold, hard to identify, let alone to inhabit and dwell within, and yet one which signalled the very productivity of the assembly as a political form. It became the default theoretical space from which to think politics as both impasse and potentiality. For instance, at the public reading of a manifesto at the first Inter-Neighbourhoods Assembly on 5 November 2011, the notion of exhaustion was explicitly foregrounded as the fulcrum of political hopefulness and action:

> Following the enthusiasm and multitudinous attendance of the first assemblies in May 2011, we are now going through a deflationary stage. Those of us who remain involved in the assembly movement, although tired (*cansados*), we are still committed and willing to work even harder.
>   We are exhausted (*cansados*) because we are struggling to open up spaces of creativity at the same time as we have to confront extreme situations that constrain us and demand immediate reaction on our part. We are exhausted because we have no time for reflection and serious debate, because we are not content with what we have achieved despite the fact that we have only been at it for five months. We are babies and yet we want to run the 100 m hurdles race. (Asamblea de los Barrios del Sur 2011: 1)

At other times, however, exhaustion was invoked as a space of joy, an experience of physical exhilaration, where finally one's relation with the world was felt to be unbounded. 'We have been here, sitting outdoors in the burning sun, for over three hours now', Adolfo noted in his fieldwork diary a year into his weekly attendance of assembly meetings. 'People come and go and I stay put. It's been a long time since I last spent a morning like this, doing nothing. It must be apathy or because I'm exhausted (*debe ser la desidia o el cansancio*), but otherwise I feel as if I'm in a state of grace'. The assembly bracketed the world outside for a while, and although debates and discussions would occasionally turn rancorous or inconsequential, some people relished the idea of spending a few hours 'doing nothing' (*sin hacer nada*) whilst enjoying the morning sun.

There is another sense in which exhaustion became productive for assembly-goers. In November 2012 a group of activists from the Lavapiés assembly camped in front of Bankia's headquarters in Madrid. (Formerly a private bank, Bankia was partially nationalized by the Spanish government in May 2012 following a requested bailout of €19 billion.) One day, one of the bank's employees, having to negotiate her way to the main entrance, commented, 'You are nice people but you are *cansinos* (exhausting)'. The guerrilla artivist group GILA[4] thence adopted the theme of '*cansinismo*' to launch a campaign that aimed to paralyse the bank's activities for one day by developing a 'creatively exhausting' style of sociability. Under the rubric 'Creativity, camouflage and exhaustion' (*Creatividad, camuflaje y cansinismo*), GILA called assembly-goers to walk 'camouflaged as clients' into Bankia's branches all over Spain and subject the bank's employees to endless information requests. 'We want to bring the operations of the bank to the point of collapse by the sheer forces of pacification and exhaustion', noted one of GILA's members.

Journal of the Royal Anthropological Institute (N.S.), 110-123
© Royal Anthropological Institute 2017

Experiment

Although 'exhaustion' has rarely been accorded any centrality in political theory, there is in fact a distinguished tradition in the history of science that awards it a prominent place in the configuration of the modern ontology of politics. We are referring to Steve Shapin and Simon Schaffer's celebrated account of the controversy surrounding the nature of experimental work in seventeenth-century England, and in particular their description of the polemic between Robert Boyle and Thomas Hobbes over the capacity of air-pumps to produce real vacuums (Shapin & Schaffer 1985; on the role of the controversy in the making of the 'moderns', see Latour 1993). As we shall see shortly, the history of the production of the vacuum – of the 'exhaustion of air' – was fundamentally entangled with the 'assembling' of genteel witnesses, who were, by their presence, said to lend political and epistemic credibility to the practice of experimentation. In the rest of the essay we wish to draw a provocative analogy between the role that 'exhaustion' played in this seventeenth-century scenario and in the Madrid Occupy movement. We are aware of the analogical risk we are taking here. We would like to suggest, however, that there is scope for exploring the historical and cultural role accorded to 'exhaustion' as a *tabula rasa* from which novel assemblages of relations and knowledge are said to rise. What kinds of relations are summoned to inhabit an 'exhausted' space or body, and why do such spaces become springboards for political hopes and fears? In particular, we are intrigued by the role assigned to assemblies in both the circumscription and mobilization of exhaustion to political and experimental uses. Let us return to the seventeenth century.

Not a few of the famous discussions that Boyle and Hobbes had over the ontology of the vacuum centred on the quality of the exhaustion in the pump: how 'the constitution of the air', as the experimentalists talked about it, depended in great measure on the integrity of the air-pump and whether the apparatus leaked or not. Thus, Boyle once noted that it was 'nonsensical for Hobbes to maintain that "our receiver, when we say it is almost *exhausted*, is as full as ever (for he will have it perfectly full) of common air"' (cited in Schaffer & Shapin 1985: 180, emphasis added). For Boyle, the exhaustion-vacuum complex was fundamentally a 'matter of fact' to be produced and tested experimentally. He was less interested in endowing the world with particular metaphysical qualities than in opening up a space in which to keep producing experimental knowledge. As Shapin and Schaffer put it:

> The finite leakage of the pump was not, in [Boyle's] view, a fatal flaw but a valuable resource in accounting for experimental findings and in exemplifying the proper usage of terms like 'vacuum'. The 'vacuum' of his exhausted receiver was thus *not an experiment but a space in which to do experiments* and generate matters of fact without falling into futile metaphysical dispute. And it was *an experimental space about which new discursive and social practices could be mobilized to generate assent* (1985: 46, emphasis added).

Hobbes, on the other hand, abhorred the idea that the air-pump could be exhausted of air. For him, the idea of a vacuum was abominable, a *horror vacui*, for it was conducive to a world of wide, open dissent, populated by objects and phenomena (ghosts, spirits, witches) of disreputable ontological provenance. A vacuum was a source environment for ontological chaos. Indeed, this was the ontological mayhem that Hobbes thought the priestcraft had long parasitized upon and benefited from, and for which he held the Church responsible at the advent of the Civil War.

Journal of the Royal Anthropological Institute (N.S.), 110-123
© Royal Anthropological Institute 2017

Hobbes' political ontology may therefore be cast as a formula against exhaustion. Insofar as Hobbes is the father of modern political theory (Skinner 2008), we may therefore say that exhaustion played a crucial formative role in the ontology of modern politics. *It was against exhaustion that the ontology of politics took shape.* However, exhaustion also played a formative role in the ontology of modern experimentation, for of course it was the orchestration of exhaustion as a matter of fact that Boyle worked so hard to produce in his air-pump trials. We may say analogously that in *searching for exhaustion, the ontology of experiment took shape.*

Air-pumping assemblies

Our argument rises from this dual and ambiguous (against/for) role of exhaustion as an ontological engine of both politics and experiment. We want to suggest that there might be scope for a conception of *exhaustion as political experiment*, where exhaustion need not be conceived solely as a deterrent of agency (something to work against) nor as a goal in itself (something to work for). The concept of exhaustion as a form of political experiment dwells instead on the ambiguity of its ontological affordances as now a vital source, now an ominous threat, of potential energies.

Yet how to hold exhaustion stable as an analytical figure across such widely divergent historical and social contexts, from seventeenth-century England to twenty-first-century Spain? In the English context, as we have seen, the Boylean 'vacuum' was 'not an experiment', as Shapin and Schaffer put it, 'but a space about which new discursive and social practices could be mobilized to generate assent' (Shapin & Schaffer 1985: 46). Therefore, to be for or against exhaustion was not simply a matter of being for or against the ontology of the vacuum. It mobilized, also, an accompanying argument about the political ontology of *dissent* itself.

So what about the Spanish context? What epistemic and political bodies did Madrid's assemblies air-pump into the vacuum spaces of plazas and streets? We have already seen the efforts that the assemblies put into designing spaces of hospitality and conviviality conducive to the production of *consensus*. The 'methodology of care' (*metodología del cuidado*) was construed as both political epistemology and sociology: a tool for eliciting the assembly as an *organon* of collective thought and reason *and* a design for the socialization of stranger-relationality in public space. Indeed, right from the outset, there was an understanding that the assemblies' location in the open air opened up novel spaces for political action and knowledge, that there was a particular way in which politics was exhausted through the occupation of public space. For instance, at an assembly meeting of Sol's encampment's Commission on Thought (*Comisión de Pensamiento*), there was a specific debate on the use of the term 'popular' to refer to the assembly movement (fieldwork diary, Adolfo, 16 June 2011):

> *Young man*: Right from the very first day ours has been an attempt at rescuing plazas, at opening up spaces (*abrir espacios*) for anyone's use . . .
>
> *Woman*: We are driven by a desire to exhaust democracy (*el deseo de agotar la democracia*), to radicalize the experience of democracy, for ours is a society that falsifies what democracy is about, that misrepresents democracy for capitalism.
>
> *Young man*: Ours is a structure of neighbourhood assemblies . . . We are all neighbours (*vecinos*), we are a *topos*, a place . . . We are proposing a place for everyone and anyone. That's what's meant by 'popular', a space for all, where a neighbour need not have the same ideas as I do but she feels the place is hers too.

The exchange shows the extent to which assemblies were imagined as a practice for the exhaustion of politics 'as we know it'. Such an exhaustion opened up a vacuum (*abrir espacios*, in the idiom used above) for novel forms of social and political association: a tentative and uncertain *topos* of neighbourly relations. The vignette captures also, however, the hesitation and ambiguity in naming these novel forms. Thus, whilst over the following months the word 'neighbour' (*vecino*) gained traction when referring to the constituency of assemblies, the term 'neighbourhood assemblies' was always rejected in favour of 'popular assemblies'. It is perhaps not too far-fetched, then, to think of assemblies as air-pumps for the exhaustion of classic representational politics, as instruments 'for exhausting capitalist democracy', as the woman put it in the vignette above. Assemblies exhausted the 'public' out of public space and the 'neighbourhood' out of the 'neighbour'. They gave new valences to these terms by re-signifying the kinds of knowledge and acknowledgements guiding the assembling of strangers in public space.

As an ethnographic category, then, 'exhaustion' at Madrid's popular assemblies movement provided a placeholder for a shifting complex of sentiments regarding physical fatigue and exhilaration, a social praxis of care, nurturance, and hospitality, and a creative manipulation of the material conditions of space. Exhaustion signalled a culture of political transformation whose centre was 'assembled', also, as an exhausted space: a space that was perceived as being 'emptied out', such that people's relations to each other as neighbours could be entangled anew into a specific experience of democracy.

When seventeenth-century natural philosophers first started congregating to share their mutual interests in and findings about experimental practices, their 'assembling' into a physical space and social body became no trivial matter either. The location of these 'houses of experiment', as Steve Shapin calls them (1988), was of great consequence to the types of knowledge that experimentalists were entitled to lay claims to. Experiments took place in a variety of venues,

> from the apothecary's and instrument maker's shop, to the coffeehouse, the royal palace, the rooms of college fellows, and associated collegiate and university structures. But by far the most significant venues were the private residences of gentlemen ... The overwhelming majority of experimental trials, displays, and discussions that we know about occurred within private residences (Shapin 1988: 378).

The location of experimental work in the privacy of the home, argued Shapin, determined crucial questions of epistemology, such as the shaping of curiosity as a solitary enterprise, modelled after the 'models of space' of the 'monastic cell and the hermit's hut', where one could insulate oneself 'from distraction, temptation, distortion and convention' (1988: 384). Yet it also demanded that the threshold of privacy and intimacy of the home be negotiated such that certain witnesses were allowed inside the house in order to validate and lend credibility to the experimental findings. 'If experimental knowledge did indeed have to occupy private space during part of its career', observed Shapin, 'then its realization as authentic knowledge involved its transit to and through a public space' (1988: 384).

Knowledge was therefore attested to be valid, valuable, and creditworthy when assembled in the presence of gentlemen of good standing. The nature of this 'assembly' became absolutely central to the experimental project. Thomas Sprat, the Royal Society's first historian, already described as early as 1667 the importance of the role of the 'Assembly' in 'resolv[ing] upon the matter of *Fact*' (Shapin & Schaffer 1985: 58). The sociology of this assembly, the trustworthiness of its membership, helped define the reliability and objectivity of experimental knowledge. Although there were of course a number of referents of social intercourse that the assembly of experimentalists modelled itself after,[5] much was made of the importance of its members standing in no relation of servitude, of them being free from 'sordid Interests' (Joseph Glanvill, cited in Shapin 1988: 396), including, for example, freedom from mercantile relations, or freedom from labour relations, such as was the case with the technicians who aided in the experimental set-ups, whose labour was paid for. Freedom from relations, in other words, was a warrant for the assembling of knowledge anew, and it was the nature of this 'assembly' of knowledge and people that was self-consciously perceived as a singularly unique and novel social space.[6]

The coupling of 'relations' and 'knowledge' across social domains in seventeenth-century England is also the subject of a recent series of articles by Marilyn Strathern (e.g. 2014; 2017), part of her long-standing inquiry into the duplex nature of the relation as an epistemic and social figure. Strathern is particularly interested in the 'widening ethos of association' that led to the articulation of 'society' as a novel discursive object of public consciousness in that historical moment (2014: 11). One example of such novel use would be the Royal Society's corporate self-designation as a 'society', that is, an assembly of people that experimented not only with matters of fact but also with their own sociality as a matter of concern – a matter of trustworthiness, credibility, and, as noted above, *freedom of and from relation*.

Yet, according to Strathern, there might be room for exploring a parallel source of epistemic creativity in the seventeenth century, one that heeds attention to the 'abstraction' of knowledge not just from the *societies of experiment* (the houses and assemblies of genteel natural philosophers), but also from the *experiments of society*: from the creativity that familial and interpersonal networks invested in the use of novel generic terms for designating kin and affinal connections, paramount amongst which was the term 'relation'. 'The precise significance of generics, such as "relations" and "friends" (and later "connections") for kin ties', she writes, 'was that they combined recognition – acknowledging the kinship of this or that person, that is, choosing to know them – without specifying degree, without, in short, specifying the nature of the tie, and thus the kinship "properties" embodied (my phrasing) in those who were related' (Strathern 2014: 10). As such a generic term, 'relation' thus captured a sense of openness regarding kinship connections that echoed the epistemic uncertainty and possibility at play in experimental trials. This capacity of relations to 'abstract' knowledge of people and the world has proved extremely fertile since. So much so, Strathern suggests, that it makes one wonder how anthropology has come to the language that makes all theories and discourses about 'kinship to be about relations' (2014: 13).[7]

Here we wish to follow Strathern's inspiring analysis and ask whether we might not consider Madrid's popular assemblies as experiments of society in their own right. These are *experiments of street*, where the assembly migrates the thresholds of witnessing, trustworthiness, and credibility to the open air, and where relations of knowledge and familiarity are cast anew among strangers and neighbours. As noted above, the word 'neighbour' (*vecino*) was self-consciously adopted by assemblies to designate the congregation of souls they bodied forward in space. The assembling of neighbours was an experiment in abstraction with effects not unlike those ascribed by Strathern to the 'relation'. In this usage, *vecinos* were not simply spatial or territorial subjects, but political and epistemic agents too. Assemblies provided a *topos* for a form of knowing and recognizing one's political and social surroundings, of which the *barrio* (neighbourhood) and the *vecino* became at once specific and generalized terms of reference.

Conclusion: at the end of the assembly

Byung-Chul Han has recently written a philosophical meditation on what he calls our 'burnout society' (Han 2015). Han seeks to refute a widespread philosophical thesis that characterizes our age as an 'immunological' era, where concepts of identity take shape through dynamics of rejection, negativity, or enmity. In other words, where the 'other' is defined by the imagination of immunological invasion. But our society, Han suggests, is no longer defined by the pathology of viruses and bacteria, by immunology. We are no longer moved by a compulsion towards expulsion and negativity. Ours is rather a society that runs on an excess of positivity, where there is too much of everything: production, performance, information (Han 2015: 5). The violence and exigencies of positivity have driven the self to the point of exhaustion. We have been drained by an ever-accelerating compulsion for self-enhancement. We are a 'burnout society'.

There might be a way out of burnout society, however, that draws on fatigue's own existential resources for escaping the culture of positivity. Seeking inspiration in Peter Handke's 'Essay on tiredness' (1994), Han identifies a more fundamental form of tiredness, a feeling of abandonment that takes residence in the world without calling for differentiations. Instead, this form of fatigue dwells in a space of in-betweenness, a 'space of friendliness-as-indifference' where the self 'abandons itself' to the world around us and the things of the world lose their sharpness and distinctiveness, their otherness, and give way to an 'aura of friendliness' (Han 2015: 31, 33). This abandoning further opens up the self to the tactility of the world: we surrender our self to the 'touch' of others (Han 2015: 32). 'This tiredness', writes Han, 'founds a deep friendship and makes it possible to conceive of a community that requires neither belonging nor relation' (2015: 33). Instead, it is founded on an experience of pacification that grows out of 'a particular rhythm … that leads to agreement, proximity, and vicinity … without familial or functional connections' (Han 2015: 34).

The experience of tiredness and pacification that Han talks about echoes aspects of the politics of exhaustion that we have described in this essay. This is the feeling of abandonment and exhilaration that Adolfo noted in his fieldwork diary, or indeed the hopeful melancholy invoked in the last sentences of our opening vignette: 'We sit, and we listen, and we witness, and sometimes we touch something, we find something, someone. In honesty, it is not always clear what remains at the end of the assembly (*al final de la asamblea*)'. Yet the form of exhaustion that conjures the 'end of the assembly' as an image of political hope moves also beyond the romantic ethos and political communitarianism implied in Han's analysis. Indeed, it has been our intention in this essay to show the extent to which political exhaustion 'exhausts' the political as we know it. Assembly politics certainly draws on the cultural and historical resources of deliberative and representational democracy: the politics of oratory and rhetoric; the boundaries of communicative action in public space; the theatrics of agonism and antagonism; the normative 'veil of ignorance' through which we are all made into strangers (Rawls 1999). But if there is a community – a vicinity, Han calls it; a neighbourhood, in the idiom used by assemblies – that this political exhaustion calls into existence, it is not one that is canvassed from the resources of political theory. Rather, this is a politics born in the vacuum of politics, outside the ontological spaces that Hobbes first inaugurated for it. The ontology of this politics is to be found

Journal of the Royal Anthropological Institute (N.S.), 110-123
© Royal Anthropological Institute 2017

elsewhere, in the spaces of experiment. For if exhaustion was something abhorred by the Hobbesian imagination of political agency, it was, on the contrary, something to look for in the manufacturing of experimental knowledge. In opening up a space for exhaustion, seventeenth-century natural philosophers such as Boyle were making room for novel 'assemblies' of instruments, people, and relations. 'At the end of the assembly', then, might be a fit image for both: a limit space where exhaustion finally yields a political deed, but also an ever-receding horizon of experimental trial. At the end of the assembly, Boyle meets Hobbes in the experiment of street.

NOTES

Our deepest and heartfelt thanks to the members of Lavapiés and Prosperidad's Popular Assemblies, whose generosity, hospitality, and intellectual and political sensibilities 'enlisted' us as witnesses into a vibrant cultural moment of experimental transformation in the city. This text is only possible thanks to them. We are also grateful to Hannah Brown, Adam Reed, and Thomas Yarrow for the care and insight with which they edited our text. The names and identities of all informants have been anonymized as per their wishes and/or to protect their privacy.

[1] We can hardly provide here a sociological overview of the hundreds of assemblies that popped up in Madrid. Generally speaking, assemblies reproduced the demographic and socioeconomic backgrounds of the neighbourhoods wherein they took residence. In response to the specific needs of each neighbourhood, some assemblies developed 'stronger' working groups than others. For example, in Prosperidad, a neighbourhood at the epicentre of a large and socially diverse district (Chamartín), where there are known to be large differences in the quality of education provided by local state schools, the assembly became known across the city for its 'Education' working group. The Lavapiés assembly, on the other hand, became well known for its 'Immigration' and 'Housing' working groups. On the whole, assemblies reproduced the rich heterogeneity of urban life.

[2] *Agotamiento* offers us in this guise a phonetic and conceptual counterpoint to Chantal Mouffe's distinction between 'agonistic' and 'antagonistic' political traditions (2005).

[3] *Mirón* stands for 'he or she who looks at', that is, a 'seer' or 'onlooker'. *Mirones* are also said to use their detached position to '*mirar por encima*', to over-see. In this sense *mirones* may be said to oversee or supervise that which they are looking at. They occupy an ambiguous position between observers and witnesses, hence our referring to them as 'passer-by witnesses'.

[4] An acronym for *Grupo de Intervención de Lavapiés*, Lavapiés Intervention Group.

[5] As Shapin puts it, 'The relationship between the proceedings of the early Royal Society and the Interregnum London coffeehouse merits extended discussion, most particularly in connection with the rules of good order in a mixed assembly. Other elements resonate of the monastery, the workshop, the club, the college, and the army' (1988: 393).

[6] Shapin cites Thomas Sprat's description to this effect: 'Sprat said that the "cure" for the disease afflicting current systems of knowledge "must be no other, than to form an Assembly at one time, whose privileges shall be the same; whose gain shall be in common; whose Members were not brought up at the feet of each other"' (Shapin 1988: 397).

[7] Because, of course, kinship is a form of knowledge that preceded this *new* relationality, and that, subsequent to these seventeenth-century shifts, became conditioned by it.

REFERENCES

ACAMPADASOL 2011. Guía rápida para la dinamización de asambleas (available on-line: *http://madrid.tomalaplaza.net/2011/05/31/guia-rapida-para-la-dinamizacion-de-asambleas-populares/*, accessed 23 January 2017).

ASAMBLEA DE LOS BARRIOS DEL SUR 2011. Acta de la Asamblea de los Barrios del Sur, sábado 5 de noviembre del 2011 (available on-line: *http://madrid.tomalosbarrios.net/249936/acta-i-asamblea-de-los-barrios-del-sur/*, accessed 23 January 2017).

CORSÍN JIMÉNEZ, A. & A. ESTALELLA 2014. Assembling neighbors: the city as hardware, method, and 'a very messy kind of archive'. *Common Knowledge* **20**, 150-71.

GERBAUDO, P. 2012. *Tweets and the streets: social media and contemporary activism*. London: Pluto.

GRAEBER, D. 2011. Occupy Wall Street's anarchist roots – Opinion – Al Jazeera English (available on-line: *http://www.aljazeera.com/indepth/opinion/2011/11/2011112872835904508.htm*, accessed 20 January 2017).

HAN, B.-C. 2015. *The burnout society.* Stanford: University Press.

HANDKE, P. 1994. Essay on tiredness. In *The jukebox and other essays on storytelling* (trans. R. Manheim & K. Wilson), 3-46. New York: Farrar, Straus and Giroux.

HARVEY, D. 2012. *Rebel cities: from the right to the city to the urban revolution.* London: Verso.

LATOUR, B. 1993. *We have never been modern* (trans. C. Porter). Cambridge, Mass.: Harvard University Press.

LEONTIDOU, L. 2012. Athens in the Mediterranean 'movement of the piazzas': spontaneity in material and virtual public spaces. *City* **16**, 299-312.

LORENZO VILA, A.R. & M.Á. MARTÍNEZ LÓPEZ 2005. *Asambleas y reuniones: metodologías de autoorganización.* Madrid: Traficantes de Sueños.

MARTÍNEZ, G. 2012. *CT o la cultura de la transición: crítica a 35 años de cultura española.* Madrid: Penguin Random House.

MORENO-CABALLUD, L. 2014. Cuando cualquiera escribe: procesos democratizadores de la cultura escrita en la crisis de la Cultura de la Transición española. *Journal of Spanish Cultural Studies* **15**, 13-36.

MOUFFE, C. 2005. *The return of the political.* London: Verso.

POLLETTA, F. 2002. *Freedom is an endless meeting: democracy in American social movements.* Chicago: University Press.

POSTILL, J. 2014. Freedom technologists and the new protest movements: a theory of protest formulas. *Convergence: The International Journal of Research into New Media Technologies* **20**, 402-18.

RAWLS, J. 1999. *A theory of justice* (Revised edition). Cambridge, Mass.: The Belknap Press of Harvard University Press.

RAZSA, M. & A. KURNIK 2012. The Occupy movement in Žižek's hometown: direct democracy and a politics of becoming. *American Ethnologist* **39**, 238-58.

SENNETT, R. 1977. *The fall of public man.* Cambridge: University Press.

SHAPIN, S. 1988. The house of experiment in seventeenth-century England. *Isis* **79**, 373-404.

——— & S. SCHAFFER 1985. *Leviathan and the air-pump: Hobbes, Boyle and the experimental life.* Princeton: University Press.

SIMMEL, G. 1972. The stranger. In *On individuality and social forms* (ed. D.N. Levine), 143-50. Chicago: University Press.

SKINNER, Q. 2008. *Hobbes and republican liberty.* Cambridge: University Press.

STRATHERN, M. 2014. Reading relations backwards. *Journal of the Royal Anthropological Institute* (N.S.) **20**, 3-19.

——— 2017. Connections, friends and their relations: an issue in knowledge-making. In *Comparative metaphysics: ontology after anthropology* (eds) P. Carbonnier, G. Salmon & P. Skafish, 61-82. London: Rowman & Littlefield International.

VERTOVEC, S. & R. COHEN 2002. *Conceiving cosmopolitanism: theory, context and practice.* Oxford: University Press.

Épuisement politique et expérimentation de la rue : Boyle rencontre Hobbes chez Occupy Madrid

Résumé

Le présent essai décrit les négociations complexes entourant la sociabilité entre inconnus, l'espace public et les connaissances démocratiques qui ont marqué les assemblées populaires dans le sillage du mouvement 15M/Occupy en Espagne. Le travail de rassemblement a été « épuisant » selon les participants, ce qui peut vouloir dire deux choses : dans un sens, les réunions se sont souvent avérées usantes pour la patience et la résilience des participants. Dans un autre sens, elles ont été décrites comme des espaces « d'épuisement » de la chose politique, décortiquée et remplacée par de nouvelles possibilités démocratiques. Les auteurs proposent ici un récit de l'épuisement comme catégorie ethnographique, en s'intéressant en particulier au rôle qui lui est accordé comme vide permettant l'apparition de rôles sociaux et politiques nouveaux. Ils élaborent leur argument par le biais d'une analogie provocatrice avec les premières expérimentations scientifiques, dans lesquelles la nature d'une « assemblée » de pairs de confiance et sa localisation dans l'espace profane sont devenues constitutives d'un nouveau type de connaissances expérimentales. Quelles figures sociales et épistémiques les assemblées populaires incarnent-elles aujourd'hui ?

7

Minutes, meetings, and 'modes of existence': navigating the bureaucratic process of urban regeneration in East London

GILLIAN EVANS *University of Manchester*

Inspired by Latour's aim to restore balance to the anthropological project by exoticizing the artefacts and procedures of so-called 'modern knowledge', this essay gives an ethnographic description of emergent processes of knowledge production in the context of the planning and development of urban regeneration in London. Bureaucratic meetings are described as part of the organizational infrastructure that enables the crafting of new urban futures, and it is argued that, because the making of reality is always seen to be forward moving, there is a need, as in navigation, to plot a course. The essay focuses on the subversive potential of informal meetings, and argues, more generally, that meetings are the materially social, and affectively technical, manoeuvres that make possible direction-finding and contestation about the way forward.

> Bureaucracy develops the more perfectly, the more it is dehumanized, the more completely it succeeds in eliminating from official business love, hatred, and all purely personal, irrational, and emotional elements which escape calculation.
>
> Weber 1968: 273

The haunting: East London, November 2014

Mark looks gaunt this time: he is worn down and worn out: weary with battle. One won. One lost.

On my way to meet him, I see the evidence of his victory: an open space – bare earth, and black topsoil – in plots. Underneath darkening skies, a crop of lonely looking sheds stands out, brand-new, incongruous against the cluttered backdrop of more usual urban forms. Faded high-rise council flats, bright new apartments, and a hotchpotch of Victorian industrial buildings make a skyline for the ground. And, leading the eye away, the tangled traces of infrastructural flows – canal, railway, and road.

The significance of this – this scratch of earth – is not lost on me. As the train I am travelling on goes by, I want to stand up, cry out loud, declare Mark's victory to fellow-passengers: 'He did it; they've done it: they won. Look at the sheds! Look at the plots!' But I say nothing, and sit quietly, containing my excitement as the train passes, and I look backwards, until the space is out of sight.

Journal of the Royal Anthropological Institute (N.S.), 124-137
© Royal Anthropological Institute 2017

When I see him, I want to celebrate with Mark, but for the moment, he thinks only of the defeat he has suffered. Trying to make sense of it, he talks it through, and we walk, in a light rain.

The minutes

Mark is meticulous: the minutes of each meeting of the Manor Garden Allotment Society are kept carefully in individual, transparent wallets, and all of them are contained, in date order, in bright Lever-Arch files whose weight substantiates the passage of time: duration marked, one gathering after another. In amongst other business, a fight is documented: the evidence of a long struggle. Seven years, and counting ...

Mark wants me to see everything: to bear witness. Not to take sides, but to explain, and make public. He is a good secretary: exceptional, consumed by an order of business that far exceeds the administration of the day-to-day activities of the Society. Increasingly complex technicalities make it hard for Mark to keep pace with, and adapt to, the evolution of the conflict that members are engaged in, but he is relentless, determined, in a voluntary capacity, to serve the members well, manage his day job – crafting the wooden containers in which priceless works of art are transported from London galleries around the world – and, meanwhile, to tend his own plot, and make time for family life. His efforts are heroic.

To be sure, the usual, summarized account of the management of the decision-making process is there, the evidence recorded of the standardized repetition of rules that, as if by magic rite, allows the Society, comprising eighty-one members, to know itself as a single entity, a collective body, acting as if one (Schwartzman 1989). However, what strikes me is the personalization which punctuates the standardized formality of the minutes: ghosts of dead members hang about the pages, and in between the lines there is a lament about insufferable displacement from the land. For example, the spring 2015 AGM reports: 'A minute's silence was held in tribute to Reg. Hawkins who passed away recently. President remarked on how Reg. had been one of MGS' [Manor Gardens Society's] longest standing members, and noted the excellence of his allotment gardening'. Similarly, at the Extraordinary AGM in the winter of 2013, to discuss how to respond to confirmation of the breaking of the promise by the London Borough of Waltham Forest to provide land for the allotment-holders within the Olympic Park, priority is first given to respect for deceased members:

> A minute's silence was held in tribute to Pat Lemming who passed away recently. Chair remarked on how Pat had always put the Society's survival at the forefront of the agenda. Pat will be remembered for her stoic support of the Community, and for carrying the sound of laughter wherever she went. RIP Pat.

And, at the AGM, in the autumn of 2012, when first mention is made of the notification that the planning obligation may not be honoured by the London Borough of Waltham Forest to provide 2.1 hectares of allotment land at Eton Manor in the northeast of the Olympic Park, Mark notes in the minutes that the Manor Gardens Allotment Society 'had fought for five years to be relocated back into the Legacy Park as per the approved plans and through our own consultations had a Manor Gardens Society members' mandate which cited return to the Park, in 2.1 hectares as mandate'. Mark notes in the minutes that in a meeting with Waltham Forest he had 'expressed no room for negotiation', and, immediately after, he records the sad passing of Charlie Wilbourne and Ron Webb, 'both of whom will be remembered as seasoned members of our gardening community for many years. RIP'.

Journal of the Royal Anthropological Institute (N.S.), 124-137
© Royal Anthropological Institute 2017

Because we, too, are modern subjects of the polite procedures of congregation, we all of us understand these rules, and embody the stylization of the elite about what constitutes proper conduct in social gatherings (van Vree 1999). *Of course*, people take it in turns to speak, discuss one issue at a time, hold back from personal attack, and, in formal meetings, where collective goals, and ways of achieving them, are to be decided upon, they assume, on matters about which there is disagreement, that a majority vote will be taken whose outcome is to be accepted, in good faith, as the shared will of those assembled. In this way, modern meetings, in contrast to the proceedings of the early modern and medieval courts that preceded them (Elias 1994 [1939]), make parliamentarians and good citizens of us all. Through the cultivation of democratic processes of self-inhibition, meetings contain the time-consuming chaos of contestation, and disorganized discussion, so as to manage, non-violently, the social process of decision-making as the proper expression of a polite society organized in terms of civility and rational efficiency (van Vree 1999). In this sense, meetings are an essential part of the material organization of the modern 'mode of existence' (Latour 2013).

Ideally, by leaving out the personal details of who said what to whom, minutes of meetings purify the written record. Emotional content is eliminated from the description of the meeting; so, too, are the subjective vagaries of interpersonal dynamics. The record shows, instead, a summarized set of collectively agreed decisions about those specific issues which, at any time, preoccupy an assembled group whose members have in common shared goals linked to a specific environment external to the group itself, which, in this case, is the land – the plots, the garden allotments.

On this basis, anyone inspecting the minutes ought to be able to conclude not only that those assembled, through the documentation of meetings, are held accountable, retrospectively, for what they decide, but also that under the same conditions it comes to appear to be the case that any other reasonable group of people would have reached the same decisions. The meetings, then, constitute the Society – here, the Manor Gardens Allotment Society – as a collective body, a single entity, and the minutes, through a de-personalizing process of purification (Latour 1993), ideally ascribe to that entity the modern capacity to act objectively.

'Meeting-ization'

What van Vree (1999) describes as the history, in Europe, of the 'meeting-ization' of society is also, then, the objectification of society; it is part of what made possible the formation of the nation-state as a certain kind of territorial amalgamation. The meeting, as the means for the standardization and formalization of what counts among citizens as appropriate decision-making behaviour, proliferated throughout an integrated territory (as the state assumed the monopoly over legitimate violence), and this enabled the regularization of procedures for the non-violent adjustment of citizens' actions and intentions towards each other. As they learnt novel methods for the negotiation of conflict, and adapted to the conditions for the possibility of more peaceful interdependence, and coexistence, citizens came to negotiate conflict collectively, in new ways. In essence, van Vree (1999) outlines how, under conditions of nation-state formation and the democratization of the political process, words became the new weapons, meetings the new battlegrounds, and the sword and the dagger (among the general population at least) were laid to rest.

Journal of the Royal Anthropological Institute (N.S.), 124-137
© Royal Anthropological Institute 2017

Following Thompson (1966), van Vree (1999) shows how, during industrialization in Britain, the distribution of the meeting through all classes of society, as the most effective and most acceptable means for the organization and government of collective efforts of all kinds, led to a proliferation of places for the working classes to meet and do the work of transforming politics for themselves: for example, in industrial work associations, guilds, unions, and societies of all kinds. This development of a 'meeting class' implied not just the 'civilization' of certain sections of the working classes through reform of the means for assembly, but also, overall, that citizens' conflicts with the state itself were more likely to be civil, polite, and especially non-violent. Thus, the civilizing process (Elias 1994 [1939]) with respect to the manners cultivated in modern meetings not only militates against violent resistance (making violence one of the most exceptional phenomena in contemporary times), but also acts to constitute society as the object of an integrated set of collective actions that, throughout the nation, are constantly in the process of being negotiated.

The case of the Manor Garden Allotment Society is illustrative of this: in its battle against the state it has behaved impeccably – too politely, some might say – and the meeting has undoubtedly been the means for the containment of the violent emotions generated by the conflict. This is true both within the Society itself, where meetings have contained the endless contestation among members about how to proceed, and without, in the meetings with state authorities whose actions towards the land of the allotments have rendered uncertain the common future towards which allotment-holders had been working for almost a century. The meeting is seen, in this light, to be a mechanism of adaptation as negotiations are made between different organizations about conflicting actions concerning the same object of concern – the land – and unequal power relations are thereby made manifest in the moment-by-moment materialization of the decision-making process.

The Manor Garden allotments

I am amazed and tell Mark, straight away, about my interest in the souls of the dead that inhabit the pages of the minutes. I have no intention of undermining his skills as secretary, but there is no denying it: the minutes are suffused with emotion. The lament for the land is inescapable; it creeps through the lines like ivy through concrete, and makes of the minutes a surreal exercise in rational accounting.

Impressing upon me the degree of connection to place that has been forged through three generations of devoted cultivation and participation in the social life of the gardens, Mark explains that deceased allotment-holders' ashes were often scattered on the land. A lifetime of dedicated cultivation and involvement in an intimate community of 'diggers' meant that the very substance of the gardeners – as persons – became inseparable from the soil. Unsurprisingly, many of the 'old timers' had chosen the allotment, and, more specifically, their own plot, as their final resting-place.

It is no surprise either that the displacement of the Society from the land of the Manor Gardens to make way for the construction of London's Olympic Park in the East End of London, and the fight to hold the authorities to their political promise to reinstate the allotments after the Games, have been experienced by the gardeners as a deeply traumatic and disorientating series of events. A gardening couple, now restaurateurs, described their impending loss, in 2007, as follows:

Journal of the Royal Anthropological Institute (N.S.), 124-137
© Royal Anthropological Institute 2017

We needed courage to find our allotment for the first time. The vast area of Victoria Park has a dusty bleakness, unusual for London. If bicycling there, we have to keep away from the kerb, to avoid broken glass and rusty metal. The smell of burnt cow hair from the meat processing plant adds to the atmosphere. The only clue that there is any gardening life in the area is the wild rocket pushing out of the cracks in the pavement. Beside the bus depot, out of sight of the road, is a barbed rusty gate, behind which things change dramatically.

You can't help but gasp when you open the gate and find yourself standing at the foot of a 70-metre bridge high over the river, looking across to a bank of wild plums, elderflower and blackberries. There is not a building in sight, just the odd proud shed. Here are the land and the community that have been so important to us over the past seven years.

When we think of our first season on the allotment, we are reminded of cooking for friends and family when we were young. Bright-eyed, eager, we spent vast amounts of time preparing food, with very mixed results. In our modern lives, whether growing our own vegetables or cooking elaborate meals, it just doesn't add up. It's irrational. But why does it give us so much damn pleasure?

The first person we met was our neighbour Hassan: kind Mr Charisma, who was to become our friend and mentor. He introduced us to other people on the allotment – Cypriots, Kurds and Turks. We soon realized that we were among special people who thought differently about growing and could teach us much about cooking too. Our eyes were opened to things such as frying green tomatoes, cooking artichoke leaves, braising wild poppy leaves, and much more. The Eastern Mediterranean was alive in Hackney Wick, [East London].

Last year our crops suffered an unusual amount of damage from rabbits. We were puzzled as to the reason, but then it clicked: the Olympics were coming. Like a scene from *Watership Down*, the bulldozers were encroaching and the rabbits were escaping and settling where they could. By the time you hear about this, our century-old allotment will have been replaced by a vast, concrete pathway. We will have been moved on …

So now we must start afresh, scratching around in a new patch of earth (Clark & Clark 2007: vi-vii).

Sparking a fierce resistance in the gardeners, the imperative for them to move was first fought in spectacular fashion: Friends of the Earth made global the local support for a campaign called Life Island. The fight was taken to the High Court, and the argument was made that the gardeners had every right to remain on the land, because the soil they worked was given to them as a gift.[1] The land was inalienable, and, therefore, not to be bought at any price. That is to say, the allotments were not translatable in commodity terms: the gardeners were, literally, in their persons inseparable from their plots. It is no surprise, then, that the emotional traces of the violent upheaval to their lives caused by displacement from the land could not reasonably be purified from the minutes, or that, in general, decisions pertaining to inalienable objects, land and materials, do not lend themselves easily to bureaucratic procedure, which depends on 'calculable rules without regard to persons' (Weber 1968: 269).

Finally, after a protracted and high-profile battle against eviction, it was agreed that the allotments would be destroyed, but they had to be reinstated somewhere in the Olympic Park after the Games were over. The promise, materialized and made law as a planning obligation, was that after temporary removal, during the Games, to a site north of the Olympic Park called Marsh Lane, all the plot-holders would be re-allocated, by December 2014, to a new, larger plot on 2.1 hectares of land inside the boundary of the Olympic Park. As time went on, the 2.1 hectares was divided into plans for two separate allotment sites, one in the south and one in the north of the park, at Eton Manor, a site significant to many of the diggers because land here was also gifted to them, at the beginning of the twentieth century, for sporting facilities, playing fields, and club houses.

Journal of the Royal Anthropological Institute (N.S.), 124-137
© Royal Anthropological Institute 2017

Pudding Mill Lane, November 2014

Following the curve of the path around the Olympic Stadium, commenting, without malice, on the creative planting of the borders and canal sides, and the tasteful preservation of an old iron bridge over the canal, Mark is ready to take shelter from the rain. Over coffee, he finally speaks of his victory, a victory of sorts for the Society. First, he pays homage to the diggers, the old timers:

> These guys, they'll turn up a piece of land alongside a railway to grow their spuds, you know, they accommodate, and that's one of the great things about allotments: they're kind of marginalized lands, but people make good value from it. They will recover a piece of land and make something really good from it, and that's kind of like, you know, an old cockney kind of thing: all the old fellas are saying, you know, give us a bit of land to scratch around in and we'll make it work, we'll make it great.

Dedicated to these 'old fellas', and determined to make good on the bitter disappointment of their displacement, Mark describes the positive experience of collaborative design at the new allotment site, called Pudding Mill Lane, just inside the southern perimeter of the Olympic Park. He describes, in joyful terms, the outcome of his long-term liaison with Vincent Bartlett, a planner from the Olympic Park Legacy Company (OPLC), which was the organization tasked by city and central government with planning and delivering an Olympic legacy for London from the 2012 Games. Mark's account complicates the typical story of a straightforward Olympic land grab, and the intimate life of the state (Bernstein & Mertz 2011) is revealed in the articulation between allotment society and city government, which transforms the local scale of allotment cultivation into a larger story about London's economic growth.

> Once they [the OPLC] had come up with the first designs I went back to them, and I set out a plan of action, and sent it to Vincent, saying, 'We've done really well so far and we're really pleased especially with . . .', you know, it was still up in the air, they didn't want to talk about Eton Manor, but Pudding Mill Lane they wanted to talk about, and I said, 'We were really pleased that we seemed to be moving in a direction that's really positive, people are starting to get excited about it. I've got this idea of making it even better', and I told them the results of my survey and I had a plan of how they could incorporate that information into making things better.
>
> Vincent immediately arranged for me, and Pat Burcham [one of the old timers], to go down and meet with him. I cleared that at our AGM with the broader Society. They all felt that was a really good idea. I said that I would take it forward and they agreed to that. I went to the designers and the main guy that was doing the design, this German fella, Christof Brintrop [from LDA Design, the landscape architects commissioned by the Olympic Delivery Authority], really good listening designer, I explained to him what I'd done and he was so excited about it, and he was saying, kind of like, 'the raw material that you have to design something like a set of allotments' which he's never done before, he said, 'it suddenly realized some kind of clarity for him, because he's got real data to work with'.
>
> I gave him the information, I talked to them about percentages and land use and stuff, they went away, they came back and they put all of those changes in, they changed the plots' sizes, they put bends in the path to give it more character, just subtle little things that I know make a big difference, so I was really pleased with that. And when we went back to the meeting, where they had begun to incorporate those ideas into the designs, I can remember a guy from the Olympic Park Legacy Company Parks Design team said, 'You can't change the spine path at Pudding Mill Lane', and Pat said, 'It's ok, it's not that bit we want to change, it's what's going on around it'. The guy from Park Design said, 'That's fine'. Pat then said, out of interest, 'Why can't you change that, is it to do with some kind of planning regulation about what's on the plans?' And he said, 'No it's cos they've already built it'.
>
> We had no idea they'd already started construction at this point, and me and Pat looked at each other and Pat said to them, 'You mean you've started it?' They said, 'Yeah'. We said, 'Well, what have you done?' And they said, 'Well, we've put the footprint in, we've put the hard standing in, and', he said, 'we've dug down, we've put the path in'. And, it was just so lovely: Pat Burcham, who is this big bruising East End boy, he's one of those guys that's got a silent laugh, and it's all in his body kind of

thing, and there were tears coming down his face, just the joy, seeing this realization. That year his grandfather had died; he was the guy, he's on the plot next to mine, and last year there would have been his grandfather, his mum and dad, him, his brother, his brothers' kids, four generations working the plot, so for someone like him … He was the guy who used to play rugby for the major, Arthur Villiers, for Eton Manor and stuff like that, so it was such a big deal for him, so joyful.

Here, Mark describes how profound cynicism about the intentions of the city government and the Olympic planners turned to delight among the allotment-holders as it became clear that at least part of the promise – not just to reinstate, but to increase allotment provision, and for it to be resituated within the boundary of the Olympic Park – was seen to be coming to fruition. Not only was part of the land being made available, as promised, but the planning and design of the site were being carried out in a genuinely collaborative way, through informal meetings, with plenty of scope for reflection and the expression of emotion. And the diggers themselves, and their spokesperson, Mark, were treated as experts, with the German designer acknowledging his own inexperience, and Vincent, the government planner, fulfilling his commitment to the allotment-holders, working with them to realize their vision of twenty-first-century allotments to be proud of.

In contrast to the earlier mass mobilizations of the Society, Mark's success at Pudding Mill Lane marks a new kind of political action. It takes the form of years of painstaking work, cultivating a behind-the-scenes, informal relationship with the planner inside the OPLC. The dramatic material transition in the gardeners' tools of trade, and particularly Mark, as secretary/spokesperson/activist, could not be more pronounced: from spade and hoe to documentary and diplomatic tools, Mark has acquired a differentiated set of skills essential to the cultivation of successful political manoeuvres in the complex context of urban planning in London.

The personable relationship between Mark and Vincent allows for a properly collaborative process, one that recognizes the emotive context in which the OPLC is operating and that arrives at an effective decision for all concerned precisely because the process of planning through relationship-building has led to an affective and therefore meaningful outcome. This is not to say that relations between Mark and Vincent have always been harmonious: Mark is the first to admit that Vincent has, in his dealings with the allotment-holders, soaked up his fair share of anger, resentment, and frustration. What matters is that Mark met in Vincent a planner capable of and interested in listening to, properly consulting with, and defending the interests of the Society. Here, Vincent is to planning and the state what Mark is to gardening and the Society: a leading figure with a genuine sense of personal responsibility and a strong sense of public service duty. It is this mirroring of intention (Robbins 2012) that has allowed for the productive articulation of the two organizations, and the successful forging of a relationship between two men, who are now responsible for growing a new piece of city together.

The effectiveness here of the informal meeting is significant: decisions about the future are still being made, conflict resolution is still happening, but there is the potential, outside of official protocol and consequent documentation, for the outcome of the meeting to be something other than a rationally calculable, 'objective' determination; it is, rather, in this case, the obviously relational product of an ongoing, intersubjective, highly emotive, but nevertheless non-violent negotiation about the best course of action to take. This more experimental and innovative way of working says something, too, about the OPLC as a new kind of governance organization, one that is both committed to relationship-building with 'local communities', and genuinely, in some work teams, like Vincent's, interested in urban 'regeneration' not as simply 'top-down' or 'trickle-down', but as a potentially transformative tool for change in post-industrial neighbourhoods. Perhaps it is because it stands outside of the usual bureaucratic structures of public sector governance that the OPLC is able to occupy a transitional space – somewhere between an anti-bureaucratic private sector disinterest, and the procedural obsessiveness common to newly formed organizations – and individuals like Vincent are able to manoeuvre in the interstices between what is in the Company's best interest and what is for the public good. Others in the organization describe this kind of manoeuvring with some pride as being able to operate like 'ghosts in the machine'.

Eton Manor

Reflecting with Mark on why he has not enjoyed the same kind of success with the second allotment site in the north of the Olympic Park at Eton Manor, in relation to which he feels utterly defeated, I suggest to him that the explanation might partly be to do with the lack of development of any personable relationship with key players behind a very different set of city government scenes. Moreover, I argue, the loss of global attention to and support for their cause since the original mass mobilization with Friends of the Earth must also have been significant for the Society.

I ask Mark to explain what has gone wrong at Eton Manor, and he relates how the complicated issue of land ownership has got in the way: the OPLC does not own the land in the north of the park where the second allotment site was always supposed to be located. Lea Valley Regional Park is the owner, and the land is located in the London borough of Waltham Forest. Out of all the four host Olympic boroughs – Newham, Hackney, Tower Hamlets, and Waltham Forest – Waltham Forest always felt short-changed by the legacy plans, and, so it seems, was never properly supportive of the idea of hosting half of the re-located allotments. As time went on, the powers-that-be at Waltham Forest began to make clear that they did not want their small legacy gain to be compromised by having to yield land, now growing in monetary value, to community purpose. On the contrary, the stated aim became to create a globally significant Olympic legacy in Waltham Forest, with a focus on sports provision centred on the elite provision of cycling facilities at the Velodrome. And so, without also irreparably damaging their relations with the OPLC, who were all the time pressuring Waltham Forest and Lea Valley Regional Park to 'meet their planning obligations', the planners at Waltham Forest quietly began to alienate the allotment Society from the proposed site.

Mark describes how, without a significant ally behind the scenes at Waltham Forest, he was drawn into and, eventually, lost in the labyrinth of planning decisions. Isolated and exhausted, he felt powerless in the face of legal technicalities, and frustrated by the endlessly evasive manoeuvres of the authorities. I suggest, too, that Waltham Forest has been successful in its campaign against the Society precisely because it has been able to use the bureaucratic process of official meetings to make its planning decisions appear to be objective. Over time, the minutes have effectively erased from the record the original legal obligation to the allotment-holders; the long history of their emotive resistance to the subtle shifts in the urban planning field of play; and the trauma caused to the Society by the unjust collusion of all parties in their alienation from the land promised to members.

Journal of the Royal Anthropological Institute (N.S.), 124-137
© Royal Anthropological Institute 2017

Working ethnographically with meetings and minutes is, then, anti-modern: it means attempting to restore to the written record the full history of disorder, to reincorporate the emotionally charged, chaotic contestation of inter-subjective dynamics and material manoeuvres; to purposely contaminate apparently objective decisions with impolite objections to the civilized production of matters of fact.

The contrast between the two cases, one victory, one defeat, suggests that in the very act of planning and organizing place-based projects, the categories of community and state are mutually constituted in highly specific and unpredictable ways (Robertson 1984). This helps us to understand, firstly, that the state exists objectively only in the endlessly emerging moments of contested articulation between government, territory, and population (Bourdieu 2014), and, secondly, that ethnography is perhaps the only method that allows us to study these processes of articulation as they emerge, so that we can speak critically and constructively to the practice of state craft in contemporary times (Bernstein & Mertz 2011).

Acts of enclosure

Polanyi (1944) taught us long ago that wherever we see a new enforced enclosure of land, we ought to expect an articulation of market forces with state intervention. Confronted with the extraction of value to which the creation of a market in land potentially gives rise, the local populace rail against their exclusion and/or displacement from this value-creation process. In the light of a long history of land enclosure in Britain, the government has to work hard to convince the public that it is working in the interests of the greater good. This is especially the case in the East End of London, because the last major act of enclosure, in the 1980s, was Canary Wharf, a new financial district formed out of the post-industrial docklands, which became notorious for employing 90,000 prospering white-collar workers, whilst on the surrounding housing estates unemployment rose steadily through the period of construction and development, and these neighbourhoods remain, today, some of the most disadvantaged in the country.

Tsing (2005), writing about the creation of a market for land and other commodities at the frontier of logging and metal extraction in Indonesia, describes as 'haunting' the troubling of market forces with alternative ideas of value. She shows how attracting global capital flows to new sites of development requires both a spectacular drama, a fantastical 'economy of appearances', and cultivation of the false idea that the new frontiers of capital expansion, in any time and place, are formed by the heroic conquering of wild places and wastelands devoid of human history. Psychogeographer Iain Sinclair (2012) describes as 'ghost milk' the urban planners' fantastical imaginations of a post-Olympic Games future in the East End of London, visions of an imagined time and place that, he argues, similarly rely on the notion of a wasteland and bear no relation to, and have no respect for, the historical significance of what has been displaced from the Lower Lea Valley to make way for the Olympic Park.

Crying out against the imposition of the grand projects of a state oblivious to the cultural histories of small-scale, historically specific, and locally meaningful action, Sinclair echoes James Scott's concerns (1999) about what it is for a state to act. In a sense, I think he is right, but it is not at all straightforward. On the one hand, the displacement and improper treatment of groups like the Manor Garden Allotment Society by Waltham Forest and the Lea Valley Regional Parks Authority will haunt the Olympic legacy for a long time to come. This should be understood, especially after the 2008 financial crisis, in terms of the critique of a market-driven notion of society where global aspirations for city competitiveness eclipse and evacuate the lived experience of people inhabiting diverse urban environments. On the other hand, however, the ethnographic problem in the post-industrial urban neighbourhoods of Britain and elsewhere in the world, in cities like Detroit in the United States, is precisely to do with the question of how to seduce capital to flow back to cities in decline, and then how to irrigate that flow for particular productive purposes. The commercial imperative cannot be ignored, and the success of the process of regeneration depends, therefore, on the effective articulation of government projects of urban transformation with commercial and community interest, which brings our attention, as anthropologists, to what I have described above, which is the ethnographic details of what, in practice, effective articulation might look like.

Conducting fieldwork within the OPLC itself, I also had the opportunity to participate in and observe the struggle to make of bureaucratic process a practice of effective articulation. Over a period of three years, I bore witness to the endless determination of Vincent's like-minded colleagues, such as Emma, Senior Manager of the OPLC's Community Engagement Team, as she fought to stay true to public service ideals, and maintain her allegiance to local community interests as the priorities of the Company shifted, too heavily, over time, and at the expense of community interests, towards the commercial imperative. I show below how at a time of perceived crisis and instability in the OPLC, Emma and her immediate colleagues in the Community Engagement Team attached increased significance to their 'team meeting'. This, too, like Mark's artful resistance from below, was a subtle and effective form of political action, one that revealed to me the radical potential of the informal meeting to act as an effective strategy for skilful subversion, especially when the way ahead has become uncertain.

Regeneration: coming back to life, September 2009

Emma leads one of the four sub-groups, including Public Relations, Press, and Marketing, which make up the OPLC Communications Team (Comms). Overall, the role of the Comms Team is to maintain and manage communications both internally, within the Company itself (across its various work streams, and with its parent organization, the London Development Agency (LDA), and 'owners' – the Mayor of London, the Department of Culture, Media, and Sport, and the Department of Communities and Local Government), and externally, with the general public, media, politicians, stakeholders, and community groups in East London, about how London's Olympic legacy is being planned.

In material terms, this means crafting the 'messages': coming up with 'lines' and designing the 'look and feel' of a rhetoric that, from one week to the next, produces and stabilizes a persuasive narrative to the OPLC and the world about the existence and purpose of the Company. Through the production of a surface impression of itself (Evans 2012; 2014), the OPLC convinces itself and the world that it exists as a viable entity, and in so doing, it grows in confidence as a new organization and begins to develop and sustain a network of relations with important allies (Latour 1988) – adherents, if you like – whose belief in the Company lends momentum to the cause. These allies have to be 'kept on board' and careful communication is critical to this task.

Emma leads the weekly 'team catch-up' meeting. Clearly worried, she explains that the board of the LDA, at their last meeting, refused to sign off on the transfer of Olympic land and associated debt to the newly formed OPLC. Emma's small team

Journal of the Royal Anthropological Institute (N.S.), 124-137
© Royal Anthropological Institute 2017

of four (including myself) knows full well that the refusal to transfer Olympic park lands and associated debts means that the Company, in the process of being formed at this time, would become a toothless tiger, a 'useless entity' not to be taken seriously by investors or property developers, and doomed, therefore, to fail: the whole legacy project would be jeopardized.

Emma explains that the formation of the OPLC itself, out of the Legacy Directorate that preceded it as part of the LDA, signifies a new legacy direction of travel, away from former Mayor Ken Livingstone's left-wing communities-focused view of regeneration, and more commercially focused, property and enterprise development perspective of the Conservative Mayor, Boris Johnson.[2] An atmosphere of anxiety and uncertainty hangs over the meeting. Rebecca, Emma's second in command, protests and says that, meanwhile, during this transitional hiatus, the team has 'run out of messages', 'run out of story', and there is no sense of what the new narrative about legacy will be for the new company under the newly appointed Chief Executive. Rebecca wonders how they can go on doing their jobs, and, by implication, how the momentum of the Olympic legacy can be sustained. She worries that the most important political stakeholders – the Olympic host boroughs in the East End of London – have no idea yet about who the new Chief Executive is, and what it is he has to say about 'the direction of travel'. If there is no 'message', how will the Comms. Team keep the host boroughs 'on board'?

Emma agrees with Rebecca that they have nothing to go on, and no sense of direction while new priorities are worked out from above. She warns that it is going to be an awkward few months. She then explains that they have been told to start working with the Marketing Team to also engage with 'international business communities' and no longer focus solely on 'local communities' in the East End. At this, Samantha, Emma's second assistant, despairs, saying simply, 'how disappointing': Samantha knows full well, like her close colleagues in the Community Engagement Team, that years of invaluable effort have already been put into building relationships of trust and open communication with stakeholders and local communities in the East End, and that it will be a serious threat to the project if that trust is broken. With an air of futility, she says that their work is beginning to feel like what she had always imagined and dreaded government bureaucracy to be, which is 'layers and layers of uselessness'.

Emma then reassures her team that the new idea is to use the excitement from the Games, and the development of each permanent sporting venue left on the park after the Games, as well as an 'events' strategy, to 'buy people into the Park' and 'build community up'. Meanwhile, while the new Chief Executive works out what his new 'top line' messages about the Olympic legacy are going to be, Emma suggests that by producing a 'core presentation' for him to use in his public engagements, they can surreptitiously attempt to align what he says in the world with their existing understandings of what is considered to be important about the Company's work streams.

By putting their 'lines' into his mouth, the Comms Team attempts to exert its influence over the new Chief Executive. It is no surprise, therefore, that the new Interim Director of Communications for the OPLC is extremely wary of the existing Comms Team. She worries that their lines and messages speak of what she calls 'The Old World', and she emphasizes at every opportunity that she is trying to usher in a new world with different priorities. However, neither she nor the new Chief Executive knows anything about the East End, and with no project knowledge at all, they are, in the end, at the mercy of Emma and her team, who prove to be indispensable, because they are the only ones who have the necessary expertise to chart the existing terrain.

Navigational techniques

The meeting that I focus on above took place at a time of serious uncertainty in the planning of London's Olympic legacy. Not surprisingly, the transfer of precious political cargo from one organizational vehicle to another caused a great deal of anxiety for people like Emma and her team, who, with considerable dedication, had already been working on and driving the project forward for several years.

I focus on uncertain times to make a more general point, which is that all organizational forms are inherently unstable. This has important implications for the analysis of organizational practice, not least because the formal meeting can then be understood in a number of ways as a stabilization device. You could say that the bureaucratic meeting is the organizational means for distributing cognition (Hutchinson 1995) about navigational matters.

In the uncertain world of state-funded urban regeneration, where political and economic currents are extremely treacherous, it is no surprise to me that before it was ever called the Olympic Park Legacy Company, the organization designed by government to take over the sole task of planning and delivering the Olympic legacy was called an SPV, a Special Purpose Vehicle. The metaphor of motion suggests that for a new reality to come into being, the idea of it has to be given organizational form and moved forward, which requires a clear and strong sense of direction as well as effective mechanisms for navigation. One such mechanism, I suggest, is the bureaucratic meeting: it is the means for steering the course towards a common future, and for plotting how to proceed, especially in moments when the way forward is unclear.

The never-ending array of meetings at the OPLC function to constitute the new organization as a continuously articulated whole, a viable entity with a particular purpose, and the meetings allow for the adaptation of work teams internally, so that each member's actions are aligned with the overall purpose of the team, and then the teams' actions are aligned with each other. What is most interesting about this taken-for-granted organizational infrastructure, however, is how at times when there is a sense of mutinous subversion, when disputes arise from within about which direction the Company ought to be taking, managers lower down the hierarchy, like Emma, who have all the expertise, but none of the authority, can, through the possibilities provided by informal, undocumented meetings, exert their power and influence surreptitiously, manoeuvring to gradually force adjustments to be made to the direction of travel even at the very top of the organization.

Either way, formally or informally, the negotiations of the bureaucratic meeting aim expertly towards a steadying of the ship through a continuously contested decision-making process about what needs to be done to hold or change course. Here, what Tsing (2005) describes as the 'about to be present' emerges in relation to protracted battles about the vision of the future which the projects of the state substantiate, in this case in the post-industrial East End of London. The ethnography reveals that the future of East London is not crafted by any easy equation between government and capital, or characterized by a straightforward dichotomy of insurmountable difference between the bureaucratic process of governance and what counts as community interest. Indeed, it is heartening to have witnessed that inside the bureaucracies of urban government there are warriors, people who are prepared to use each and every meeting as the place to (non-violently) do battle for a public service version of the common good. This endless struggle, over a number of years, to define what urban regeneration means, in terms of transformation for people living in relative poverty, exhausted Emma and her colleagues, but led, ultimately, to the appointment of a new Director of Regeneration with the necessary experience of local, community-led planning. He was able to take up the challenge from more junior colleagues and redouble the efforts of the team to steer the course towards a transformative Olympic legacy for the people of post-industrial East London.

NOTES

I am grateful to all those at the Olympic Park Legacy Company, between 2009 and 2011, who gave permission for and supported my research. Special thanks are due to Emma Wheelhouse, now Frost, for her tolerance of my presence in her team, and to Richard Brown for giving me access to the behind-the-scenes planning operation. Mark Hartton, Secretary of the Manor Gardens Allotment Society, has been a patient interlocutor, and I am thankful for the support of the 'diggers' who gave permission for me to access the minutes of their meetings. The research for this essay was conducted as part of an RCUK Fellowship held between 2007 and 2012, and I am grateful for the support and intellectual environment of the Centre for Research on Socio-Cultural Change at the University of Manchester, which hosted my research. A version of this essay was presented at the seminar in the Department of Social Anthropology at Manchester, and comments made by staff and students led to improvements. Thanks are also due to the anonymous reviewers, whose notes and queries were invaluable. Finally, I am grateful to the editors of this collection of essays, Hannah Brown, Adam Reed, and Tom Yarrow, for the vision and commitment that have inspired this essay.

[1] Established in 1900, the 1.8 hectares of land for the allotments was gifted to the East End by Major Arthur Villiers, an old Etonian, son of the seventh Earl of Jersey, a descendant of the Duke of Buckingham, and director of Barings Bank, the oldest merchant bank in London. The gift of land was a philanthropic act to provide small parcels of land for working-class people living local to that area to grow vegetables and, in the face of real deprivation, obtain a degree of self-sufficiency and improved quality of life. The land was bequeathed 'in perpetuity', and allotments flourished by the River Lea, in Hackney.

[2] Boris Johnson was Mayor of London from 2008 to 2016, when he was succeeded by Labour's Sadiq Khan.

REFERENCES

BERNSTEIN, A. & E. MERTZ 2011. Introduction: bureaucracy: ethnography of the state in everyday life. *PoLAR: Political and Legal Anthropology Review* **34**, 6-10.

BOURDIEU, P. 2014. *On the state: lectures at the Collège de France, 1989-1992* (trans. D. Fernbach). Cambridge: Polity.

CLARK, S. & S. CLARK 2007. *Moro East*. London: Ebury Press.

ELIAS, N.E. 1994 [1939]. *The civilizing process* (trans. E. Jephcott). Oxford: Blackwell.

EVANS, G. 2012. Materializing the vision of a 2012 London Olympics. In *The Routledge 2012 Olympics special issue* (ed.) V. Girginov, 45-61. London: Routledge.

――――― 2014. What documents make possible: realizing London's Olympic legacy. In *Objects and materials: a Routledge companion* (eds) P. Harvey, E.C. Casella, G. Evans, H. Knox, C. McLean, E.B. Silva, N. Thoburn & K. Woodward, 399-408. Abingdon, Oxon: Routledge.

HUTCHINSON, E. 1995. *Cognition in the wild*. Cambridge, Mass.: MIT Press.

LATOUR, B. 1988. *The Pasteurization of France* (trans. A. Sheridan & J. Law). Cambridge, Mass.: Harvard University Press.

――――― 1993. *We have never been modern* (trans. C. Porter). Cambridge, Mass.: Harvard University Press.

――――― 2013. *An inquiry into modes of existence: an anthropology of the moderns* (trans. C. Porter). Cambridge, Mass.: Harvard University Press.

POLANYI, K. 1944. *The great transformation: political and economic origins of our time*. Boston: Beacon.

ROBBINS, J. 2012. Some things you say, some things you dissimulate, and some things you keep to yourself: linguistic, material and marital exchange in the construction of Melanesian societies. In *The scope of anthropology: Maurice Godelier's work in context* (eds) L. Dousset & S. Tcherkézoff, 25-45. New York: Berghahn Books.

ROBERTSON, R. 1984. *People and the state*. Cambridge: University Press.

SCHWARTZMAN, H.B. 1989. *The meeting: gatherings in organizations and community*. New York: Springer.

SCOTT, J. 1999. *Seeing like the state: how certain schemes to improve the human condition have failed.* New Haven, Conn.: Yale University Press.

SINCLAIR, I. 2012. *Ghost milk: calling time on the grand project.* London: Penguin.

THOMPSON, E.P. 1966. *The making of the English working class.* New York: Vintage Books.

TSING, A. 2005. *Friction: an ethnography of global connection.* Princeton: University Press.

VAN VREE, W. 1999. *Meetings, manners and civilization: the development of modern meeting behaviour.* London: Leicester University Press.

WEBER, M. 1968. *Economy and society: an outline of interpretive sociology* (eds G. Roth & C. Wittich). New York: Bedminster Press.

Procès-verbaux, réunions et « modes d'existence » : tracer le processus bureaucratique de la régénération urbaine dans l'est de Londres

Résumé

Inspiré de la démarche de Latour visant à rétablir l'équilibre du projet anthropologique en exotisant les artefacts et procédures du savoir dit « moderne », le présent essai donne une description ethnographique des processus émergents de production de savoir dans le contexte de la planification et du développement de la régénération urbaine à Londres. Les réunions bureaucratiques y sont décrites comme une composante de l'infrastructure organisationnelle qui permet de créer de nouveaux futurs urbains. L'auteure avance que puisque la fabrique de la réalité est toujours décrite comme « en marche », il faut que l'on trace sa route, comme en navigation. L'essai se concentre sur le potentiel subversif des réunions informelles et fait valoir, plus généralement, que ces réunions sont des manœuvres sociales (concrètement) et techniques (affectivement) qui permettent de trouver un cap et aussi de contester la direction adoptée.

Journal of the Royal Anthropological Institute (N.S.), 124-137
© Royal Anthropological Institute 2017

8

Ideological twinning: socialist aesthetics and political meetings in Maputo, Mozambique

MORTEN NIELSEN *Aarhus University*

Based on recent ethnographical data from Maputo, Mozambique, this essay examines the revolutionary aesthetics of political meetings in a sociopolitical environment marked by the collapse of a national socialist ideology. Local political meetings in Mozambique articulate a paradoxical tension between *sacrifice* and *revolution*. While socialist rule disintegrated in the mid-1980s, most local political meetings allow for the actualization of the revolutionary socialism which the governing Frelimo party was forced to sacrifice in order to remain in power. In the essay, it is thus examined how the enactment of a revolutionary aesthetics successfully exposes what Frelimo was incapable of realizing and thus momentarily captures the party's ideological legitimacy. Taking my inspiration from Roy Wagner's recent work on holography and invention, I explore the relationship between *sacrifice* and *revolution* as an articulation of a symmetrical 'twinning' of seemingly contrastive political principles that are held together by a singular political aesthetics that is actualized only at political meetings.

Shortly after being sworn in as Mozambique's president on 2 February 2005, Armando Guebuza embarked on a nation-wide tour to thank his supporters and mobilize the population around the political agenda that would guide his presidency. Having commenced the tour in the far north in early May, he reached Maputo, the country's capital, in the south a month later, where he made a victorious return when visiting Mulwene, a peri-urban neighbourhood on the northern outskirts, on 6 June. The visit in Mulwene took the form of a political meeting with collective singing in praise of the governing Frelimo party followed by speeches by national and local party cadres on the need for popular mobilization and unconditional support for the incumbent president. Not surprisingly, the meeting reached its climax with the presidential speech, where the new political agenda was introduced and described at length. Until that moment, the presidential visit in Mulwene had followed the formula for political meetings used in Mozambique since the country gained independence from its Portuguese colonial oppressors in 1975. Halfway through Guebuza's speech, however, the meeting took a surprising turn. In front of the huge gathering and standing no more than 10 metres from the raised wooden platform where the president was delivering his speech, a tall and sinewy man suddenly took out a large poster and raised it over his head. In sizeable block letters, the banner text expressed an unequivocal critique of the governing regime: 'Mozambique: a backward country' (*Moçambique: um pais atrasado*). Having faced the increasingly agitated crowd, the man turned towards the president and held the banner high for a few minutes before folding it away when approached by an official from the president's staff. Surprisingly, the protester was not immediately reproached for having made a public critique of the governing party. In a cordial tone, the official wrote down the man's contact information and promised to return within a week in order to know more about the cause of his dissatisfaction.

What is particularly interesting about the brief disturbance of the political meeting is how the local protester managed to successfully turn the government's rhetoric against itself. On 25 June 1975, Mozambique's new president, Samora Machel, declared the 'total and complete independence of the People's Republic of Mozambique', in which, 'under the leadership of the worker-peasant alliance, all patriotic strata would commit themselves to the annihilation of the system of exploitation of man by man'.[1] And, to be sure, the 'annihilation of the system of exploitation' implied that all traces of 'backwardness' and 'obscurantism' (e.g. ancestor worship, spiritual healing, and oppressive feudal structures) should be irrevocably removed from society (Isaacman & Isaacman 1983). While the Frelimo government's ideological vision of establishing a 'worker-peasant alliance' based on a nationalist version of Marxism-Leninism collapsed during the economic crisis of the 1980s, in many local communities its legitimacy still derives from activating a revolutionary socialist 'political aesthetics' at present-day local political meetings. Taking my cue from Jacques Rancière, I understand aesthetics to be 'a system of a priori forms determining what presents itself to sense experience. It is a delimitation of spaces and times, of the visible and the invisible, of speech and noise, that simultaneously determines the place and the stakes of politics as a form of experience' (2004: 13). Hence, if aesthetics defines and delimits a field of the perceptible by determining what is visible and invisible within it, *political aesthetics* refers to the conditions of sharing a sensorial experience and to the sources of disrupting that same order. It is, and here I again follow Rancière, a redistribution or interruption of the sensible; 'a reconfiguration of the given perceptual forms' (2004: 63). Returning to the incident in Mulwene, then, it was by publicly confronting the government with its political rhetoric (e.g. the need to transcend 'backwardness' and obscurantism) and, implicitly, with its fundamental shortcomings that the protester effectively turned the revolutionary political aesthetics of the former socialist party against itself.

In this essay, I chart the revolutionary capacities of formalized political aesthetics activated at political meetings in a sociopolitical environment imprinted by the effects of a national ideological collapse. Through an extended case-study analysis of a political meeting held in a neighbourhood on the outskirts of Maputo in the spring of 2005, I discuss how a nationalist ideology came to act upon itself through the staging of a surprisingly robust socialist aesthetics that has survived the disintegration of socialism in the mid-1980s. As I will describe, the carefully orchestrated meeting elicited a pristine political cosmology with a revolutionary force that the governing and former socialist party has never managed to harness.

One may rightfully ponder why the revolutionary socialist aesthetics of the early post-Independence era continue to be activated at political meetings in local communities. It could be imagined, for example, that the potency of socialist aesthetics and therefore also of the formula for political meetings that has been used since Independence would gradually wane following the collapse of socialism as a guiding ideology. As I will argue,

Journal of the Royal Anthropological Institute (N.S.), 138-152
© Royal Anthropological Institute 2017

however, political meetings in local communities endure as potent vehicles for activating socialist aesthetics that stretch what might be contained by an all-encompassing political system. Crucially, it was at political meetings and rallies that Frelimo's ideological vision of a modernist socialist society was most forcefully promoted and contrasted with the 'obscurantist beliefs and practices' of traditional communities (Honwana 2003: 62; see also Cahen 1993: 54). With the collapse of socialism as a national ideology in the mid-1980s, however, the socialist aesthetics activated at political meetings in local communities seem to articulate a different tension. While the formula for political meetings has remained intact since the initial post-Independence years, it no longer elicits a collective vision of a pure socialist society. Rather, at the heart of contemporary political aesthetics is a paradoxical tension between *sacrifice* and *revolution*: since the late 1980s, the aesthetics of political meetings in many local communities has been structured around the recollection of a socialist utopia that is widely acknowledged as having fundamentally collapsed. In a sense, the staging of meetings such as the presidential visit in Mulwene thus articulates what the Mozambican nation-state had to sacrifice (i.e. socialism) in order to become what it is today. Still, given that the Frelimo government has never deliberately distanced itself from socialism, a revolutionary residue remains, which can be activated at political meetings.[2] Taking inspiration from Roy Wagner's more recent work on holography and invention (2001; 2010; 2011*b*; 2012), I explore the transformation of political meetings as an articulation of a symmetrical 'twinning' of seemingly opposing political principles that are held together by a singular and robust political aesthetics actualized only at political meetings. Hence, the initial and fundamental tension between an 'obscurantist' past and a modernist future is gradually 'twinned' outwards into a new tension between sacrifice and revolution. In a sense, the latter opposition (sacrifice::revolution) is the *expersonation* (Wagner 2001: 51) of the original tension (obscurantism::modernity) returning with a vengeance.

If, as I argue, political meetings in contemporary Mozambique are apt media for stretching the limits of all-encompassing political ideologies, this might have significant implications for our anthropological understanding of meetings writ large. In closing the essay, I will therefore suggest that certain forms of political meetings balance out society's key political paradoxes; not because they adhere to a static ritualized formula (cf. Moore & Myerhoff 1977), but because they change as rapidly as the world of which they are part.

The election of a new quarter chief in Mulwene

Since the birth of the neighbourhood in 2000, Mulwene had been governed by one neighbourhood chief (*secretário do bairro*) and fifty-two quarter chiefs (*chefes de quarteirões*), who administer individual quarters, each comprising approximately 150 households. In Quarter 20, the residents had become increasingly dissatisfied with the erratic and allegedly corrupt behaviour of their local quarter chief and wanted to nominate a new one. A small group of residents from the quarter therefore decided to organize a formal election process in order to find a better successor. While knowing that the neighbourhood chief in Mulwene would probably disapprove of their initiative, they summoned all residents for an initial meeting where candidates would be given the opportunity to present their political agendas to the public.

Early in the morning on 12 March 2005, the promoters went through Quarter 20 blowing whistles in order to summon all residents for the meeting that was planned to begin at 9 o'clock in one of the quarter's public squares. The neighbourhood chief had been informed of the meeting and, while sceptical of the initiative, agreed to participate as the municipality's official representative, together with his notary and a local delegate from the governing Frelimo party. After a delay of fifteen minutes while awaiting their arrival, the meeting began when the promoters asked all participants to sing two communal songs in praise of Frelimo's socialist victories. Encouraged to do so by one of the promoters standing to his right, the portly neighbourhood chief then stood up in front of the forty-odd participants attending the meeting and raised his right hand towards the sky. 'Mulwene *hoye*!' he shouted three times, each exclamation immediately followed by a repeated response shout from the participants. 'You all know what Frelimo is?' he rhetorically asked, and proceeded to respond: 'Frelimo is progress. Only Frelimo will be able to remove the evils that prevent us from reaching a collective future and destroy the individualistic and greedy behaviour that corrupts the Mozambican nation'. During the neighbourhood chief's ten-minute-long monologue, he repeatedly emphasized that the election was not a collective process and that he was only there as a state representative to witness the procedure. 'This is your process; not ours!' he thundered out each word separately, and left a theatrical pause before returning to his seat next to the Frelimo representative. 'And this is not how it should be done', he concluded.

The promoters then asked the six candidates to present their political programmes and sketch out how to tackle the pressing problems that residents in Quarter 20 were facing. All but one of the candidates structured their contributions as a crescendo towards a high-pitched critique of the weak collective morale. 'The quarter chief was the embodiment of the spirit of apathy', one of the candidates argued.

> But that spirit has to be eliminated. We need to be strong and brave enough to denounce those who promote chaos and confusion. In this quarter, we will never be able to live in peace if we are afraid of reporting on our neighbours. Denouncing a neighbour is not equivalent to killing a brother; it cures bad morale.

When all candidates had presented their political programmes, the promoters announced the date for the election and thanked the neighbourhood chief and the local Frelimo member for attending the meeting. The gathering slowly dissolved and people returned to their homes to resume their weekend activities.

Political meetings as ideological delivery rooms

After the celebration of Independence in 1975, it took Frelimo two more years to build the ideological skeleton of an alternative state (Coelho 2004: 4). At the Second Congress in 1977, a development strategy was formulated that was intended to guide Mozambique through the next decade. Most importantly, Frelimo was constituted as a vanguard Marxist-Leninist party which was to act as the primary force pushing the nation towards a socialist reconstruction (Dinerman 2006: 50). This ambitious objective would be achieved by adopting a planned economic strategy and, even more profoundly, through a 'decolonization of individual minds' leading to the complete eradication of all ethno-cultural differences (Meneses 2006: 65). Traditional practices such as spiritual healing and ancestor worship were consequently condemned as obscurant remnants of the kind of backwardness that the new socialist nation would leave behind. From the late 1970s, the political rhetoric of the new government was further sharpened and it was increasingly emphasized how internal enemies were hindering the socialist process through rumours, conspiracies, and economic sabotage (Hall & Young 1997: 48). In

Journal of the Royal Anthropological Institute (N.S.), 138-152
© Royal Anthropological Institute 2017

his detailed analysis of the so-called 'Meeting of the Compromised' in 1982, where accused opponents of the socialist revolution were questioned and scorned in public, Victor Igreja (2010) exposes the violence and ruthlessness with which the Frelimo government wanted to transform Mozambican society. Focusing on one particularly brutal encounter, Igreja describes how 'the way in which Machel [the Mozambican president] created the context for this interrogation demonstrated that he desired to humiliate [the accused person]' (2010: 793).

During the initial post-Independence period, Frelimo's legitimacy was relatively uncontested, with ties to the population based on a strongly felt 'wartime affection' (Ottaway 1988: 217). 'To die a tribe and be born a nation' (Henriksen 1978: 455), Frelimo's slogan during the struggle against the Portuguese colonizers, was carried into the post-Independence era as a guiding vision for a unified nation that was determined to use 'scientific socialism' to eliminate ethnic differences and heal the wounds afflicted by colonial suppression (Saul 1985). In the late 1970s, Kathleen Sheldon was doing ethnographic research on gender relations in Beira in the central Mozambican province of Sofala. Her unpublished memoirs from that period beautifully capture the intense atmosphere at local political meetings among activists who were intent on building a unified nation liberated of the vices of the past. Sheldon (2014) eloquently describes a series of meetings with the 'Organization of Mozambican Women' (*Organização da Mulher Moçambicana*, OMM), beginning with communal singing of socialist songs in praise of Frelimo ('Frelimo sings with us, you can't sing alone'), followed by endless sessions of analytical self-criticism where traditional practices were rejected as being morally abhorrent before the denunciation reached a crescendo at the final gathering. At the meetings' closing stage, the need for continuous revolutionary progress towards the realization of pure socialism was collectively formulated and written down in memoranda for the organization's growing archive.

Sheldon's memoirs give a passionate glimpse into a decisive period of Mozambique's recent history when political meetings served as delivery rooms for a socialist ideology that was to catapult the country into a modernized and independent future. If we then compare the meeting Sheldon describes in the 1970s with the meeting held in Mulwene in March 2005, it does seem as if the ideological drive has maintained its pace throughout the intervening forty-odd years. In both instances, political meetings reflect strikingly similar aesthetics framed by communal singing in praise of Frelimo's socialist victories followed by sessions of analytical self-criticism and mutual allegations of moral deviancy, before concluding with a ritualized recital of the need for collective progress towards a modernized future liberated from the vices of the past. Returning to Rancière, we might argue that despite the apparent differences in objectives at the two meetings (the short-term objective of electing a new quarter chief versus the long-term objective of transforming the Mozambican state into a socialist democracy based on a 'worker-peasant alliance'), they both seem to articulate similar forms of political aesthetics aiming to reconfigure 'what is given to sense perception', which, in both instances, is a particular configuration of 'domination and subjection' (Rancière 2009: 13). The problem is, however, that Mozambique is no longer 'a bellwether for the future of socialism in Africa' (Young 1982: 89). Despite the ambitious goal of rapid development, Independence did not mark the beginning of a period of reconstruction for Mozambique. Only two years after Independence, the already sorely tried country was cast into a regional conflict between the ruling Frelimo party and Renamo,[3] a guerrilla movement supported first by Rhodesia and later by South Africa.[4]

Journal of the Royal Anthropological Institute (N.S.), 138-152
© Royal Anthropological Institute 2017

As the fighting escalated, the limits of Frelimo's programme of modernization and secularization as well as the incapacity of its ideology to respond to people's actual problems became obvious. With an increasingly paralysed state organization without the necessary resources to carry out even minor administrative tasks, in 1987 the government made a definitive 'turn towards the West' (Devereux & Palmero 1999) and decided to undertake far-reaching economic reforms orchestrated by the International Monetary Fund and the World Bank (Hanlon 1996). The ideological shift was apparent at Frelimo's Fifth Congress held in 1989. All references to Marxism-Leninism were carefully removed from official documents, along with any associated phrases, such as 'scientific socialism'. The party's new political key terms were significantly less clear and some almost vacuous, such as the ideal of creating a 'democratic society of general well-being' (Hall & Young 1997: 202; Nielsen 2014a). In 1990 Mozambique took a final step away from its socialist past by adopting a new constitution that enshrined the principles of multi-party democracy. From the first democratic elections in 1994 and until today, Frelimo has nevertheless been elected as the majority party in the national parliament. At the general elections in 2014 it thus won 144 (58 per cent) of all 250 constituencies.

Considering the radical political and ideological transformations that Mozambique has undergone during the last forty years, it does seem strange that participants at political meetings today, such as the election meeting in Mulwene, continue to actualize a socialist aeshetics that is uncannily similar to that of the initial post-Independence era. Could it not be imagined, for instance, that contemporary Mozambique would follow other postsocialist nation-states in sub-Saharan Africa and Eastern Europe in rejecting socialist values and rhetorics through an unambiguous adoption of economic liberalism (cf. Pitcher & Askew 2006)? Hence, while the socioeconomic transformations can be read in terms of the recent 'turn towards the West', it is the unchanging and robust aesthetics of political meetings that warrant further analytical investigation.

Political meetings: an ideological terminus?

A few days after the presentation of the candidates in Quarter 20, I visited the neighbourhood chief to discuss the procedure. I had barely sat down before my interlocutor voiced his dissatisfaction. 'It's all wrong, Morten'. The neighbourhood chief leaned back and sighed. 'This is not at all how it is supposed to be done. Why didn't they just approach me?' He gave a small theatrical pause before continuing to respond to his own question. 'It could have been so easy. If they want a new leader, let me nominate a new one. But they wanted to prolong the process; they wanted to complicate things . . .'.

And, indeed, the election process in Quarter 20 was more complex and time-consuming than previous elections in the neighbourhood. Two weeks after the initial meeting, the formal election was held in a vacant plot in Quarter 20. An election committee was appointed, and during the course of two consecutive days they organized an election process that involved the large majority of residents in the area. The neighbourhood chief attended the final session, accompanied by his notary and the local Frelimo delegate, and when all votes had been counted, he officially announced the name of the winner. Defeating the only female candidate with only a handful votes, Faruque Abdalá, a newcomer who had lived in Mulwene for four years, won the election. While looking a bit taken aback by the situation, he thanked the neighbourhood chief for the honour of representing his community.[5] The following weekend, the inaugural ceremony was held marking Abdalá's assumption of the office held by his unpopular predecessor. After the initial songs in praise of Frelimo, the neighbourhood chief announced that all responsibilities had been transferred to Abdalá and he was now the official representative of Quarter 20. Turning towards the promoters of the election process, the neighbourhood chief expressed his continued dissatisfaction with the process. 'I am only here as formal representative of the state', he declared in a loud and clear voice. 'And what you have done is not right. It should have been done differently. It is not in the revolutionary spirit of the party to commence a political process without involving your leader' (lit. 'your father', *o seu pāe*). Still, as he continued to explain, the process was well organized and supported by the majority of residents in the quarter and therefore it had to be accepted as formally legitimate. The promoters thanked the neighbourhood chief, and after a few statements in praise of the party, the meeting was over.

The basis for the popular participation that was so crucial to Frelimo's nationalist project during the late 1970s has gradually been eroded and today political meetings are considered as anachronistic remnants from an era that has little or no relevance to the present. While Frelimo's initial programme clearly defined the procedures for securing independence, it was considerably more vague about how to draw benefits from popular involvement in the process of creating a progressive socialist nation-state. All too quickly, mass organizations (such as OMM) that were established as mechanisms of popular empowerment 'became more like transmission belts for delivery of the party line' (Saul 2005: 313), with the consequence that those critical debates that should have been the life-blood of a revolutionary process gradually dried up.

This historical account does nevertheless seem to be at odds with the situation in Mulwene, where the possibility of an important political transformation arose from the activation of a political aesthetics that originated in the initial post-Independence era (Nielsen 2011; 2014b). In order for participants to engage in debates during the meeting, a complete assimilation was required so that bodily postures (e.g. sitting up straight when listening to the neighbourhood chief's initial discourse and standing up while singing the communal songs in praise of Frelimo), verbal phrasings (e.g. the very formalized structures of sentences and individual statements), and argumentative structures (e.g. the recurrent self-criticism) seemed to arise from a socialist ideology that everyone present also acknowledged as having fundamentally failed. Somehow, a radical alteration occurred when participants allowed themselves to become assimilated by this political aesthetics. During the meeting, the difference between then and now – between a proto-socialist past and a capitalist present – ceased to exist and all that remained was an endless repetition of a single eternal moment.

A few weeks after Abdalá had been elected as quarter chief, I sat down with old Boavida Wate, a former Frelimo activist and community chief in Mulwene during the 1980s, to discuss the process. Having been quite vocal in his criticism of the neighbourhood administration in Mulwene, Wate was clearly satisfied with the way things had turned out. I asked him how the promoters had managed to successfully organize the elections despite the overt hostility of the neighbourhood administration. 'Well, Morten, you have to know how to do things properly. I knew how to organize the meeting, so I helped them. You need to do the "Mulwene *hoye*" …'. Wate raised his right arm as if in praise of Frelimo and smiled. "If you let people sing their songs, they feel as if they are at home (*eles chegaram em casa*)". In 'Power, poets and the people',

Jeanne Marie Penvenne and Bento Sitoe (2000) analyse Frelimo's salutations and praise etiquette. Since the armed struggle against the Portuguese colonizers, Penvenne and Sitoe tell us, Frelimo has used political meetings to 'consolidate and expand its base'. Typically commencing with a 'rousing sequence of exhortations in support of Frelimo's goals (*Viva!* – Long live!) and against Frelimo-defined "enemies" (*Abaixo!* – Down with!)' (2000: 72),[6] a shout-and-response session ensued where the leadership called out phrases for the audience to respond to: 'Long live Frelimo!' and 'Long live the struggle against imperialism!' As Wate emphasized, the promoters of the elections were not only conscious of the party's salutation and praise etiquette; they knew that in order for them to successfully organize an election process that was from the outset explicitly opposed by the neighbourhood administration, they would have to work through the political aesthetics of their immediate opponents. As it turned out, the activation of the socialist aesthetics made the ideology act upon itself and thereby stretch what could be contained by an all-encompassing political system. Significantly, it was at the meeting that the revolutionary force associated with the staging of Frelimo-like aesthetics both (re)actualized the failures of the governing party and precisely for that same reason gave the local residents a unique opportunity to reclaim political legitimacy: They were essentially being more Frelimo-like, as it were, than the party itself had ever managed to be. In the final section of this essay, I will discuss how the stretching of the political ideology produced what Rancière has defined as a '"double effect": the readability of a political signification and a sensible perceptual shock caused, conversely, by the uncanny, by that which resists signification' (2004: 63). As I shall argue, this double effect emerged when the tension between obscurantism and modernity was 'twinned' outwards as a relationship between sacrifice and revolution.

Ideological twinning

In *An anthropology of the subject* (2001), Wagner examines the 'twinning' of bilateral symmetry and sexual dimorphism as a fundamental form of 'appositional self-knowledge'. The human body is connected to the external world through a double process of twinning. All that might serve to model extension or relations in the world is twinned *inwards* in the body's laterality (walking by putting one foot in front of the other, co-ordination of hands and feet, etc.), which is again twinned *outwards* as two distinct gender types defined as male and female (Wagner 2001: 42). Hence, as emphasized by James Weiner (1998: 26), gender and laterality are used to 'code' each other in a symmetrical relationship between two genders, external to each other, and two sides of the body, internal to each other. Twinning is not equivalent to mirroring, however. What is twinned is also transformed in the act of its own replication: male is not female's identical twin, just as the two genders do not reproduce the two sides of the human body. Wagner defines this appositional pairing of gender and bilaterality as 'anti-twins' of each other. They are, he tells us, 'distinctive in relation to the generic animal form by underdetermining the physical body and overdetermining its attributes. As disembodied concomitants or gender symmetries, they are one-sided beings' (2001: 49). Hence, gender always involves a certain kind of underdetermination of its inherent laterality (male as internal to female, and vice versa). What is revealed to others is one's 'own gender' in contrast to some 'other gender'. Still, as a genderless 'sexual desire' (Dalton 2002: 58), one's 'own gender' (also defined by Wagner as 'supergender') is not an impersonation or replication of an inner counterpart but, rather, an *expersonation* of the hidden laterality (Wagner 2001: 51; 2012: 162-3). While *impersonation* involves a 'mere copying of its subject, an act of *mimesis* in Aristotle's terms, and thus necessarily an exaggeration of some features and consequent omission or downgrading of others', *expersonation* 'reverses this process, and registers more concrete particularity than is found in the original … so that the original becomes a *de facto* impersonation of it' (Wagner 2012: 162; see also Wagner 2001: 48-66). As a 'form of abstraction' (Holbraad 2013), impersonation subtracts the unique particularities of things in order to establish stable and conventionalized social forms.[7] Expersonation, by contrast, adds to the things upon which it operates, 'rendering them more particular than it found them' (Wagner 2012: 162). In a sense, anti-twinning (or expersonated twinning) characterizes the appositive knowledge of twinning itself. Almost like the Möbius Strip, the anti-twins are 'subject-object shift agencies that either turn us inside out or show us to be one-sided' (Wagner 2010: 51). With explicit reference to Gregory Bateson's (1979) perplexing analysis of lateral asymmetry when looking in a mirror, Wagner thus concludes that the effect of anti-twinning is an acute insight as if the mirror had borrowed one's eyes in order to view itself. 'It is the "sense" of a picture that contains its own depictive (and hence pragmatic "understanding") capabilities that is at issue' (Wagner 2001: 54). We achieve this acute and inverse insight, Wagner might say, when briefly sensing that our own gender (our 'supergender'!) is structured by the laterality of the physical body, which is otherwise underdetermined.

What I find particularly illuminating in Wagner's exposition of twinning as appositional self-knowledge is the paradoxical insight that knowledge might act upon itself through recursive (holographic) self-replication. He thus invites us to consider the purchase of keeping an analytical 'double-focus' on twinness and unity *at once* (Wagner 2012), which folds within the object the knowledge about its internal composition (e.g. the twinness to every 'one' and the unity to every twinness).[8] This is a particularly rewarding approach, I propose, when studying contemporary reverberations of an ideological collapse within a political system that claims to be all-encompassing. For could it not be that political disruptions in such environments arise precisely by 'expersonating' the ideological premise which, although having collapsed long ago, still orientates its internal organization? If so, the twinning of an ideological collapse is not merely an imitation of a fractured utopian imagery; it might equally articulate the emergence of a pristine revolutionary sensibility.

While Mozambique is not a socialist nation-state and probably never has been (cf. Cahen 1993), its nationalist ideology is today structured around the painful recollection of having sacrificed socialism in order for the nation-state to survive. Today, there is no distinction between the Mozambican state and the Frelimo party, whose interest groups and affiliated associations dominate civic life in both urban and rural areas throughout large parts of the country (Nielsen 2007; Sumich 2015). Indeed, as argued by Michel Cahen, '*the site of production of national sentiment is the party*. The party *is* the nation in this country without a nation' (1993: 56, italics in original). At the heart of this nation, however, is no longer a shared ideology that outlines the guiding principles and moral values of the collective. Rather, what unites and binds people together as a collective is the congenital collapse of the ideological project from which the nation was born (Nielsen 2014*a*; cf. Pitcher 2006). In other words, this nationalist imagery in 'a country without a nation' is, paradoxically, configured in terms of an imagined future that disintegrated long before it could be implemented.

The activation of a political aesthetics that everyone acknowledged as having already collapsed should therefore not be considered merely as a caricature of socialism, or, to use Alexei Yurchak's apt term, a parodic 'overidentification' with an ideological idea (2006; see also Boyer & Yurchak 2010) structured around a leap from 'obscurantism' to modernity. Rather, what I wish to suggest is that political meetings in local Mozambican communities articulate a symmetrical twinning of the latter into the seemingly contradictory ideological principles of *sacrifice* and *revolution*. Official state-authored rhetoric is structured around the recollection of a socialist utopia that is widely acknowledged as having fundamentally collapsed. Even public gatherings in local communities, such as the meeting in Mulwene, are permeated by a nostalgic sadness that takes effect through the staging of an allegedly defunct socialist aesthetics. Sustaining a political aesthetics that is acknowledged as having collapsed long ago is, however, an operative lever for reproducing the party's political legitimacy and continued relevance. Through the repetitive staging of the 'socialist drama' at political meetings, Frelimo reminds the Mozambican population of what it was prepared to sacrifice in order to salvage a decaying nation-state. From this perspective, the government's 'turn towards the West' in the mid-1980s was not caused by an ideological rejection of socialism but, rather, by an all-consuming love for the nation, which, at the crucial moment of dire national crisis, infused the political elite with the strength to sacrifice its socialist soul.

At local meetings, such as the one that occurred in Mulwene in March 2005, state-authored rhetoric structured around the painful recollection of an ideological sacrifice confronted by seemingly contradictory political principles that operate through the resuscitation of a revolutionary potential that the governing Frelimo party never managed to harness – let alone realize. No wonder, then, that the neighbourhood chief was reluctant to acknowledge the legitimacy of the election process. By allowing the enterprising promoters to organize the election procedures in conformity with the ordering of political meetings organized during the initial post-Independence era, he invariably confronted the incapacitated Mozambican state with its own weaknesses. With brutal clarity, the election process revealed not what the former socialist government had been willing to sacrifice in order to salvage the weakened nation but, rather, what it had been incapable of delivering. Returning to Wagner, we might argue that the promoters of the election 'expersonated' themselves by imitating a version of the socialist ideology that had never existed before. By so doing, the perspective was essentially taken out of the perceiver (promoters, residents, and neighbourhood cadres) (Holbraad 2013) and the ideology came to operate on itself to such an extent that the state-authored mourning of the socialist ideology that was sacrificed in the mid-1980s paradoxically appeared as an impersonation of its symmetrical anti-twin (the resuscitated revolutionary potentials actualized by the promoters).[9] Held together by a singular and surprisingly robust socialist aesthetics, the two pairs of ideological principles can thus be seen as a symmetrical twinning of what the potentials and implications of political meetings might be. They disrupt the internal organization of a political system not by positing an opposition or radical outside but, rather, by operating as what Wagner (2010) calls a 'subject-object shift agency' that allows a momentary and, indeed, unsettling gaze at the holographic self-scaling capacities by which the political imagery is stretched.

In sum, a reading of the political meeting in Mulwene by way of Wagner's analysis of twinning suggests that the socialist aesthetics was activated not merely as a (re)enactment of a collapsed utopian ideology in order to destabilize the Frelimo government. The ambition was not at all to overthrow an all-encompassing political system but, rather, to allow the socialist aesthetics to recursively operate on itself and thereby generate a 'double effect' (Rancière 2004: 63): the political aesthetics was immediately readable while at the same time acting upon itself in an uncanny twinned-out version. With Wagner, I will consequently argue that the appositional self-knowledge that was thus produced (i.e. the expersonated version being ideologically stronger than the 'original') is what allowed a stretching of an all-encompassing political system. While all participants undoubtedly knew that socialism will never again come to as serve as the ideological basis for a national project, its momentary force arose from the successful activation of the tension between two latent oppositions, namely obscurantism::modernity and sacrifice::revolution.

Conclusion

In 'Forgetting from above and memory from below', M. Anne Pitcher (2006) contrasts 'forgetting' among state officials and businesses with 'remembering' among urban workers in Maputo. In the attempt to build a national identity that rests on 'entrepreneurialism, social harmony through market participation, and the shared goals of business and the state' (2006: 106), state officials and financial entrepreneurs are strategically attempting to eradicate the traces of the country's socialist past. By contrast, urban workers are reviving the political sensibility of the early post-Independence era in order to articulate their dissatisfaction with the effects of neoliberalism:

> In the urban areas, some workers are expressing their discontent in a language that draws on the promises made in the past, the right accorded to them under socialism, and the principles articulated by the previously Marxist-Leninist party. By employing these symbolic frameworks, workers are not attempting to return to that historical moment just after independence ... But their discourse does serve as a powerful reminder to the ruling party that it stills depends on workers for political support... This may constitute a *political awakening* in Mozambique, where collective desires instilled in workers during the socialist period are rescued from certain oblivion in the new era (2006: 99, 105, italics added).[10]

What Pitcher considers as a 'political awakening' among urban workers, I take to constitute an 'interruption of the sensible' (*pace* Rancière 2004) at political meetings in local communities. While it may rightfully be argued that socialism in Mozambique never was properly implemented, the activation of its political aesthetics by a collective acting in opposition to a local municipal administration did, for a brief moment, elicit the revolutionary capacities contained in that ideology. To be sure, none of the participants at the meeting had ever experienced the realization of the socialist ideal; still, the staging of its political aesthetics clearly manifested what implications it could have. It might therefore be argued that the political meeting in Mulwene was a potent way of making ideology act upon itself. Through a singular and surprisingly robust political aesthetics, the socialist ideal turned upon itself and 'twinned' out into a symmetrical relation between its sacrifice and revolutionary potentials. A revolutionary potential was 'expersonated', in other words, by imitating a version of the socialist ideology that never existed. Paradoxically, then, what political meetings in contemporary Mozambique seem to generate is a mode of appositional self-knowledge where a revolutionary potential contains and is contained by its own collapse; not a 'perspective seen twice' (Strathern 1991: 113) but, rather, a twinned-out perspective seen as one.

In Sally Falk Moore's classic analysis of a citizens' political meeting in Kilimanjaro, Tanzania, she shows how unanimity is achieved through 'style and form, rather than substance' (1977: 152). Carefully examining the repetitive formalities of the meeting,

Moore traces the contours of a 'doctrinal efficacy' that works by recursively legitimizing the 'unquestionable' and timeless qualities of its socialist ideology. In order to 'carry the new political faith far into the countryside', political meetings are used 'to define and teach an official version of social reality while acting it out' (1977: 170). Returning to the political meeting in Mulwene in May 2005, it was the seemingly timeless character of the socialist aesthetics that allowed for a transformation to occur on the 'inside' of an all-encompassing political ideology. In both instances, therefore, political meetings serve as vehicles for coming to terms with considerable sociopolitical transformations through the making of a seemingly timeless aesthetics. Let me then finally propose that political meetings, in this regard, seem to exhibit certain fundamental qualities that are not unlike those of certain Amerindian myths (Lévi-Strauss 1970; 2001; see also Gow 2001). According to Lévi-Strauss, myths are 'instruments for the obliteration of time' (1970: 16), which exist to lessen the effects of radical societal transformations. Hence, in *The naked man*, he argues that the Amerindians 'have conceived their myths for one purpose only: to come to terms with history, and … to re-establish a state of equilibrium capable of acting as a shock absorber for the disturbances caused by real life events' (1981: 607). Myths appear timeless precisely because they change at the same pace as the world of which they are part. They 'readjust' themselves, Lévi-Strauss explains, in order to produce the 'least resistance to the flow of events' (1981: 610). In a certain sense, political meetings in Mozambique and Tanzania seem to operate as 'instruments for the obliteration of time' which undergo transformations as rapidly as the societies of which they are part and therefore, paradoxically, appear to be timeless. Considered as such, meetings are to politics what myths are to cosmology.

NOTES

This article is based on ethnographic fieldwork carried out between 2004 and 2015 in Maputo, Mozambique. I am truly grateful for the insightful and challenging comments and suggestions from Jason Sumich, the three editors of this volume, and the anonymous *JRAI* reviewers.

[1] *http://vozdarevolucao.blogspot.co.uk/2009/06/mensagem-da-proclamacao-da.html* (accessed 24 January 2017).

[2] It could even be argued that the tension between sacrifice and revolution reinvigorates an ideological force that has been at the heart of socialist movements throughout the last century, namely the need to sacrifice existing value regimes in order for a revolution to occur. In this particular instance, however, the relationship between sacrifice and revolution constitutes an oppositional (synchronic) tension on the 'inside' of an all-encompassing ideological system and not a progressive (diachronic) movement in time.

[3] Renamo (The Mozambican National Resistance, *Resistência Nacional Moçambicana*) was initially a rebel movement, but after the peace treaty in 1992 it was transformed into a political party (Vines 1996). While Renamo 'desperately searched for a political ideology' (Honwana 2003: 62) to constitute a nationalist vision in opposition to Frelimo, it is doubtful whether it succeeded. In the attempt to muster popular support, Renamo has consistently emphasized its respect for those traditions and religious beliefs which were rejected by Frelimo as manifestations of 'obscurantism'. As a political party, however, Renamo has been less successful in formulating an ideological programme.

[4] Before the war reached its conclusion in 1992, a million Mozambicans had lost their lives, one-third of the population (i.e. five million people) had been forced to leave their homes, and 60 per cent of all schools had been destroyed (Vitanen & Ehrenpreis 2007). According to recent estimates, the total cost of the conflict was US$20 billion, which roughly equals five years' GDP for the country (Christie & Hanlon 2001: 6).

[5] As I was later told, Abdalá had recently bought a truckload of grit to stabilize the dirt road outside his house and, on that account, had apparently gained a certain degree of popularity.

[6] According to Jason Sumich, Frelimo was even known by the nickname '*abaixo com*' (pers. comm., 6 May 2016).

[7] In *Coyote anthropology*, Wagner thus argues that '[t]he secret of everyday values and normal life is just simply that of impersonation … We copy, mimic, and imitate one another every day, in fun *or* in abject seriousness, including our ideas, body movements, and especially our feelings, and have learned to do so since the day we were born, or before' (2010: x, original emphasis).

[8] Here, we might recall Turner's aphoristic comment that 'twinship presents the paradoxes that what is physically double is structurally single and what is mystically one is empirically two' (1991: 45).

[9] As such, expersonation reverses conventional forms of imitation and mirroring so that 'the one you see in the mirror steals your act of looking but only to see itself' (Wagner 2011a: 173).

[10] It might be argued that the recent series of popular uprisings and lynchings that have unsettled several Mozambican cities articulate a similar, albeit more violent, form of 'political awakening' (Bertelsen 2014). Hence, in February 2008, groups of angry citizens took to the streets of Maputo to manifest their anger about the government's plan to increase transportation costs by between 50 and 100 per cent. During the riots, there were at least sixty-eight cases of popular lynchings, where individuals accused of misconduct of office and other forms of crime were informally sentenced during processes of popular justice (Lubkemann, Kyed & Garvey 2011). Significantly, these processes clearly resembled the practice of public flogging and beating of thieves that was implemented during the initial post-Independence era (Bertelsen 2009; see also Sachs & Welch 1990).

REFERENCES

BATESON, G. 1979. *Mind and nature: a necessary unity*. New York: E.P. Dutton.

BERTELSEN, B.E. 2009. Multiple sovereignties and summary justice in Mozambique: a critique of some legal anthropological terms. *Social Analysis* **53**, 123-47.

——— 2014. Effervescence and ephemerality: popular urban uprisings in Mozambique. *Ethnos* **81**, 25-52.

BOYER, D. & A. YURCHAK 2010. AMERICAN STIOB: or, what late-socialist aesthetics of parody reveal about contemporary political culture in the West. *Cultural Anthropology* **25**, 179-221.

CAHEN, M. 1993. Check on socialism in Mozambique – what check? What socialism? *Review of African Political Economy* **57**, 46-59.

CHRISTIE, F. & J. HANLON 2001. *Mozambique and the great flood of 2000*. Oxford: The International African Institute in assocation with James Currey and Indiana University Press.

COELHO, J.P. 2004. The state and its public: notes on state ritualization in the transition from socialism to neo-liberalism in Mozambique. Paper presented at the international workshop on 'Ritualization of the State: Neo-popular State Rituals in Mozambique and South Africa', Wits Institute for Social and Economic Research (WISER), Wits University, Johannesburg, 3-4 June.

DALTON, D. 2002. Recursive tricks and holographic infinities: the invention of culture and after. *Social Analysis* **46**, 51-61.

DEVEREUX, S. & A. PALMERO 1999. *Mozambique Country Report: creating a framework for reducing poverty: institutional and process issues in national poverty policy*. Maputo, Institute of Development Studies, University of Sussex.

DINERMAN, A. 2006. *Revolution, counter-revolution and revisionism in postcolonial Africa: the case of Mozambique, 1975-1994*. Abingdon, Oxon: Routledge.

GOW, P. 2001. *An Amazonian myth and its history*. Oxford: University Press.

HALL, M. & T. YOUNG 1997. *Confronting Leviathan: Mozambique since Independence*. London: Hurst.

HANLON, J. 1996. *Peace without profit: how the IMF blocks rebuilding in Mozambique*. Oxford: James Currey.

HENRIKSEN, T.H. 1978. Marxism and Mozambique. *African Affairs* **77**, 441-62.

HOLBRAAD, M. 2013. How myths make men in Afro-Cuban divination. Paper presented at the Workshop in Honour of Roy Wagner, Trujillo, Spain, 20-4 May.

HONWANA, A. 2003. Undying past: spirit possession and the memory of war in southern Mozambique. In *Magic and modernity: interfaces of revelation and concealment* (eds) B. Meyer & P. Pels, 60-80. Stanford: University Press.

IGREJA, V. 2010. Frelimo's political ruling through violence and memory in postcolonial Mozambique. *Journal of Southern African Studies* **36**, 781-99.

ISAACMAN, A. & B. ISAACMAN 1983. *Mozambique: from colonialism to revolution, 1900-1982*. Boulder, Colo.: Westview Press.

LÉVI-STRAUSS, C. 1970. *The raw and the cooked* (trans. J. Weightman & D. Weightman). New York: Penguin.

——— 1981. *The naked man* (trans. J. Weightman & D. Weightman). London: Jonathan Cape.

——— 2001. *Myth and meaning*. London: Routledge.

LUBKEMANN, S.C., H.M. KYED & J. GARVEY 2011. Dilemmas of articulation: customary justice in Transition. In *Customary justice and the rule of law in war-torn societies* (ed.) D.H. Isser, 13-76. Washington, D.C.: United States Institute of Peace Press.

MENESES, M.P. 2006. Toward interlegality? Traditional healers and the law. In *Law and justice in a multicultural society: the case of Mozambique* (eds) B. de S. Santos, J.C. Trindade & M.P. Meneses, 63-88. Dakar: Council for the Development of Social Science Research in Africa.

MOORE, S.F. 1977. Political meetings and the simulation of unanimity: Kilimanjaro 1973. In *Secular ritual* (eds) S.F. Moore & B.G. Myerhoff, 151-72. Assen: Van Gorcum.

——— & B.G. MYERHOFF 1977. Secular ritual: forms and meaning. In *Secular ritual* (eds) S.F. Moore & B.G. Myerhoff, 3-24. Assen: Van Gorcum.

NIELSEN, M. 2007. Filling in the blanks: the potency of fragmented imageries of the state. *Review of African Political Economy* **34**, 695-708.

——— 2011. Inverse governmentality: the paradoxical production of peri-urban planning in Maputo, Mozambique. *Critique of Anthropology* **31**, 329-58.

——— 2014*a*. The negativity of times: collapsed futures in Maputo, Mozambique. *Social Anthropology* **22**, 213-26.

——— 2014*b*. A wedge of time: futures in the present and presents without futures in Maputo, Mozambique. *Journal of the Royal Anthropological Institute* (*N.S.*) **20**: **S1**, 166-82.

OTTAWAY, M. 1988. Mozambique: from symbolic socialism to symbolic reform. *The Journal of Modern African Studies* **26**, 211-26.

PENVENNE, J.M. & B. SITOE 2000. Power, poets and the people: Mozambican voices interpreting history. *Social Dynamics* **26**: **2**, 55-86.

PITCHER, M.A. 2006. Forgetting from above and memory from below: strategies of legitimation and struggles in postsocialist Mozambique. *Africa* **76**, 88-112.

——— & K. ASKEW 2006. African socialisms and postsocialisms. *Africa* **76**, 1-14.

RANCIÈRE, J. 2004. *The politics of aesthetics* (trans. G. Rockhill). London: Continuum.

——— 2009. *The emancipated spectator* (trans. G. Elliott). London: Verso.

SACHS, A. & G.H. WELCH 1990. *Liberating the law: creating popular justice in Mozambique*. London: Zed Books.

SAUL, J.S. (ed.) 1985. *A difficult road: the transition to socialism in Mozambique*. New York: Monthly Review Press.

——— 2005. Eduardo Mondlane and the rise and fall of Mozambican socialism. *Review of African Political Economy* **104**, 309-15.

SHELDON, K. 2014. Selections from the mackerel years: war, hunger, and history in Mozambique. Unpublished manuscript.

STRATHERN, M. 1991. *Partial connections*. Totowa, N.J.: Rowman & Littlefield.

SUMICH, J. 2015. The uncertainty of prosperity: dependence and the politics of middle-class privilege in Maputo. *Ethnos* **81**, 821-41.

TURNER, V. 1991. Paradoxes of twinship in Ndembu ritual. In *The ritual process: structure and anti-structure*, 44-93. Chicago: Aldine.

VINES, A. 1996. *Renamo: from terrorism to democracy in Mozambique?* London: James Currey.

VITANEN, P. & D. EHRENPREISYOUNG 2007. *Growth, poverty and inequality in Mozambique*. Country Study, No. 10. Brasilia: International Poverty Centre (available on-line: *http://www.ipc-undp.org/pub/IPCCountryStudy10.pdf*, accessed 24 January 2017).

WAGNER, R. 2001. *An anthropology of the subject: holographic worldview in New Guinea and its meaning and significance for the world of anthropology*. Berkeley: University of California Press.

——— 2010. *Coyote anthropology*. Lincoln: University of Nebraska Press.

——— 2011*a*. The chess of kinship and the kinship of chess. *HAU: Journal of Ethnographic Theory* **1**: **1**, 165-77.

——— 2011*b*. Vújà de and the Quintessentialists' Guild. *Common Knowledge* **17**, 155-62.

——— 2012. 'Luck in the double focus': ritualized hospitality in Melanesia. *Journal of the Royal Anthropological Institute* (*N.S.*) **18**: **S1**, 161-74.

WEINER, J. 1998. Hand, voice and myth in Papua New Guinea. In *Fluid ontologies: myth, ritual and philosophy in the Highlands of Papua New Guinea* (eds) L.R. Goldman & C. Ballard, 16-30. Westport, Conn.: Bergin & Garvey.

YOUNG, C. 1982. *Ideology and development in Africa*. New Haven: Yale University Press.

YURCHAK, A. 2006. *Everything was forever, until it was no more*. Princeton: University Press.

Jumelage idéologique : esthétique socialiste et meetings politiques à Maputo au Mozambique

Résumé

Sur la base de récentes données ethnographiques recueillies à Maputo au Mozambique, l'essai examine l'esthétique révolutionnaire des meetings politiques, dans un environnement sociopolitique marqué par l'effondrement de l'idéologie socialiste nationale. Au Mozambique, les meetings politiques locaux manifestent une tension paradoxale entre *sacrifice* et *révolution*. Bien que le gouvernement socialiste se soit désintégré au milieu des années 1980, la plupart de ces meetings permettent l'actualisation du socialisme révolutionnaire, auquel le parti Frelimo a dû renoncer pour rester au pouvoir. L'auteur examine ainsi comment la mise en actes d'une esthétique révolutionnaire donne à voir ce que le Frelimo a été incapable de réaliser et saisit ainsi, le temps d'un instant, la légitimité idéologique de ce parti. Tirant son inspiration du récent travail de Roy Wagner sur l'holographie et l'invention, il explore la relation entre *sacrifice* et *révolution* comme l'articulation d'un « jumelage » symétrique entre des principes politiques apparemment contradictoires, retenus ensemble par une esthétique politique singulière qui ne se manifeste que lors des meetings politiques.

9

Ethics in rehearsal

BERNARD KEENAN & ALAIN POTTAGE *London School of Economics and Political Science*

In this essay we explore a rather spare kind of meeting: a conversation between three people with minimal facilitating equipment. The stakes are high because these are meetings in which the barrister in an asylum or immigration case first meets with a client who is at risk of deportation. We focus on two dimensions of these encounters. First, we identify the aesthetic that configures and animates most asylum cases: the aesthetic of inconsistency. The meetings we observed were all about inconsistency; about working out how to respond to actual and anticipated challenges to the coherence of a refugee or migrant's personal narrative. The logic of inconsistency is so persistent and so corrosive that the exercise of anticipation – 'rehearsal' – is essentially open-ended. This leads to the second dimension of our meetings. Barristers who work in this area of law develop a particular style or ethos, which allows them to accompany vulnerable clients through the rehearsal and also to make sense of their own involvement in the machinery of deportation. In these two aspects we find the basic choreographic principles of our meetings: the articulations which shape their material and affective ecology, and which inform the barrister's interpretation and performance of his or her professional role.

According to a practitioner who had recently left the fold, lawyers who dedicate their professional lives to representing refugees risk becoming 'either martyrs or ironists'. How does one engage with a system in which a popular discourse of radical suspicion functions as bureaucratic infrastructure? And how is a lawyer to deal with the routine documentary products of this machinery: letters of refusal in which selected parts of a refugee's story are arbitrarily recomposed so as to suggest logical contradiction, inconsistency, and lack of credibility? We know that these letters have little to do with the lived experiences of refugees; for the lawyer, the problem is how to bring law to bear on texts that are often just pastiches of legal logic. It seems that for the bureaucrats who compile these letters the ritual formula of refusal – 'it is not accepted that' – is all the argument that is needed. And to some extent that is so, because in the UK the refusal of an asylum application by a Home Office caseworker leaves the refugee with recourse to an appeal mechanism whose effectiveness has been compromised by reforms which were expressly designed to expedite deportation, and by cuts to the legal aid budget

Journal of the Royal Anthropological Institute (N.S.), 153-165
© Royal Anthropological Institute 2017

which have further reduced the involvement of lawyers.[1] In terms of the broad structure of the asylum process, the role of lawyers was already more marginal that one might have supposed, but the effect of these changes is further to reinforce a structural effect of alienation.

Many lawyers were drawn to working with refugees because they wanted 'to make a difference'. The barrister who convened the meeting around which this essay is framed expressed this vocation very eloquently:

> I had no doubt in my mind about it being the right thing to do, in every case. Even if people were crazy rapists or whatever, I didn't think it was better to send them to Congo, for example, where women live without proper police or probation services or whatever a rapist needs [to not reoffend]. So even in the worst immigration cases, I still always felt that what I was doing was right.

How does one work out a professional style that reconciles this kind of normative commitment with the indifference of bureaucratic machinery? This is a classically ethical question, which we explore by way of a study of a particular kind of meeting: the case conference in which the barrister retained to represent a refugee at a forthcoming hearing meets the client and the solicitor.

The lawyer's mode of engagement, his or her ethical style, will depend in the first instance on which branch of the profession he or she inhabits. In the English legal system, the solicitor will accompany the refugee from a relatively early stage in the case through to the final disposition, and may become much more familiar with the refugee, with their circumstances, and perhaps their broader community. The barrister will usually meet the refugee for the first time in the case conference, which, now that access to legal aid is so severely restricted, is likely to be held in the moments before the hearing itself. There is some latitude in the way that lawyers use the term 'conference', but most of the practitioners we observed insisted on using it only for the classic encounter between solicitor, client, and barrister. This is a simple form of meeting, which rarely involves more than four people (the client, two lawyers, and an interpreter), and which is contextualized by the most minimal equipment. But our hunch is that some interesting insights into law and lawyering emerge from the observation of these encounters.

Case conferences might be unfolded as sociotechnical assemblages. They involve the repertoire of frames, infrastructures, and techniques that has been anatomized in recent ethnographies of legal form (see notably Riles 2010), and analysis might be scaled up or down, from the procedural regime of asylum law to the now-classic form of the file. In the course of our observations, two forms emerged as particularly intriguing principles of articulation. First, taking our cue from Thomas Scheffer's discussion of 'styles' of lawyering, we started out with the notion that ethics played an interestingly complex role in the articulation of the conference. In his study of how case files function as infrastructure for very distinct professional styles,[2] Scheffer notices how ethics (in the sense of an affective or normative disposition) is wired into contexts: '[H]abitus turns into a disposition that is supported by a local infrastructure of corresponding artefacts' (2007: 71). Style is 'infrastructured' by, and in turn acts as infrastructure for, the elements that are 'convened'[3] in a case conference.[4] Ethics in this particular sense remains the 'medium' of our study. At the same time, however, we noticed the persistence of a particular legal aesthetic – inconsistency – which seemed to be articulated into almost all the observable elements of the conference, from the materiality of the documentation to the ethos of the practitioners. This aesthetic is interesting because it suggests a mode of technicality which is distinguishable from sociotechnical inflection. So although we retain 'ethics' as the rubric of our study, we take lawyering style as a medium in which the agency of this technical armature becomes manifest.

Inconsistency

The only evidence that many asylum seekers can offer in support of their application is a story held in their head – a recollected narrative of persecution and flight.[5] There is no witness evidence to enrich or corroborate their version of events, and no contextualizing evidence other than official compilations of information about the political situation in the 'country of origin'.[6] For refugees seeking asylum in the United Kingdom, the procedural chain that leads to the appeal tribunal (and hence the kind of case conference that we observed) begins with a screening interview, either with an Immigration Officer at a port of entry or with a Home Office official at the central office of the UK Immigration Service. The training given to immigration officers emphasizes the forensic significance of contradictions or inconsistencies: 'Point out the discrepancies, that is your job, find out the discrepancies in what they say and decide' (cited in Jubany 2011: 80). The screening interview, which is supposed to be about gathering information rather than making decisions, is followed by an interview with a Home Office caseworker, who will make a decision on the application. In the letters of refusal which follow most of these interviews, grounds for refusal of an application are typically elicited from the tissue of the story itself, and formulated in terms of 'inconsistency' between different parts or iterations of the narrative. Indeed, the rhetoric of inconsistency has become so automatic that Home Office caseworkers often characterize propositions as inconsistent when they quite plainly are not. Of course, legal cases usually turn on judgements as to the consistency, plausibility, or credibility of a factual narrative, but in asylum procedure 'inconsistency' becomes a particularly persistent and pernicious device.

Inconsistency is carried forward throughout the case as a device that functions at once synchronically and diachronically; it articulates the elements within each phase (interview, consultation, conference, hearing) and relays each phase to the next. So, for example, the object of the conference is to formulate, within the temporal frame of the meeting, a witness statement which retrospectively engages the arguments made in the Home Office letter of refusal, and which does so in terms which also anticipate the rejoinders that are likely to be made in the tribunal by the Home Office advocate and the inquiries that the judge might pursue. In that sense, inconsistency is always 'in rehearsal'. Inconsistency, and the hermeneutical style that actualizes it, is apt to disclose gaps and contradictions anywhere and everywhere. Indeed, in asylum cases the bottom line is a tragic irony: an account of persecution that presents no obvious inconsistencies will itself be said to be inconsistent with the traumatized state of the 'real' refugee. So no narrative can ever be intrinsically complete. When it happens, the 'resolution' of inconsistency is often the effect of a singular event which eclipses the narrative as 'a whole': on one side the 'gotcha'[7] moment in which the applicant is betrayed by a flagrant contradiction; on the other, the moment in which a single detail emerges from the narrative so as to 'absolve' inconsistency (here we fuse the familiar meaning with the archaic sense of absolution as resolution).[8]

How is ethics implicated in this machinery? To begin with, there is a rather obvious sense in which the subjectivity (or ethos) of the refugee is implicated in the discourse of gaps and contradictions. The barrister who convened the conference that serves as the narrative frame for this essay told us that she saw her role as being to detach the refugee from the logic of the letter of refusal:

> [A] surprising number, given the culture of disbelief, most people are telling the truth in their cases, you know? And the problem is that they're battered down by this system. And often the more important thing is about not getting people to respond to the ridiculous logic of refusal letters. The problem is people take it on, they take on the wild crazy reasons for why they're not ... then they try to explain them, and trying to explain them, that's what makes them sound not credible.

The barrister insulates the client from the Home Office narrative by characterizing the allegation of non-credibility as a technical problem to be addressed and resolved through the presentation of the evidence. The case, which centres on inconsistency, is a matter of legal technicality and therefore the business of the advocate as champion. And, if the basic strategy is to anticipate and defuse potential allegations of inconsistency, then the 'case' is crafted by drawing the potentialities of the refugee's narrative, the self-presentational competences (or limitations) of the refugee, and the form of the witness statement into the aesthetic of inconsistency. But this ethical style works only if the client gives the barrister something to work with. In some situations the client is 'inconsistent' even in the case conference, and it becomes almost impossible for the barrister to develop a strategy that connects the witness statement to the self-presentation of the client. In extreme cases, where the refugee's case is publicly funded, the barrister may have to form a professional judgement as to whether the case justifies further funding.

Inconsistency also articulates the professional relationship between the barrister and the solicitor. Many barristers assumed a posture of detachment or relative objectivity, and hence claimed a particular insight into the documented case – or, more precisely, into the way that the contents of the file might play out in the agonistic frame of inconsistency. From this perspective, one question as the conference unfolds is whether a particular solicitor can be relied upon to have drafted a decent witness statement. As one barrister observed to us:

> If you've got a solicitor you trust, you think, 'You've done all this. I know these are all the grounds and I don't need to poke or prod to find some more'. There are some solicitors where you think, 'I don't think these are all the grounds'. So actually in the conference you spend time poking and come out with two or three grounds that weren't there before.

The encounter between barrister and solicitor, which may be just one phase of an ongoing relationship, is inflected by the barrister's sense of how the solicitor's competences 'measure up' to the logic of inconsistency.

Ecology

Most case conferences take place in barristers' chambers, in rooms dedicated to the purpose. In less fancy chambers the conference room often doubles as a library or filing room; and, for clients at least, the experience of being enfolded in an archive has its own aesthetic effects. The conventional ecological formula for the conference is simple: three people sitting around a table. In one rather extreme situation, this prototypical infrastructure is expressed as hard architecture. The room set aside for lawyer-client meetings in the High Security Unit of HMP Belmarsh (the maximum-security prison used to hold a number of those facing deportation or extradition for reasons related to national security) imposes a particular frame for interaction. The 'table' is a solid cuboid structure that runs the entire length of the room, effectively dividing it in two. The lawyer, having been driven from the secure visiting area of the prison to the maximum-security unit in a van with darkened windows, enters the meeting room from one 'side', the client from the other. The solid table ensures that nothing can be passed between lawyer and client without being visible through the windows that run the length of each side, and who knows whether what is transacted verbally is not also open to scrutiny.[9] In yet other situations, the conventionalized form of the conference has to be actualized in a context in which few or none of the usual props are available. One barrister with experience of working in both refugee law and criminal law told us of some of the peculiarities of criminal cases:

> It's slightly different, yeah, and a huge percentage of those conferences take place when you're interviewing somebody in a room not much bigger than a disabled toilet, with no obvious furniture and a terrible smell. The first thing I was told, or one of the first things I was told when doing conferences in crime, is that when you open the wicket [the hatch on cell door], to speak to your client, make sure your face isn't in front of the wicket because who knows what's going to come out of that thing first. It might well be a fist, even if they know it's you.

So what is involved in sitting three people around a table? The 'arrangement of people' (Sommer 1967: 145) is an obvious infrastructure of interaction, so obvious that it is easily overlooked. It is also, as it turns out, a resource for ethical performance. Even the most minimal equipment – again, a table and a few chairs – allows for degrees of proximity, opacity, or engagement, whether material or discursive, to be mobilized strategically. The case conference that we take as a narrative frame for this essay offers a particularly interesting example. The case in question was not a matter of refugee law because there was no question of persecution, but it mobilized the forms and strategies that we observed in other conferences. The client was facing deportation from the United Kingdom on the ground that he was a foreign national who had been convicted of a criminal offence. He had a British partner with whom he had two children, so deportation would have resulted in the separation of the family. The question, then, was whether deportation would amount to 'disproportionate' interference with his rights and the rights of his family within the terms of the European Convention on Human Rights. One of the children had learning difficulties, so the family had been supported by social services for some time. This kind of case no longer falls within the scope of legal aid provision, so the client was paying for representation himself, on the basis of a fixed fee arranged with the solicitor.

About ten minutes after the client, his partner, and the solicitor arrive at the chambers, the barrister comes to the waiting area next to reception. She introduces herself very warmly; she smiles and addresses the client and his partner directly, shaking their hands. She and the solicitor know each other well, and they acknowledge each another very briefly. The barrister leads the solicitor and clients a short distance to the conference room, in which a large table is surrounded by a number of chairs. Water, biscuits, glasses, cups, and saucers are assembled on the table, and the barrister relays requests for tea and coffee to someone outside the room. The barrister is carrying the papers with her and she sets these up in front of her as she sits down. She asks the client to sit next to her – 'Why don't you sit here?' He does so, and his partner takes a seat adjacent to him. This is perhaps the most interesting moment in the meeting. In most conferences the barrister automatically sits opposite the client and solicitor. This may be a vestige of tradition; some of our barristers referred to the solicitor and client as, respectively, the 'professional client' and the 'lay client'. The usual seating arrangement is not inconsistent with expressions of empathy. One barrister suggested to us that she always sat opposite the client and the solicitor because 'it would be a bit intimidating to have both lawyers on the other side of the table from you. It looks a bit like we're opposed to them really'. But the ethical ecology of this particular conference is significantly different.

After the meeting, the barrister told us why she preferred to sit next to her clients:

> I don't want to be an aloof barrister. I feel like, without fail, the clients I mainly have, you want to be as unintimidating and as much like a 'real person' as possible. So I think you want to be next to them. And it will be like this in the hearing, it will be me, and you, and that's what you want to make them feel. You have to be like, I am going to be there, I am going to say this, you want them to feel like, oh my God, thank goodness she's going to be the one, the wall, like the kind of solid … I don't know, you've really got to try and make sure your clients feel confident in you. And you've got to know their case well before you meet them. Because if you don't know … I think it really reassures a client when you come to your conference and you're able to say it's obvious that you know their whole case already. That makes them feel like, OK, she understands it …

Although her professional profile was similar to that of other asylum law barristers – young but relatively experienced, trained in the public service-orientated repertoire of public law, immigration law and criminal law – this barrister had (somewhat unusually) started out as a junior caseworker in a solicitor's firm. As much as possible, she tried to model her professional style on this formative experience:

> I think when I started in some ways I would have been better [at conferences] because as a caseworker I was very used to having client contact, and sometimes now I have to remind myself to slow down and explain, it can't be me talking to another lawyer, and that's so much of your time as a barrister is just talking to another lawyer, or a judge, and writing things.

This contrasts quite sharply with the style of the lawyer for whom the work of accompanying refugees, or of gaining their trust, was not part of her role, and who might well take a case without ever meeting the refugee him- or herself:

> If credibility's not an issue, I don't ever want a conference. If [the Home Office] accept everything that's been said, then it's legal stuff, and unless [the client] can contribute to that, which is quite rare, there might be two or three questions they can help with but I'd always ask the solicitor for those, just phone them.

Of course, there is more to an ethical style than the axis of proximity. In dealing with the client, one is also relating to the solicitor and documentation, and to each of these elements through the other. And a sustainable ethical style is one that holds together all these dimensions of the conference.

In some of the conferences that we observed, the basic felicity condition for the barrister's participation was opacity rather than proximity. Some practitioners preferred to sit opposite the client and the solicitor so that in the course of the conference they could discreetly check their email, or perhaps work on a more urgent case. One of our barristers deployed the material form of documents to strategic effect. Using a trick learned from his mentor, he would forest the papers with randomly placed Post-it notes to suggest close reading of the file, and he would seek to compound that impression by evoking one or two of the more obscure details of the case. He explained to us that 'a real part of conferences is giving the impression of knowing the case better than the client. And clients are always in my experience impressed if they can see how well you've prepared for the meeting'. From the client's point of view, the difference between opacity and proximity may not be decisive. After all, the barrister who made defensive use of Post-it notes also came up with the one of the more spectacular 'resolutions' of inconsistency in the course of a conference: noticing that a refugee had scars on his head which substantiated his story of having been beaten by police officers, and which explained why he was unable to recall his experiences in any consistent way.

Agenda

To return to the conference that frames our discussion, the barrister begins by describing the spatial layout of the courtroom to the client: the judge will sit facing the other participants. The Home Office will have a table on one side of the room, and the client and the barrister will have a table on the other side. She explains the order in which each party will speak, summarizes the roles of the Home Office Presenting Officer and the Immigration Judge, and explains her own role in the hearing. She emphasizes to the client that she is there to deal with all procedural issues and that if he has any questions or concerns during the case he can confer with her at any time. She then goes on to identify the central issue in the case: 'credibility'. She tells the client that although the issue has been explored quite extensively by the solicitor, it remains problematic: 'Basically, it means whether or not the judge accepts the facts as you put them, your version of events. In this particular case, your big credibility issue is going to be about the offence, so we'll focus on that today, because it will be difficult at the hearing'. Having flagged the question, the barrister then turns to a part of the file that contains a report by the social services on the children's needs. She goes through the facts in the report with the client and checks that they are correctly recorded. The client's partner adds some more details to the issues discussed in the report and the barrister makes further notes.

This phase of the conference is quite conventional. It is usual for the barrister to set the agenda by identifying the central issue, and to spend the first few minutes checking certain details in the paperwork. In most of the conferences that we observed, the questions or issues to be covered in the conference were written on the last page of a (new and freshly opened) notepad, and from time to time the barrister would suspend the flow of note-taking and turn to this page to check the agenda. The (invariably blue) notepad mediates between the bundle of documents (which might be marked with Post-it notes to identify the most crucial parts) and the course of the conversation as it unfolds in the conference. The central document is a work in progress – the witness statement in which the contents of the refugee's narrative are tuned and retuned in the light of a strategic judgement of how the narrative (and the narrator) might stand up to the forensic questioning of a Home Office Presenting Officer. At least for one barrister, the witness statement was the essential actor in the conference:

> I don't like conferences unless there's already a witness statement. I know some solicitors like to take the client along in order to get a witness statement . . . I prefer to have a statement in front of me so I can cross-examine, effectively, the witness statement, check for gaps, errors, issues.

In cases where the participation of the refugee might give greater latitude to the Home Office, the barrister might seek to let the statement stand in for the client.

The rather spare image in Figure 1, which is a photograph of the back page of one of these blue jotters, depicts a somewhat idiosyncratic conference plan.

Instead of writing out an agenda, or a list of questions, on the last page of her notepad, this barrister draws a map of the courtroom. She then reproduces the image for the client in the course of the conference, step by step. As she draws each figure, and positions them in relation to the place that will be occupied by the client, she

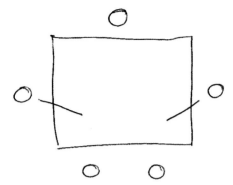

Figure 1.

explains the role of each actor in the hearing, what they might be likely to do or say, and sounds out the client's likely reactions or responses. This procedure works as a kind of mnemonic device for the barrister: from her perspective, each figure stands for a part of the case that is likely to be put to the client, so that the re-animation of the map within the frame of the conference recalls the points that she has identified in her reading of the draft witness statement. But the map is also an exemplary piece of ethical machinery. It is a device for rehearsing the experience of the trial with the client, for 'walking them through' the forthcoming hearing. The process of drawing out these minimalist figures, of situating, contextualizing, and explaining, brings the time of the hearing into the process of the conference. Rehearsal through topography casts the lawyer as empathetic champion, assures the client of her competence and mastery of the case, and realizes an affect of proximity that is, if anything, more intense than what is achieved by sitting alongside the client.

To return to our conference, the barrister concludes the first phase of the meeting with a brief review of a further set of reports from social services about the likely effects of deportation on the welfare of the children. And here she addresses the solicitor directly:

> These reports are good but we could use more. How many reviews were done in total? We should try to get the whole file – normally it is possible. Call up and request it from legal department, say you urgently need the file. There might be helpful notes. The problem is that the current report doesn't show the timing.

The solicitor, who has been keeping notes on her laptop, makes a further note and agrees to look into the matter. The barrister goes on to remind her of the implications of a recent decision in which it was held that children might eventually adapt to life without a deported parent, and observes that it would be important to use psychological assessments of the family to meet that argument. In this collegial exchange, the solicitor figures as a productive collaborator, but it is clear that the barrister has the better insight into the case as it goes forward to the hearing.

The barrister then turns to the crucial part of the case: the client's account of the criminal offence. She automatically turns to the relevant pages of her file, but she proceeds to ask a series of focused questions without ever consulting the papers. Her tone remains friendly, but the tempo of the conference changes. In response to a question about a specific aspect of the conviction which had led to these deportation proceedings, the client offers a non-committal answer: 'Not really'. At this point the barrister responds with a firm but non-confrontational challenge:

> What do you mean by 'not really'? Look, the problem is that you are minimizing your role . . . In your statement, it sounds like you didn't even do anything. In the sentencing remarks from the trial, the judge says that you describe yourself as having let yourself be brought into a situation, but that you are not naïve . . . So it was clearly not accepted that your basis of plea was just that you had no idea. So if you say it now, they won't trust you. You obviously admitted something different before the court. It's better to take full responsibility – and leave it at that. You did the sentence, you're not going to reoffend, it was clearly a mistake. At the moment, your statement says something different.

This is the point at which the aesthetic of inconsistency emerges most clearly in the course of the conference. The Home Office Presenting Officer or the judge will pick up on this contradiction between what the client admitted at his trial and what he says in the witness statement. The barrister begins the process of reformulating the statement by going back to the beginning, the better to satisfy herself of the possible grounds of inconsistency: 'What happened with the offence? Start at beginning. How did you get into it?' The documents drop away, and the conference turns into a rehearsal of cross-examination.

Ethics

All of the barristers we talked to emphasized that they were bound by rules of professional conduct which prohibited the 'coaching' of witnesses – essentially, telling witnesses what they should say in court. The barrister who convened our sample conference offered us the clearest explanation of the rule:

> You can always tell someone what to leave in and what to leave out of a statement, and what evidence will help their case and what won't. What you can't do is tell them to change their evidence. If they say, I said the car was black, and it would be better if it was blue, you can't tell them to say it's blue. You have to say, tell me the truth and I'll tell you whether the truth is helpful or not helpful. And when the client asks, well what should I say, that's when you have to be like, no I can't help. I don't think it's that difficult. I don't. I think that line is not that difficult to navigate.

When pressed on the question of where this rule was inscribed, or what its contents were, she responded somewhat vaguely: 'Yeah, I think it is in . . . I don't know where'. This is intriguing: the rule is recognized to be essential and binding, it is consistently practised, and yet none of the practitioners we worked with felt impelled to verify its provenance, content, or scope.

The rule that proscribes rehearsal is indeed found in the Bar Council's Code of Conduct: 'You must not rehearse, practise with or coach a witness in respect of their evidence'. The handbook in which the Code of Conduct is contained runs to 277 pages, of which only six are devoted to the rubric 'Behaving ethically'; and whereas other rules in this rubric are glossed with commentaries and illustrations, this particular rule stands unadorned (Bar Standards Board 2014: 27-30). So even if practitioners were to look for a formal specification, they would not find very much. Here, we should recall what sociologies of the so-called 'self-regulating' professions have long suggested: that ethical rules function as a corporate parure, a documentary get-up by which the professional body impresses itself and others (see here Strathern 2006). We are interested in the sense in which 'ethics' as a corpus of deontological principles is articulated by 'ethos' in the sense of professional style. We know that rules are learned through being lived, but these ethical rules of conduct are not lived (or mastered) in the same way as the technical rules of law or procedure that barristers mobilize in textual or oral argument.

Our hypothesis is that the rule takes on a different depth or texture depending on the articulation of the logic of inconsistency with the perceived competences of the client and the ethical style of the lawyer. A number of barristers drew a distinction between the experts who are sometimes consulted in asylum cases and the regular refugee. Whereas experts were able to infer from a barrister's line of questioning how they should deal with a Home Office Presenting Officer, many refugees lacked the competences to do this. So, as one put it, 'You do try and fix that stuff as much as you can'. What are the limits to 'fixing stuff'?

At the point in our conference when the barrister's questioning turns into a mode of cross-examination, the client's answers become increasingly terse. When asked whether he was paid for his role in the offence of which he was convicted, he replies, 'Not really'. At this point, the barrister offers further advice:

> Just answer the question; stop trying to minimize. Let someone else judge it. Imagine how it comes across. You can be embarrassed, you can say you were embarrassed, but there is no point minimizing or misleading. You got a five-year sentence because it was a serious offence. You admitted you knew what you were doing. You can't make it sound better now. It sounds best to say you accept it ... The judge's mind-set is constantly tuned to lying or not lying. And if you suggest in any way that you're not being 100 per cent honest, they won't like you; it's insulting to them, and they won't be sympathetic to your stressful situation and that you were motivated by your family.

After this, the client relaxes a bit. He admits that some cash was seized, and that it was forfeited. Once this has been discussed, the barrister also seems happier. She has convinced the client to be more forthcoming; the statement can be redrafted and hopefully the client will offer more expansive and forthright answers if or when he is called to give evidence at the hearing. What has been negotiated here is the line between familiarization and inadmissible 'rehearsal' or 'coaching'.

How does one 'fix' inconsistency while remaining on the right side of the rule? One fairly consistent theme emerged from our conversations with barristers: 'There's a difference between familiarizing someone with the likely procedure and the likely way that the evidence is going to be presented by the other side, and saying, "Look, you're going to say x, y, and z'. Perhaps this can be construed as a difference between two modes of rehearsal: between putting the client in the picture about how things will unfold in court and instructing them on how to perform once they get there. For one of our barristers, telling a client how to dress for their appearance would count as coaching. Many of our informants invoked a criterion of truth: so, for instance, it would be permissible to say to a client, 'Tell me the truth and I'll tell you whether the truth is helpful or not'. Rehearsal would be anything that prompted the client to change a 'true' story. But the nature of inconsistency is such that what is in play is not truth as such but the 'truth' that emerges from the agonistic exchange of hypotheses and allegations. Again, inconsistency is 'resolved' not by 'completing' a narrative but by finding a strategy that anticipates and defuses the aspersion as to credibility that is implied by an allegation. In our conference, the barrister feels that she has properly judged that line.

Concluding the conference, the barrister addresses the solicitor with a list of points that need further work. First, she recapitulates the elements of the case and identifies additions or amendments that should be made to the witness statement. Then she asks the solicitor to procure a full set of records from the social worker, to obtain a letter of support from a prospective employer, and to get hold of the children's medical files and letters from their teachers. The conference concludes on a less than optimistic note: the

Journal of the Royal Anthropological Institute (N.S.), 153-165
© Royal Anthropological Institute 2017

barrister advises that although some Presenting Officers are fair, others are not, and although some Immigration Judges are sympathetic, the family should also 'prepare for the worst'. When the clients have left, the solicitor and barrister fix a time for their next conversation about the case.

Passing

In his account of law-making in the Conseil d'État, Bruno Latour observes that law is not truly a sociotechnical enterprise. The media of lawyering – speech and text – have remained essentially the same for two millennia, and these media lack the capacity to 'inflect' action in the manner of even the most basic technological artefacts (Latour 2006: chap. 5). One might suggest in response that communicative media – in law as elsewhere – have precisely the capacities of inflection that Latour reserves for technological devices. An example can be found in his ethnography of the Conseil. In the course of rendering judgement, the *conseillers* felt obliged to respect a time-honoured convention of hesitation: 'for [justice] to speak justly, she must have hesitated' (Latour 2006: 152). In debate, the judges sought to convince themselves that they had hesitated for long enough to sound out the full scope for decision that was afforded by precedent and policy, or to ensure that the decision was properly reasoned. It would be interesting to pursue Latour's analysis somewhat further, and to explore the variability of the convention. How does the duration of hesitation vary, how does its inflection of the decision change, according to the character of the tribunal or the case? What of those cases in which judges do not hesitate, the better to affirm the rightness of the decision or the more peremptorily to reject the pretensions of one of the parties? But the essential point is that the time of hesitation, its measure or texture, is not chronometric: 'long enough' is not a matter of minutes or seconds.

The forensic sense of time emerges from the way that the judges, as agents of the convention, 'perform' duration so as to engage the expectations of the public, and these expectations are ethopoietic artefacts – effects of the way that the judges see themselves being seen by this (virtual) public. In the process of hesitating, the judges mobilize or inflect time in such a way as to turn it into something other than itself. The 'time' that functions as a variable or emergent felicity condition for the formulation and enunciation of judgement is generated by the process of communication, by the reflexive performance of hesitation for an addressee (the virtual 'body' of the court, or a public). This is inflection within the ancient medium of 'talk'. It is interesting to dwell on the formula that Latour uses to characterize the moment of decision, or the moment in which an ethical moment is capitalized to the benefit of a mode of enunciation: 'law passes'.

In asylum and immigration cases, the machinery through which law 'passes' is configured by the aesthetic of inconsistency; documents, ecologies, ethical dispositions, professional strategies, and conceptual forms are actualized and connected along lines of force or tension that are generated by 'inconsistency'. The ethos or style of the barrister, which is manifested in such things as the disposition of chairs, the handling of files, or the ethical care with which clients are engaged, evolves as a resource for making this machinery more 'liveable' for both the lawyer and the client. But, as in Latour's example, the lawyer's ethical style is itself implicated in the articulation of the protocol through which law passes. To begin with, inconsistency is the aesthetic that discloses the elements of the case to the barrister, and which conditions how she positions herself (spatially, ethically, cognitively) in relation to her client. It is the frame that prompts and shapes the evolution of a lawyerly style: 'Lawyers adjust to the procedural regimes that they regularly attend to. The regime serves as the frame that tells apart good from bad practice, successful from failing strategies, available from unavailable communications, and useless from useful information' (Scheffer 2007: 71). And, within the frame of a particular case or a particular conference, this lawyerly ethos conditions how, in the real time of rehearsal, the barrister senses the emergence of actual or potential 'gaps' in the evidence, these 'gaps' being a function of the barrister's perception of how the material and 'human' resources that make up the evidence will play out in court. Ultimately, an ethical style is capitalized in the 'passing' of asylum procedure. This is not surprising: ethical 'equipment' (Rabinow 2003) is necessarily bound up in the world from which it seeks to take its distance. And, to return to our opening sentence, it may be that 'martyrdom' or 'irony' is just the most resilient device for acknowledging that implication.

NOTES

The authors wish to thank the participants, both lawyers and clients, for the time, confidence, and insights that made this research possible.

[1] In the United Kingdom, about 60 per cent of applications for asylum are denied by the Home Office. Of those who receive a refusal letter, most will appeal to a tribunal, where about 25 per cent are successful (House of Commons, 'Asylum statistics'; figures are for 2013).

[2] Scheffer is interested in 'the regularities and routines' of styles: 'Why, one may wonder, do lawyers sustain their respective styles across a broad range of cases, clients, and legal matters?' (2007: 70).

[3] According to an archaic sense, people are not the only agents that can be 'convened'; the *Oxford English Dictionary* (s.v. convene) offers an illustrative quotation from Robert Boyle's *The origin of forms and qualities* (1666): 'The wise Author of Things did, by guiding the first motions of the small parts of Matter, bring them to convene after the manner requisite to compose the World'.

[4] Scheffer's association of habitus with infrastructure suggests an interesting inflection of the old theme of ethos/habitus. Ethos or habitus is not a form of interiorized capitalized experience, which is actualized in engagements in a 'field'; it is an effect of the co-articulation of material, semantic, and psychic forms. This is not the sense of habitus that one finds in the work of Pierre Bourdieu. That particular sense, which has a long history, involves a particular set of tropes: in habitus, experience is capitalized as equipment for agency in the present; habitus somehow articulates potentiality into actuality, or convention into invention; habitus is observable only in its actualization, so that (sociologically or ethnographically) the 'field' functions as the medium in which virtual capacities are both actualized and disclosed to observation (see the classic analysis in Héran 1987). So in the tradition that Bourdieu draws upon, ethos/habitus becomes observable when a virtual, interior, competence is actualized in or as a set of observable transactions.

[5] The Refugee Convention provides that asylum should be granted where the applicant has a 'well-founded fear of being persecuted' (Convention Relating to the Status of Refugees [adopted 28 July 1951, entered into force 22 April 1954] 189 UNTS 137 [Refugee Convention], art. 1A). The (rarely observed) principle is that the authorities have to assist the refugee in making their case.

[6] In their analysis of how this information is actually used, Gibb and Good observe that for the Home Office the primary aim is 'to anticipate and pre-empt rival arguments rather than assess the overall country situation', so that country of origin information 'risks being treated as a set of discrete snippets, with little attempt to link one factoid to another, still less to construct a structured, multi-dimensional picture of the country situation' (2013: 303-4).

[7] For an example, see Luker (2013).

[8] In his study of appeal hearings in France, Dequen reports the observations of a judge who, having formed the impression that an applicant was too 'detached' in telling the story of how her young son had been crushed to death by a tank, was then convinced when the applicant recalled seeing next to the body a chocolate bar that the child's father had bought for him earlier that day: 'One can't invent this; these are the details that make a story credible or not' (cited in Dequen 2013: 461).

[9] In the course of the hearing in the case of *Belhadj & Others* v. *The Security Service, SIS, GCHQ, Home Office and FCO* (2015) IPT/13/132-9/H, it was revealed that legally privileged communications between lawyers and clients in national security cases have indeed been intercepted.

Journal of the Royal Anthropological Institute (N.S.), 153-165
© Royal Anthropological Institute 2017

REFERENCES

BAR STANDARDS BOARD 2014. *The Bar Standards Board Handbook* (First edition) (available on-line: *https://www.barstandardsboard.org.uk/media/1553795/bsb_handbook_jan_2014.pdf*, accessed 27 January 2017).

DEQUEN, J.-P. 2013. Constructing the refugee figure in France: ethnomethodology of a decisional process. *International Journal of Refugee Law* **25**, 449-69.

GIBB, R. & A. GOOD 2013. Do the facts speak for themselves? Country of origin information in French and British refugee status determination procedures. *International Journal of Refugee Law* **25**, 291-322.

HÉRAN, F. 1987. La seconde nature de l'habitus: tradition philosophique et sens commun dans le langage sociologique. *Revue française de sociologie* **28**, 385-416.

JUBANY, O. 2011. Constructing truths in a culture of disbelief: understanding asylum screening from within. *International Sociology* **26**, 74-94.

LATOUR, B. 2006. *The making of law: an ethnography of the Conseil d'État.* Cambridge: Polity.

LUKER, T. 2013. Decision making conditioned by radical uncertainty: credibility assessment at the Australian Refugee Review Tribunal. *International Journal of Refugee Law* **25**, 502-34.

RABINOW, P. 2003. *Anthropos today: reflections on modern equipment.* Princeton: University Press.

RILES, A. 2010. Collateral expertise: legal knowledge in the global financial markets. *Current Anthropology* **51**, 795-818.

SCHEFFER, T. 2007. File work, legal care, and professional habitus – an ethnographic reflection on different styles of advocacy. *International Journal of the Legal Profession* **14**, 57-80.

SOMMER, R. 1967. Small group ecology. *Psychological Bulletin* **67**, 145-52.

STRATHERN, M. 2006. Bullet-proofing: a tale from the United Kingdom. In *Documents: artifacts of modern knowledge* (ed.) A. Riles, 181-205. Ann Arbor: University of Michigan Press.

L'éthique en répétition

Résumé

Cet essai explore un type relativement rare de réunion : une combinaison de trois personnes munies d'un minimum de matériel. L'enjeu est important car il s'agit des réunions au cours desquelles l'avocat rencontre pour la première fois son client, au cours d'une procédure de demande d'asile ou d'immigration dont l'issue peut être l'expulsion. Les auteurs s'intéressent à deux dimensions de ces rencontres. D'une part, ils identifient l'esthétique qui configure et anime la plupart des dossiers de demande d'asile : c'est l'esthétique de l'incohérence. Les réunions qu'ils ont observées tournaient toutes autour de cette incohérence, car il fallait chercher une manière de répondre aux remises en question effectives et prévisibles de la cohérence du récit personnel d'un réfugié ou d'un migrant. La logique de l'incohérence est si persistante et si corrosive que l'exercice de l'anticipation (de la « répétition ») est pour l'essentiel ouvert. D'où la deuxième dimension de ces réunions : les avocats qui exercent dans ce domaine du droit développent un style ou un éthos particulier, qui leur permet d'accompagner leurs clients vulnérables au fil de la répétition tout en donnant un sens à leur propre implication dans la mécanique de l'expulsion. Dans ces deux aspects, on trouve les principes chorégraphiques de base de ces rencontres : les articulations qui donnent forme à leur matière et à leur écologie affective et qui éclairent l'interprétation et le « jeu » de l'avocat dans son rôle professionnel.

10

An office of ethics: meetings, roles, and moral enthusiasm in animal protection

ADAM REED *University of St Andrews*

This essay explores the relationship between meetings and organizational ethics in an animal protection charity in Scotland. Here, recent 'professionalization' has seen the late introduction of an 'ethics of office' and accompanying impersonalization of roles. A consequent struggle emerges over what the relationship should be between the core message of the organization, as an office of animal ethics, and the 'personal' principles or ethical commitment of individual staff members. All of this comes to a head when persons, and office-holders, meet.

In this essay I am interested in the relationship between formal meetings and organizational ethics. Driven by my ethnography of an animal protection charity in Scotland, it seeks to explore how the core aim of the organization – 'to secure proper respect for animals and inspire a more compassionate society' – plays out through the ordinary forms of administrative procedure in the third sector. The focus is partly prompted by recent anthropological attention to the 'ethical' as a dimension or modality of practice (Lambek 2010: 10; see also Laidlaw 2010; 2013). As its mission statement suggests, the charity views itself as values-led, involved in 'ethical campaigning'. Indeed, its use of the term draws on a common understanding of ethical practice as both the identification of a positive value to be placed on specific kinds of acts (i.e. those compassionate or respectful of animals) and a desire to situate organizational action itself within a general field of ethics (i.e. that of animal welfare and sentience debates) where criteria are laid out and judgements are exercised (Lambek 2010: 9). But as a property of action as much as thought (Lambek 2010: 14), it also implies a process by which the ethical subject of animal protection itself becomes constituted. The charity is publicly committed to the promotion of certain kinds of relationship to self, which are in turn invoked within the organization, registered and sometimes subtly refashioned at the times when staff members meet.

Describing the organizational ethics of a body that defines its rationale for existence as ethical obviously places this study in a tradition that describes and examines the institutionalization of moral concern; in this essay, for example, a background influence is the analysis provided by Hopgood (2006) of organizational development at Amnesty International. Presented as a 'fascinating story of practical morality and its possibilities and problems' (2006: 222), his book is also an account of the 'infiltration of the mechanisms and ideas of capital into all areas of not-for-profit and private life' (2006: 134). But as Hopgood's nuanced description makes clear, 'infiltration', and the general process of convergence between what were once radically distinct 'sectors' of life, impacts ethical organizations in very different ways. The indeterminacy is in part down to the kind of moral authority that such bodies historically claim and to the ethos that staff inherit and wish to struggle to maintain; but it is also due to differences in organizational size. Whereas large not-for-profit organizations such as Amnesty International started to negotiate a shift to 'modernization' and a new managerial culture in the last decade or so of the twentieth century, for a raft of small charitable organizations the pressure to modernize was considerably delayed.

A desire to respect those specificities prompts me also to engage with the re-emergent interest in the moral attributes of the concept of 'office' (Corsín Jiménez 2015; du Gay 2000; 2006; 2008; Strathern 2009). In this literature, which recombines old insights on the notion of administrative responsibility and the values of public persona from Weber and from debates in mid-twentieth-century anthropology, most notably the work of Fortes, attention falls on the specific competencies of office and on the vital quality of impersonality attached to them. The approach, I would suggest, seems to open new ways to assess the ethical mark of organizational structure and the role of the formal meeting within it. In particular, I am influenced by the observations of du Gay (2000; 2006; 2008) on dramatic shifts in the culture of public governance in the United Kingdom. Since the late twentieth century, he argues, there has been a concerted attack on the 'ethics of office', the long-standing principle that adherence to procedure and the tasks of bureaucratic roles goes hand in hand with a deliberate subordination of personal moral enthusiasms (2006: 17). The ethical commitment of the civil servant traditionally derives from this active self-denial, cultivated through a sense of duty or vocational obligation to the purpose of a higher authority. Indeed, as du Gay points out, until relatively recently the studied impersonality or indifference of the state bureaucrat was marked as a 'positive moral achievement'. Today, however, the subservience to office seems to clash with a widespread presumption that ethical action can only proceed through the exercise of moral autonomy or individual conscience-driven judgement; so that 'to hold a subaltern status and to exercise moral agency are represented as fundamentally incompatible' (2006: 2). Coupled with the introduction of new brands of managerialism, this has resulted in the increasing personalization of public offices, posing a threat, as du Gay would have it, to the constitutional performance of the civil service and its conventional concept of the moral agent.

In this account, one of the chief casualties of a weakened ethic of office is precisely the place and ethos of formal meetings in the running of governmental administration. Where politicians start introducing external 'special advisers' or encouraging an entrepreneurial spirit among senior civil servants, who consequently begin to view public offices as an 'extension of their own will and ideological commitment' (2006: 10), the procedural basis for meeting starts to break down. A new culture of informality emerges among those who attend meetings (civil servants, special advisers, and politicians), with a consequent lapse in adherence to bureaucratic due process. Careful and precise notation becomes irregular, for instance: in some meetings, minutes are no longer taken, making it hard to document who has said what and even that meetings have actually taken place (2006: 20). This is complicated by the fact that state bureaucrats no longer fully control the process or composition of those formal meetings that do occur; the latter constitute a space of redefined encounters. When reconceived as newly responsive to or representative of 'the popular will' (2006: 7), instead of subservient to the purpose of office, for example, office-holders find themselves subject to 'consumer capture', required to meet the priorities of citizen or user-group bodies outside the administration (2006: 9). Likewise, a new expectation that civil servants should be autonomous agents of conscience, prepared to act, when necessary, upon their own sense of social responsibility, leads to an assumption that meetings between office-holders will now include an 'inner moral audit' of the roles assigned them. According to du Gay, this 'personalist morality' makes it increasingly hard to sustain 'the idea that the state bureaucracy is a substantive ethical domain in its own right' (2006: 11). In this climate, the formal meeting and its accompanying technologies of procedure, such as minute-taking, tend to appear as just overly bureaucratic, outmoded, and inefficient ways of delivering the outcomes that matter.

I am not qualified to assess the historical accuracy of the narrative of public administration that du Gay provides. Nevertheless, I find his identification of shifts in organizational ethics, and the consequences for the implied ethos of formal meetings, highly provocative. This includes his observation that conceptions of moral agency based on abnegation or the subordination of the person to the higher authority of office have suffered a contemporary collapse. In particular, I am struck by the idea that in the realm of governmental and political action the personalization of roles constitutes a moral crisis, for the suggestion helps throw into relief a quite different trajectory in the relationship between formal meetings and organizational ethics, this time within the charitable sector, and more specifically the small Scottish animal protection agency I worked with. Unlike the civil service, this is an organization founded on the presumption that participation in meetings and in other forms of administrative procedure is driven by personal conviction and shared ethical feeling; the charity was established in Edinburgh early in the twentieth century, originally conceived as an anti-vivisection campaigning group and then diversifying over the years to become a generalist advocate for animal welfare. Both volunteers and paid colleagues are assumed to participate in work tasks exactly because they recognize a natural convergence of private and organizational values. In fact, the success of the charity is traditionally held to rest on the energy generated by the moral enthusiasm of its staff. In this very different organizational context, it almost appears that a counter-narrative to du Gay's tale now exists, for members of staff identify the near past as a period when they were introduced to a new principle of impersonality in their working lives, to something we might recognize as akin to an ethic of office. (While in du Gay's account new cultures of managerialism are a threat to this bureaucratic principle, I want to argue that for the staff members of the animal protection charity I worked with, managerial innovation and the ethics of office appeared somehow combined.) For many of them, the change represented their ethical organization's own historical crisis.[1]

In what follows, then, I am interested to explore what happens to formal meetings when the personalist morality that originally grounded them is challenged by an organizational ethics centred on the separation of competency or task from individual moral conscience. This includes an examination of the rise and fall of particular kinds of official meeting within the animal protection organization and a consideration of the way these meetings animate the tension between the attributes of competing moral agencies and ethical subjects. When subservience to office, and the accompanying principle of indifference or impersonality, appears as a new, alternative form of ethical labour in the charity, the question suddenly becomes who is meeting and what sort of encounter is taking place. In many ways, this essay is an old-fashioned ethnography about persons and roles.

Team meeting

At the animal protection charity I worked with, one kind of formal meeting took place every two weeks, and constituted a regular feature of the organizational calendar. At the allotted time, usually 2 p.m. on a Wednesday, Sheila, the office manager, would go round the six rooms of the charity's office gathering staff up from their respective desks and ushering them into the boardroom. The 'team meeting', as it was called, lasted about an hour, and consisted of a round-the-table report from each member of staff on their most recent work activities. It began when everyone arrived, casual chat had died down, and the nominated Chair called a start. Individuals waited until invited to report and typically spoke with the aid of prepared notes on sheets of paper or in personal organizers.

Sheila: A few quick notices [*report continues*] . . . The Staff Handbook is being constantly renewed, so can you let me know when you are ill and out of the office, to allow me to work out sick pay. Also, if you leave [the charity] it has been decided we won't give out full, personal references, just general references. Although you can of course ask colleagues to write a personal reference about levels of performance etc. on your behalf.
Right, let's hear other updates. Craig?

Craig: Thanks. I've been working on the animal sentience programme of work [*report continues*] . . . That's it.

Sheila: Mairi.

Mairi: OK. I've been mainly processing cheques coming in from the money box appeal, entering all the people in the database. We are up to 20,000 active names [*report continues*] . . . Finally, can I ask if someone takes a phone call from a supporter can you enter the details in the database too.
[*Sheila next nods to Elaine, who sits beside Mairi*]

Elaine: Right now I am trying to organize a calendar we can all use [*report continues*] . . .

Sheila: Thanks, Elaine. David.

David: We are gearing up to the Movie Viral Awards, keeping a keen eye on that [*report continues*] . . . also I've been making sure the snaring video is seen by everyone.

Eilidh: Where are we with Facebook and Twitter numbers?

David: Last look, about 500 or so followers on Twitter and 800 or so on Facebook [*report continues*] . . .
[*Sheila nods to Sarah*]

Sarah: Yup. Well I've been busy getting the funding applications out for the early years education project. And been working with the customer marketing people and on the sponsored run. I've got a couple more signed up for that . . . [*report continues until the end and then she turns to the woman beside her*]

Maggie: Not surprisingly, it's been dominated by the snaring campaign. The parliamentary briefing went well I think; good turnout of MSPs [Members of Scottish Parliament] . . . I want to do another briefing featuring gamekeepers. Hope to set that up for February 8th [*report continues*] . . . As well as the snare ban, we need to lobby on other components of the Bill, especially annual review and training. I would say the MSPs are definitely listening and definitely engaged.

Sheila: Barry.

Barry: Happy New Year, everyone! Bit late I know. But I feel it will be a good year for us. I can confirm that the snares shown in the video are now all gone from the [shooting] estate. They must have seen the film too and recognized their own traps [*report continues*] . . .

Eilidh:	Thanks, Barry. So far, the memorial appeal has raised about £3,000, which is great. I will send out a thank you and a reminder to those who have not yet responded [*report continues*] … Elaine will be trying to set up a training day; the purpose is to allow us to have time together as a team. I will also be looking a little bit into the team structure, maybe setting up supervisions or one-to-one support sessions [*report continues*] …
Sheila:	Ok, Euan.
Euan:	Three things really. We've had a lot of inquiries about the culling policy at Edinburgh Zoo. There will be something in the *Daily Mail* on the weekend and I expect to get more press on this [*report continues*] … I've been working on a story with [another animal welfare charity] around farm assurance food labelling. There will be a few teaser stories put out but once the report is published the push will get bigger [*report continues*] … [*Sheila nods to the final staff member*]
Fraser:	Right, here it is [*he tables a budget report*]. As you know, it was a tough year last year but we still increased income. I want us to keep ramping it up. You will see we had £300,000 down for Trusts and Foundations, but we had no history of making those applications [*report continues*] … I've been working with Craig on the animal sentience programme and with Barry on the funding of investigations. I think we should also do something at the training day on being a fundraiser and on donor-led organizations [*report continues until the end and meeting concludes*].

The transcript extract above is from one particular team meeting, but is typical of its reporting form. Sometimes additional business might be tagged on to the end of the meeting or points of extended clarification interjected during individual reports, but generally the structure remained constant. Indeed, barring work appointments that took staff outside of the charity's office, the team meeting was the only scheduled event that everyone attended. For me, these meetings therefore represented the best chance of catching up with the dispersed and deskbound activities of individuals, an opportunity to find out what each one had been doing for the previous fortnight. This was the case too for members of staff. Although some worked side-by-side in the same room, even sometimes in inter-dependent roles (as part of the 'fundraising team', for instance), most had only an incomplete sense of the detailed day-to-day work of colleagues. What knowledge they did have was often drawn from attendance at other smaller formal meetings called to address a specific task or project of work, or from casual conversation over lunch or tea in the staff kitchen. The team meeting, then, was viewed as a highly effective procedure for pulling colleagues together, making their individual and combined labour visible, and thus communicating what was going on across the charity.

Its efficiency was also indexed in the 'Team Meeting – Agenda' document that Sheila usually pre-circulated. A sparse and succinct – on the face of it almost pointless – text, the Agenda simply enumerated the action of reporting itself. So in the example reproduced in Figure 1, 'Updates' is agenda point one; it seems to require no further specification.[2] Point two, 'Volunteer tasks', refers to the identification of work assignments for unpaid colleagues, organizational needs that are themselves seen to only emerge out of the very process of updating. The final two agenda points are procedural to the running of the team meeting; the duty of 'Chair' is shared, all staff as members of the office 'team' taking a turn over the course of the year, and 'Any other business' leaves space for emergency discussions that exceed the remit of the individual report. It is then as updatable subjects that colleagues first and foremost come to know one another in the team meeting. They are persons assumed to have something to disclose, the embodiment of past, present, and anticipated future activity.

Journal of the Royal Anthropological Institute (N.S.), 166-181
© Royal Anthropological Institute 2017

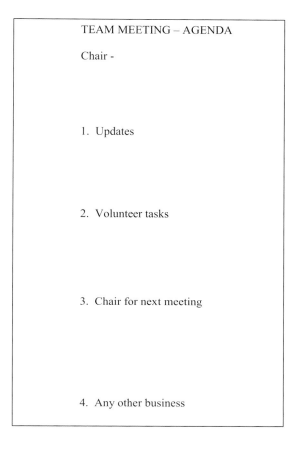

TEAM MEETING – AGENDA

Chair -

1. Updates

2. Volunteer tasks

3. Chair for next meeting

4. Any other business

Figure 1.

When I first arrived at the charity, in early 2010, the team meeting was a fairly new phenomenon. The need for regular updating was partly a result of the rapid expansion in staff numbers (the previous two years saw the number of salaried employees more than treble, from four to thirteen), which meant knowledge of collegial activity became a problem of a different scale and that there were now sufficient people that a label of association like 'team', and even the idea of there being teams within the team, might be appropriate. However, the rise of the team meeting also indexed new divisions of labour, and a new managerial emphasis on the professionalization of roles. As staff increased, so the relationship between person and role was individualized; the general competency of the original, much smaller workforce was replaced by a growing range of specialized competencies owned by or attached to named office-holders. So Sheila, as well as acting as Chair in the quoted extract above, also updates the activities and outlook of Office Manager; Craig reports on the activities of the Science and Research Manager; Mairi provides an update from Supporter Services; Elaine speaks as the Personal Assistant to the Chief Executive Officer; David responds to an interjected query and updates from the office of Movement Builder; Sarah reports on what the Assistant Fundraiser has done; Maggie accounts for the time and duties of Policy Director; Barry updates the work of the Investigations Officer; Eilidh informs and speaks from the perspective of the

Chief Executive Officer; Euan reports on the activities of the Communications Officer; and Fraser does the same from the outlook of Fundraising Director. Indeed, in many ways the team meeting existed to reflect that new reality; its round-the-table reporting scheme operating as a mechanism for formally hearing from the various offices of the charitable organization.

Just as the status of office-holder is crucial to the attributes of the updatable subject, so the team meeting is essentially, then, an encounter between or report from the perspective of those organizational roles. In these update sessions, members of staff are quite careful to connect what they have done to the remit of their professional role and to generally offer opinion on that basis. In fact, when individuals veer too far from their duties or the outlook of office, for example in offering judgement or suggestions for the activity of other office-holders, the meeting can become tense. There is a strong sense of role ownership, of pride in expertise; and a corresponding expectation that at least in the team meeting any interaction between persons will mirror the interaction between roles. This is exemplified in the ethos of complementarity. A good team meeting will involve reports that also build and respond to the accumulation of updates: the Fundraising Director, for instance, adding a fundraising component to the planned training day announced by the Chief Executive Officer, or the Communications Officer offering an idea for getting the parliamentary briefings of the Policy Director 'pushed' in the press. Likewise, part of the value of addressing 'Volunteer tasks' after the updates is attached to the notion that reports may reveal forms of 'support' needed for specific roles. Unpaid colleagues are usually slotted in in this fashion, assigned for a period to the direction of an office-holder who has recognized an activity (usually figured as unskilled) that requires labour.

It is possible, I think, to identify here the introduction of a 'frisson' (see Strathern 2009) between person and office. Indeed, the old anthropological notion, led by Fortes (1962), of an office as a generalized term for roles and status, which combine and endure in perpetuity, ritually enacted and occupied by a succession of individuals who imagine the office bestows them with power and perspective, has an interesting currency in this situation. The same applies to the argument that roles and status require a material embodiment for that power to be recognized and assigned (Fortes 1969; see also Strathern 1998). There may be no equivalent to the Ashanti stool, but it seems that the team meeting succeeds in displaying the transformed authority of staff members, offering them a space in which the incumbent's embodiment of that immaterial professional role is made visible. Certainly, there is a sense in which the contributions of staff become newly individualized through specialist offices; those who previously may have worked together, in a minimally hierarchical structure where tasks were often in practice shared, find in the expanded organization that it is now a formalized relationship to role that defines the person. But this includes, as Strathern highlights, the equivocating awareness that the concept of '"person" can in fact occupy either side of the apparent divide between self/individual and office' (2009: 133-4). In the team meeting, Maggie, for instance, can appear to herself and others as either an individual person or as a persona, someone who acts the part of Policy Director; similarly, in updating the activities of the Movement Builder, David can be taken to instantiate a source of authority beyond himself that bestows a 'personal' perspective and/or a source of authority beyond the office, which lies within the individual. It is this capacity to view the person twice, in overlapping versions, that one might claim as another product of the team meeting.

Journal of the Royal Anthropological Institute (N.S.), 166-181
© Royal Anthropological Institute 2017

Such equivocation can have interesting consequences for the notion of the 'ethical' as a modality of practice both within the person and within the organization. As previously highlighted, the history of the charity reveals a body in which private and public moral enthusiasm work in tandem. Individuals join the charity because its commitment 'to secure proper respect for animals and inspire a more compassionate society' is commensurate with their own principles. Unlike the traditional ethical labour of public administration, as described by du Gay (2006: 5), subordination to work, then, does not require an abnegation or self-denial of personal moral convictions. Indeed, it is that very conviction that is regularly seen to fuel the activity of the organization. This is because the enthusiasm of personal principle is taken not only to motivate charitable work but also to make it sustainable. (Like many other charity workers, employees often signal that they accept lower salaries as the price for doing vocational and virtuous labour.) Personal conviction, staff members claim, is also what keeps them attentive to office tasks.

Going round the table of the team meeting, one finds numerous examples of this continuity. Take Mairi, for instance, who updates from the perspective of Supporter Services; her official job title is 'Database Administrator'. Born and still living in the town of Kirkcaldy, Mairi took up her current post with the organization the year before I arrived. Previously, she had done part-time voluntary work in the charity; indeed, she has been a signed-up supporter of the animal protection organization since the early 1990s when she came across one of their campaign stalls in Edinburgh. Like many other members of staff, she connects her conversion to the principles of respect and compassion for animals with a prior childhood experience of affinity with particular creatures; in her case through a special connection with household cats and with stray dogs that she would sometimes bring back to the family home. The translation of this ethical feeling into a personal conviction would, as with many other members of staff, lead her over time to give up eating meat and wearing leather (Mairi is a vegetarian, but a lot of her colleagues are vegan), and eventually to seek out a form of work that supported and promoted what she identified as an ethical life. As Mairi put it, 'Obviously I work for [the charity] and I work to their values and their mission, but that's all part of what I believe personally'. While processing donations and entering supporter details on the office database is largely tedious work, she knows that it serves the interests of animal protection and hence her own core beliefs.

There is no immediate reason why a complexification and professionalization of roles threatens that ethical bearing. Staff may formalize the adoption of the perspective of office-holder in the team meeting, in the process newly enacting a separation between the persona and individuality of the person, but that subordination to role can still be seen to operate in the service of private moral enthusiasm. Indeed, staff members regularly connect pride in expertise and specialized competency with pride in contributing to their own and the organization's ethical goals. Being professional, disciplining the person to the impersonal and no longer explicitly ethical purpose of office-based competency, can appear as a better, more effective way of demonstrating responsibility to individual conscience.

While Mairi's work of data entry is relatively mechanical and unskilled, the role provides a means of contributing to a specific office, from whose perspective she can confidently speak in team meetings. In this regard, subordinating to Supporter Services empowers an outlook within the organization, to which she can attach, enlarging a sense of individual contribution. Those with more skilled tasks, whose job title may coincide with or encompass the status of office itself, also view the perspective of professional role as an enhancement of what personal commitment can achieve. David, for instance, who entered the charitable organization some months after me, saw the new post of Movement Builder (set up to create a digital supporter base for the animal protection charity) as an opportunity to put his specialist social media knowledge and marketing qualifications in the service of what he regarded as a good cause. Born and raised in the northern English town of Lancaster, but with both parents originally from Glasgow, David, like Mairi, reported childhood empathy for household pets as a spark to involvement in animal welfare causes. He became a junior supporter of several animal campaigning groups at the age of 11, remaining active throughout his university years, when he also took up a commitment to vegetarianism and then veganism. 'The ethical issue for me', he explained, 'is I just don't feel that animals should be there for us to abuse. You know, we don't have a right of dominion'. His compassion for animals informs his life-choices, including his decision to join the charity, but for him the capacity to speak with the authority of marketing and social media expertise, embodied in the office of Movement Builder, makes that compassion operational at an entirely new scale.

In this scenario, private moral conviction does not personalize roles, but it does make the impersonality of competency valuable to the individual person. However, as the charity grew and the number of roles expanded, the frisson between person and office also created an organizational dilemma. At its heart was a fear that not only might professionalization separate the persona of office from the individuality of person, but in addition it might allow the possibility of colleagues who met the remit of competency or office purpose but lacked a history of personal commitment to animal welfare issues: that is, someone who could fulfil the duties of role and thus effectively promote the mission statement of the charity but did not identify with that ethical purpose or hold those feelings in the individual person.

Although this anxiety was attached to the way new posts were generally advertised (mainly centred on the skill sets needed to meet the role) and to the unsettlement caused by the quite sudden arrival of a number of new colleagues, most of them strangers to existing staff, it really focused on the installation of the office of Fundraising Director. As with other specialized roles, colleagues recognized that this office could be vital to the future effectiveness of the charity. Yet, in the individual person of Fraser, a suspicion arose that the impersonality of office masked a personal indifference to many of the core values of animal protection. This was not helped by the fact that Fraser had a known professional background working in environmental charities; in many ways, conservation and animal welfare exist in tension, defined in part against each other (see Reed 2017). Suspicion also arose from his persistent failure to express sufficient outrage at cases of animal abuse highlighted in the media and from his lack of engagement in the customary enthusiastic ethical discussions that often took place during tea and lunch breaks. Fraser, it was noted, was also conspicuously silent on his personal history. (This was largely a blank to me too: although we had many conversations about the technique and strategies of fundraising, Fraser was the only member of the charity staff who refused to be interviewed.) He never, for instance, voiced a biographical narrative of the kind commonly exchanged by others (i.e. stories of awakenings through childhood encounters with pets or wild visitors to the family garden) nor offered affectionate tales of empathetic relationships with household or rescue animals today. Finally, it was widely known that he ate meat and that he wore leather shoes; in short, there was little evidence of the typical signs of an expected personal ethical bearing.

Returning to the team meeting, then, we can perhaps identify another dimension to the achievement of role perspective. As well as updating the activities and outlook of office, and in so doing opening a space for the person to occupy a position either side of the divide between role competency and principled self, the team meeting introduces the possibility of a complete disjunction between commitment to office and commitment to expected ethical feeling. This includes the possibility that, for some, serving the office and doing the job well provide their own satisfaction, divorced from either the consequences of promoting organizational values or the drive of personal conviction. For many staff, however, the likelihood that Fraser and persons like him to come may lack any private moral enthusiasm for the ethical goals they are professionally tasked to enact remained deeply troubling.[3] Sitting round the table of the team meeting, they started to wonder for the first time whether some colleagues were only fully present in their impersonal office-holding persona. The fear was not just that Fraser lacked the conscience or ethical feeling for animals that everyone previously assumed united the individuality of persons and hence established a common ethos; it was also that the personal dimension of Fraser may be entirely absent or withheld from their interactions. Could Fraser present them with an impersonal person, one without the frisson between individual and office, available to them only through the updates of the Fundraising Director? The prospect haunted many.

No AGM

If the professionalization and expansion of this organization led to the rise of one kind of formal meeting, then it also led to the demise of another. Crucially tied into its restructuring was a commitment to end the annual charge of membership dues for supporters of the charity, a decision that also meant there was no longer a need to hold an Annual General Meeting in public (the meeting notionally continued as an in-house and closed annual presentation by the CEO to the charity's Board of Trustees). The latter was a statutory requirement of organizations that formalized membership through subscription, a traditional act of charitable association that drew out an obligation to give a public account of that body's activities for each year. While the AGM followed an established procedure, it was also a notoriously uncontrolled event. Charitable bodies could never be quite sure who would turn up, what they might say, and in what directions their interventions might take the meeting. It was also an occasion that, like the expense of collecting membership dues itself, came at a financial cost for the organization; the animal protection charity was not alone among third-sector groups in concluding they were better off without it. Nevertheless, the end of the open-door AGM signalled the termination of any formal gathering between staff and the organization's supporters.

However, this curtailment of established meeting was not just a by-product of practical managerial administration; it was part of a wider radical reconceptualization of what the ethical organization was there to do. Instead of continuing to view itself as a body that looked after and represented the moral interests of a public constituency, narrowly defined as its membership, the charity now marked itself as the facilitator of a 'movement'. When I first started coming into the office, staff had only recently embarked on the transformation, which the expansion and specialization of roles was meant in large degree to enable. At its core was a desire to shift organizational attention from campaigning and lobbying on behalf of supporters to that of assisting the ethical development of individual members of the public towards animal welfare principles.[4] The movement was to be composed and led, not by the charity, but by these morally renewed and conscience-bearing subjects, chiefly defined and empowered by their status as consumers, identified as out there in the world. Part of the perceived role of the organization was to inspire 'ethical buying' or compassionate choice and to help individuals progress along their animal-friendly lifestyle, from whatever point in their own ethical journey they were at. This might mean facilitating their shift from vegetarianism to veganism, or from low- to high-welfare standard meat consumption. It might also mean converting supporters from charitable 'donors' (the restructuring of the organization was also tied to a new financial model of growth based on monthly direct debit donation rather than annual subscription and legacies) to participants in charitable 'actions', or, even better, assisting them in developing their own independent animal welfare activism. From this new perspective, the charity was there to serve the movement, a dispersed network of individual persons envisaged as acting alone, or sometimes in combination, to change themselves and hence the ethical complexion of the world around them.

So the professionalization of staff competencies embodied in the team meeting actually ran in tandem with a refocusing on or highlighting of the moral autonomy and enthusiasm of individual members of the public. While the charity might not have experienced a shift, equivalent to that described in public administration in the United Kingdom, towards the personalization of roles within the organization, it did seem to advocate for the personalization of a role outside it: that assigned to the supporter-consumer or movement mobilizer. Indeed, organizational attention fell on the moral competency of this newly visible conscience-bearing subject. In such a transformation, the charity not only facilitates the supporter's personal or lifestyle development, it and its workforce can become figured as supporters of the movement too. Seen from this perspective, the impersonalization of Fraser begins to break down a little, for the attributes (i.e. meat-eater, leather shoe wearer, environmentalist background, lack of outrage) that led some colleagues to view him with suspicion can also be seen as markers of his stage on his own personal ethical journey towards animal-friendly values. Indeed, I think Fraser joined the organization in part because he bought into the notion of a new, alternative 'mainstream' and less 'moralistic' animal protection charity, facilitator to a multi-stage movement of self-improvers that offered support from wherever the individual began. From his viewpoint, it is possible that the colleagues who sat around him at the team meeting failed to embrace the new ethos of the organization, that is, to withdraw their ethical judgement and to concentrate instead on the moral competency that each person is ready at this point in time to submit to enhancement.

Evaluation meeting

I want to conclude with an anecdote from a third kind of organizational meeting. Unlike the team meeting (and the retracted AGM), this formal gathering was a one-off affair, called to address a specific task of work, the labour of 'evaluation' (see Yarrow, this volume). However, it was not like other forms of task-orientated meetings that I attended, those typically focused on planning for a concrete activity such as composing a response to a Westminster or Scottish government consultation exercise or putting together a package of communication strategies to assist a fundraising appeal. Instead, this was a day-long event called to evaluate the charitable organization itself. Held just two years after I began my research, the meeting constituted a reaction to a very different kind of historical crisis for the charity: the imminent and quite unexpected threat of insolvency and disbandment.[5]

Journal of the Royal Anthropological Institute (N.S.), 166-181
© Royal Anthropological Institute 2017

Like many groups in the third sector in the United Kingdom, the animal protection charity I worked with experienced the effects of the Global Financial Crisis of 2007-8 in delayed form. The bite on many charitable incomes only really started to hit hard towards the end of 2010; a point illustrated by the fact that this organization felt confident enough to invest in expansion and an accompanying radical restructuring of organizational goals in the immediate years after the crisis began. By the second half of 2011, it was evident, however, that the new model of financial growth for the charity, upon which the increase in staff numbers was based, had failed to be realized (both direct debit monthly payments from members of the public and corporate donations simply didn't take off). As a result, the charity was forced to introduce harsh and quite sudden retrenchment strategies. First and foremost, this meant a severe reduction in staff numbers, so that by the end of 2011 over half of the thirteen salaried employees had left (including Sarah, David, and Fraser) and by the middle of 2012 the organization was back to a total of four employees. Each of those remaining had curtailed hours, down to working either a three- or four-day week. As a whole the charitable organization was in survival mode, reduced to budgeting for activities and looking no more than eight months ahead.

Returning to the status and professionalization of roles, the retrenchment also threw up a series of immediate dilemmas for the continuing relationship between person and office. Indeed, to me, it is hard not to read the response to retrenchment as a crisis of office; once again I am reminded of the lessons of Fortes. Most obviously, those who remained in post, albeit part-time, were faced by a challenge of motivation; not just because colleagues had lost their jobs, but also because the roles they continued to hold seemed to suddenly lack purchase with reality. As Maggie put it to me, 'I may still be the Policy Director, but of what?' The existential question of what was left for the office-holder to actually enact in an organization facing extinction was accompanied by another kind of role dilemma. As everyone pointed out, the charitable organization now had more roles or offices than office-holders.[6] Perhaps even more pressing was the recurring prospect that those office-holders who did remain might outlive their role or office in the charity!

Not surprisingly, these dilemmas had the effect of detaching persons from offices, or, more precisely, of making the individual person appear newly separated from the persona and perspective of the role-holder. If the latter appeared increasingly fragile, the former seemed increasingly durable and its visibility was heightened. Indeed, a new kind of equivalence seemed to arise between these individual persons, not so much as private moral enthusiasts or as conscience-bearing consumer subjects within a movement of self-improvers, but as vulnerable employees, each with bills to pay and families to feed. The emphasis also attached an equivalence of emotion: after the redundancies and retrenchment, these were individuals who shared experiences of sadness, resentment, anger, and frustration. The self-conscious way in which those left and still attending formal meetings identified as survivors highlighted a further kind of renewed separation, this time between the outside or external perspective on the charity (as an ethical organization continuing to register its effects in the public world of animal welfare) and the perspective from the inside, where role-holding and the activities of office appeared a precarious, ever more unsustainable outlook. It was in this atmosphere, then, that the evaluation meeting took place.

As befitting a gathering in a time of crisis, the charitable organization opted to bring in an outside expert to lead it – in this instance, someone from another Scottish charity specializing in third-sector evaluation. After 'ice-breaker' exercises between us (i.e. myself; Eilidh, the CEO; Maggie, the Policy Director; Euan, the Communications Officer; and Mairi, the Database Administrator from Supporter Services), the 'evaluator' introduced the task for the day. Our aim, we were told, was to take the charity's strategic plan, scripted two years earlier to meet the goals of the expanded organization, and to 'distil it' in order to create and agree a 'baseline of activities' for the charity going forward. The meeting, the evaluator explained, was also about re-motivating staff, team-building, and instilling new purpose in those who remained. It was made clear that in this work of evaluation everyone should contribute as an independent voice, regardless of roles or organizational hierarchy. Staff needed to come together and work as a team of individual persons before speaking once again from the perspective of office.

The rest of the day was devoted to this task. Prompted by the evaluator, we examined the strategic plan and proceeded to cut it up into little cards and then to experiment with organizing those cards in different orders on the posters provided. Relatively quickly, a principle of placement emerged. All programmes of work previously listed in the strategic plan, it was decided, were to be detached from previous allocations and reorganized into specific 'campaigns'. Indeed, the emphasis would be on the charity as a 'campaigning organization' once again, as opposed to being the facilitator of a movement. As we arranged the cards in this manner, discussion developed not just around how many campaigns a retrenched organization could realistically sustain going forward, but on what basis the relationship between roles and persons should now proceed. I think it was Euan who first pinpointed the issue as it evolved throughout the meeting. 'The problem with the way things used to be', he speculated, 'is that everyone just worked in silos, doing their own thing'. In this kind of observation, he and others meant to critique what sometimes felt like too close an attachment between the perspective of person and office. This was not so much because that individual person risked collapsing into the persona of office, but rather because the office risked being collapsed into the person. Indeed, as the evaluation meeting progressed, a consensus emerged that roles needed to be disconnected from the person of the office-holder and instead reassigned and integrated to specific campaigns. The key relationship, it was proposed, would now be between person and campaign, viewed as an assemblage of tasks with assigned roles to which individuals must respond.

One consequence of the evaluation meeting was that certain job titles got renamed. Euan, for instance, found himself no longer the Communications Officer, but rather the Press & Campaigns Officer; likewise, the Web & Publishing Officer became known as the Digital Campaigns Officer. But what happens to the office-holder, we might ask, when he or she is made to serve the campaign more than the office? Well, one outcome was that roles no longer appeared to be owned by the office; they became instead the property of each campaign. Another outcome was that certain forms of labour, those defined as outside the agreed list of campaigns, became informally reserved to the office-holder. Less roles and more what one member of the evaluation meeting termed 'private work tasks', these activities included labour left over from the strategic plan that office-holders wished or felt obligated to continue or complete on the side. From this perspective, the office remained attached to the person, even as the roles of office became reallocated to the campaigns. In fact, in a strange twist, a new kind of privacy emerged to define that work still conducted through the persona of the office-holder. After the evaluation meeting, team meetings remained as a schedule of updates, but the updating subject became newly split, offering professional outlooks both on the roles assigned him or her in particular campaigns and on the personal work of office. In this newly fluid scenario, it remained to be seen where the viewpoint of the individual person might resurface.

Epilogue: from the perspective of Office Manager

In the years following that evaluation meeting, the number of paid staff at the charitable organization has remained small. As the financial condition has eased a little, a few office-holders have gone back to working full-time. A new CEO has been appointed with no previous background in animal welfare, but with a strong professional record in charitable fundraising. (It is clear that the re-emphasis on advocacy and campaigning did not signal a return to the days before the professionalization of roles and the new managerial culture.) The organization has appointed a new Fundraising Officer, also with no previous personal commitment to animal welfare issues. The Board of Trustees or unpaid governing body of the charity has undergone similar transformations in its composition, with an emphasis on appointing those with identified professional skills (i.e. lawyer, accountant, experts in human resources and corporate charitable sponsorship). While some do have a history of private moral enthusiasm for the values that the organization promotes, others, including until recently the Chair of the Board, do not. Trustees and new members of staff, he explained to me, can always learn animal welfare principles. In this continuing emergency situation, the overriding ethical obligation of the Board is 'not to mess with people's lives' (by which he meant, the lives of employees). Giving considerable time and his labour for free, the Chair additionally invoked a broader ethical obligation to the sustainment of the charitable sector and to 'good causes' in general; indeed, these were 'personal' principles that the CEO and other new staff members also identified and claimed as the historic basis for their motivation at work.

The notion that private moral enthusiasm may be driven by a desire to be of general assistance to charitable bodies adds a further dimension, I would argue, to an ethics of professionalism. It is one way in which the individual person may reappear and the wider frisson between person and office gets rearticulated. Whether serving the perspective of office or the perspective of roles allotted to an individual campaign, all of the updating subjects of the team meeting may claim a convergence with private interest or ethical practice. The tension is now between a personal commitment to the cause of animal welfare and a personal commitment to that cause as one among many possible good causes worthy of support.

But in these twists and turns, there is one figure who remains aloof. Having worked for the animal protection charity for over thirty years, Sheila, its Office Manager, is the strongest point of continuity. Her role is about keeping the office of the charity ticking over, ensuring salaries get paid, expenses and bill payments processed, and meetings scheduled. (Her capacity to survive is perhaps testament to her functional importance.) Indeed, in many ways, Sheila has been a silent witness of all this organizational change, its ups and downs. Employed by the charity at the age of 18 on what was then known as the Youth Opportunities Programme (a UK government scheme for helping school-leavers into employment that ran during the early 1980s), she was tasked with what the organization termed 'basic office work'. Interestingly, although the charity throughout this period, and up until the appointment of Eilidh as CEO in 2007, had been run as a small body of dedicated animal welfare campaigners, Sheila was not expected to present an ethical bearing or history of personal commitment to the cause. Much like her later colleague Fraser, she has remained a consistent meat-eater; but unlike him, her lack of engagement in animal welfare debates and her failure to contribute when outrage, for instance, appeared the appropriate moral response has never been a source of comment or consternation. It may be fair or unfair to assign the difference to the workings or assumptions behind 'class', to the distinctions in expectation that accompany traditional divisions between manual or unskilled labour and mental or professional work; however, the fact remains that Sheila offers an original, solitary perspective on the ethical campaigning organization. Everyone assumes that for her work is 'just a job', and a meeting is just part of her duties, a set of observations that this time seems to be unproblematic. Sheila, then, is the Office Manager, but she is also Sheila, an individual person with a 'personal' outlook that doesn't have to matter. It may be that her anomalous status is crucial.

NOTES

I would like to thank all the members of the animal protection charity I worked with, including past and current staff (both the organization and the names of participants have been anonymized to protect privacy). Thanks to my co-editors on this volume, Hannah Brown and Tom Yarrow, and to the anonymous reviewers. I am also grateful for the informal comments and feedback provided by Alberto Corsín Jiménez, Naomi Haynes, Mette High, Shari Sabeti, Helen Schwartzman, Jonathan Spencer, and Marilyn Strathern. A version of this essay was given at the anthropology department seminar at Edinburgh, and I thank that audience too.

[1] Hopgood's description of organizational crisis at Amnesty International during the last decades of the twentieth century is interestingly different (2006: 12). There, professionalization and managerialism as espoused by 'modernizers' are also experienced as a threat by those who would claim to be the inheritors of the Amnesty ethos, traditionally grounded in a moral authority of factual or impartial witnessing and in a commitment to the 'mandate' (which limits the definition of Prisoners of Conscience to those who have not used violence). However, that crisis is complicated by a further tension with 'reformers' who wish to divest the organization of its non-political status, which to them feels like a constraint on personal moral enthusiasm, and instead commit it to wider ethical campaigning for social change. In this scenario, modernizers and reformers are sometimes in alliance, and the 'keepers of the flame' have to defend themselves against a different charge of impersonality, linked to a perceived rigidity in adherence to the mandate. Both the modernizers and the reformers attack the old moral authority of Amnesty as inflexible, slow to adapt to changing circumstances, and 'bureaucratic'; for many of them, this is said to be illustrated by the fact that there are just 'too many meetings' (2006: 179).

[2] Kirsch provides us with an interestingly different example of the assumed actions behind a sparsely constructed agenda form. Working with Pentecostal-Charismatic church bureaucracies in southern Zambia, he says that the blank spaces in the agenda form produced for church meetings was in part intended to index an 'essential unpredictability' of the meeting itself. Church meetings, like services, it was expected, must reveal themselves as divinely inspired events. A meeting that was too organized, that appeared to be too predictably conforming to a documentary structure, risked appearing uninspired. So the blank spaces on the agenda form were meant to leave open the possibility of the 'inpouring of the Holy Spirit' (Kirsch 2011: 216).

[3] Staff at the animal protection charity are well used to the idea that at times the ethical feeling of the person, and in particular his or her personal moral enthusiasm, may need to be reined in or tamed in order to ensure that high levels of crucial professional competency are maintained. This is a particular problem for the charity's field investigator, whose role includes evidence-gathering for archival purposes and sometimes for the purpose of legal prosecution (see Reed 2016). However, this is presented as a struggle or as an exercise in self-disciplining ethical emotion; there is no sense in which it is suspected that the investigator lacks personal conviction.

[4] The comparison with shifts in the organizational ethos of Amnesty International is once again illuminating. As Hopgood (2006: 202) describes it, 'reformers', in tandem with 'modernizers', pushed in the late 1980s and early 1990s for a reorientation from the traditional focus on factually researching and 'adopting victims' (i.e. individual Prisoners of Conscience) to a focus on an issues agenda (under banners such as 'women's rights' or 'economic rights') of 'empowering individuals' in the world. This integrated with modernizers' desire to produce first and foremost fundraisable programmes of work and to be seen to meet the 'needs of the [Amnesty] movement as consumers' (2006: 134). Interestingly, it also tied into the goal of reformers to replace the ethos of impartiality with that of 'advocacy' (2006: 178). In the new ethos for Amnesty,

'the logic of the campaign drives the research programme [in support of the individual cases of Prisoners of Conscience] not the other way around' (2006: 82). In the example of the Scottish Animal protection charity I worked with, the shift was very different. The introduction of a new managerial culture in the last years of the first decade of the twenty-first century, including an emphasis on fundraising and the professionalization of roles, actually coincided with a perceived move away from advocacy and campaigning, which up until that moment had been the core work of the organization. In its new role as 'mainstream' movement facilitator, the organizational concern was that it didn't alienate the conscience-bearing subjects out there in the world, at each one's diverse stage of animal welfare awareness, by forms of aggressive campaigning on single issues.

[5] If Hopgood (2006) provides an account of the moral tensions and shifts within a large and expanding organization that defines itself as ethical, then I found myself, quite unexpectedly, bearing witness to a small and ambitious ethical organization's apparently terminal decline. 'When people work in an ethical environment', Hopgood (2006: 15) observes, 'feelings run high ... Where the very ethos and functioning of the organization are constantly at issue, even as the work is done and the organization grows, they run higher still'. One might add that where that organization appears to be dramatically failing, the stakes shift entirely, opening a space for quite sudden organizational redefinition, and the further heightening but also radical redirection of staff feelings.

[6] For Fortes (1962: 68-70), the unoccupied office is not just futile but also dangerous, disrupting the ideal of succession and perpetuity that grounds it.

REFERENCES

CORSÍN JIMÉNEZ, A. 2015. The capacity for re-description. In *Detachment: essays on the limits of relational thinking* (eds) M. Candea, J. Cook, C. Trundle & T. Yarrow, 179-96. Manchester: University Press.
DU GAY, P. 2000. *In praise of bureaucracy*. London: Sage.
——— 2006. Re-instating an ethic of office? Office, ethos and persona in public management. Working Paper no. 13, ESRC Centre for Research on Socio-Cultural Change.
——— 2008. Max Weber and the moral economy of office. *Journal of Cultural Economy* 1, 129-44.
FORTES, M. 1962. Ritual and office in tribal society. In *Essays on the ritual of social relations* (ed.) M. Gluckman, 53-88. Manchester: University Press.
——— 1969. *Kinship and the social order: the legacy of Lewis Henry Morgan*. Chicago: University Press.
HOPGOOD, S. 2006. *Keepers of the flame: understanding Amnesty International*. Ithaca, N.Y.: Cornell University Press.
KIRSCH, T.G. 2011. *Spirits and letters: reading, writing and charisma in African Christianity*. Oxford: Berghahn Books.
LAIDLAW, J. 2010. Agency and responsibility: perhaps you can have too much of a good thing. In *Ordinary ethics: anthropology, language and action* (ed.) M. Lambek, 143-64. New York: Fordham University Press.
——— 2013. *The subject of virtue: an anthropology of ethics and freedom*. Cambridge: University Press.
LAMBEK, M. 2010. Introduction. In *Ordinary ethics: anthropology, language and action*, 1-36. New York: Fordham University Press.
REED, A. 2016. Crow kill. In *Animals, biopolitics, law: lively legalities* (ed.) I. Braverman, 99-116. London: Routledge.
——— 2017. Snared: ethics and nature in animal protection. *Ethnos* 82, 68-85.
STRATHERN, M. 1998. Social relations and the idea of externality. In *Cognition and material culture: the archaeology of symbolic storage* (eds) C. Renfrew & C. Scarre, 135-47. Cambridge: McDonald Institute for Archaeological Research.
——— 2009. Afterword: the disappearing of an office. *Cambridge Anthropology* 28, 127-38.

Un « office de l'éthique » : réunions, rôles et enthousiasme moral parmi les protecteurs des animaux

Résumé

Le présent essai explore la relation entre réunions et éthique des organisations dans une association de protection des animaux écossaise. Une récente « professionnalisation » de celle-ci a vu se créer une « éthique de l'office » et l'incarnation des rôles qui va avec. Les esprits s'échauffent à présent pour savoir quelle doit être la relation entre le message central de l'association, en tant qu'un « office de l'éthique » envers les animaux, et les principes « personnels » ou l'engagement éthique des différents membres. Cette agitation culmine quand les personnes, qui sont aussi les titulaires des « offices » en question, se rencontrent.

11

Outputs: the promises and perils of ethnographic engagement after the loss of faith in transnational dialogue

ANNELISE RILES *Cornell University*

This essay investigates one important artefact of meeting knowledge production: outputs. It does so through the example of the activities of the members of Meridian 180, a community of Pacific Rim intellectuals collaborating on transnational legal and policy issues. For the members, the particular kind of knowledge production facilitated by Meridian 180 constitutes a response to the failures of international bureaucracy to generate and sustain a fabric of global relationality. The group's various attempts to address the imperative for 'output' illuminate both aspects of the meeting as an organizational form, and the challenges and opportunities meetings present for ethnography. The wider underlying theme of the essay concerns the ethical purposes and promises of ethnographic styles of engagement after the loss of faith in transnational dialogue.

One way modern bureaucrats define a meeting is that it is a form of interaction that has outputs. As in the case of ritual speech, as described by Webb Keane, a meeting can only be 'recognized' as such when it is 'objectified' retrospectively in a particular form (Keane 1997) – the form of the output. Often the meeting is explicitly framed as a project to create the output. To choose an example from my prior ethnography, the UN Fourth World Conference on Women had one immediate aim: to produce a Global Platform for Women (Riles 2001). The fiction of the output in that case enabled a proliferation of meetings – a hierarchically and temporally organized series.

I focus on outputs in this essay as a way of returning with a different orientation to a familiar ethnographic place. Some time ago a number of anthropologists settled upon documents as an ethnographic artefact because of the point of commonality between practices experienced in the ethnographic trenches and the academic towers (Riles 2006). Documents embodied a critical turn on some forms of traditional ethnography that aimed to document others' practices even as they ignored others' documentary activities. Taking documents as artefacts rendered modern bureaucratic and academic knowledge strange through the analogy to others' documentary practices (Brenneis 2006; Strathern 2006). The focus on documents, then, was a methodological intervention more than a documentary one. Its success lay in its achievement of an

Journal of the Royal Anthropological Institute (N.S.), 182-197
© Royal Anthropological Institute 2017

external perspective on modern knowledge practices for which there seemed to be no 'outside'. In other words, this framing of documents was a kind of distancing move.

Although they would have shared my interest in the details of documentary practices, for example, the UN workers I studied would not have reflected on documents as artefacts. Rather than talking of documents, they would have talked of outputs. The idea, then, was to re-create the aesthetic grounds for anthropological knowledge ('distance') after the loss of faith in an 'outside' to knowledge such that distance is possible. The objective was to re-create the possibility for our own expertise (the aesthetic of distance, of context, etc.) not by discovering actual outsides but by turning our knowledge inside out, as I contended that bureaucrats managed to do through their own documentary practices (Riles 2001).

The UN meetings and documents I studied twenty years ago were robust, ambitious, global phenomena, the products of a relatively confident universalist bureaucratic moment. The faith in dialogue, in networks, in documentation projects, in globalization as a political strategy, and in social progress through law and institutions was contagious. It was so contagious, in fact, that it had emboldened a kind of renaissance of second-wave feminism that left feminists who felt discomfort with the language of universal womanhood, progress towards gender equality, and global consensus about the nature of good and evil, in intellectual disarray. This new muscular feminism – one that anticipated its own triumphant future – had ironically provided me with the critical distance I needed for ethnography: if documents and meetings were not strange to me, this empowered ethics and epistemology certainly was.

Yet today that confidence has vanished. The United Nations no longer convenes global conferences; it authorizes military action through its Security Council, that is, when that body is not blocked by disagreements among its members. Gone is the faith in progress through deliberation in the global public square. Gone is the faith in technocratic expertise that made it possible to imagine that all kinds of knowledge and political points of view might be assembled into a singular document. Gone also is the notion that there is no outside to the global form. There is absolutely no need to debunk the global meeting: we (all of us – ethnographers and our interlocutors) know how the project fails.

This raises the question of what anticipatory futures we might envision for anthropological knowledge. In this context, it may be useful to return to the now dated and discredited knowledge practices of the global meeting, not as a subject of description or critique, but as a set of practices to act through – to think with outputs rather than study documents. I am attempting to do this through a project, known as Meridian 180, borne out of this crisis of expertise – ours and theirs.

Meridian 180 began as a set of confusing and frightening conversations with fieldwork interlocutors and academic colleagues in the midst of the physical, political, and existential chaos surrounding the earthquake, tsunami, and nuclear crisis in Japan in 2011. At the time I had just completed fieldwork among financial regulators and lawyers in the financial market, and for these people the fact that Fukushima could happen was profoundly destabilizing of their faith in the market, and in the potentiality of scientific expertise.

It slowly became apparent that ethnographic skills – of hearing linkages between one set of conversations in one disciplinary or linguistic locale and another, of finding ways to transpose conversations linguistically, aesthetically, and epistemologically – could in a small way be a source of repair and insight, at least for us as interlocutors.

Journal of the Royal Anthropological Institute (N.S.), 182-197
© Royal Anthropological Institute 2017

These conversations, exploring the points at which our knowledges and commitments failed us, came to encompass a range of explicit subjects and now continue on-line and in periodic gatherings between approximately eight hundred academics, financial and legal professionals, government officials, artists, and others from thirty-nine countries. Among the distinguishing features of these discussions are that they are private (they cannot be quoted or disseminated), and that they occur in four languages at once (Chinese, Japanese, Korean, and English), such that the problems of translation and of the limitations of language are a continual challenge and presence in our minds (Riles 2013).

In some matters of form, Meridian 180 might seem to be yet another attempt to revive international dialogue through institutions. The multilingual conversation, and of course the recourse to international meetings, evoke that bygone universalist fantasy of agreement mediated through bureaucratic expertise. Yet there are also important differences. The modernist international institutional project sought to reach consensus enshrined in rules to be followed 'at the national level'. The agent of dialogue in that project was the nation-state. Meridian 180's agents, by contrast, are experts with varying degrees of confidence remaining in their own expertise, who, despite their own professional relationships to nation-states, and other established institutions, wish to act outside that context – a reflection of a collective loss of faith in nation-states and institutions as agents of change. Thus they bring to the meeting their professional backgrounds and expertise but explicitly shed their professional responsibility in order to speak only for themselves (something members repeatedly describe as refreshing and hopeful).

Gone, likewise, is the fantasy of agreement at the heart of the modernist international institutional project. Meridian 180's on-line forums and live conferences make no effort to generate consensus, and focus instead on carefully teasing out differences. The project is one of changing people's capacities to hear, empathize, and imagine, of rekindling individual and collective hope, rather than of creating rules or proposals to be implemented. Yet it retains the 'constraint of form' (Strathern 1988) that defines a bygone technocratic universalism because, as I have suggested elsewhere, that thin form can accommodate remarkable diversity in an under-the-radar, mundane way, while standing for nothing in and of itself. It may be a technology in which we have lost faith, but it is one that we already know how to use.

This project is a mutually authored rather than singular exercise and hence stretches the ethnographic commitment to collaboratively produced knowledge to its breaking-point. The intellectual, political, and ethical problems are overwhelming, and real people and institutions push back constantly in ways that create very real risks for all involved. Moreover, our particular relationship to theory is distinctively ethnographic: there are a number of theoretical problems embedded in the artefact, yet these are backgrounded as we act As If (Leach 1982; Strathern 1988; Vaihinger 2000 [1924]; Wagner 1986) we are just doing what we do. Yet I claim this project as ethnographic most of all for the following reason: Meridian 180 is both relationally produced knowledge and knowledge productive of relationality, and this knowledge is the artefact of a genuine struggle.

Yet if it is ethnographic, it is animated more by political commitments borrowed from feminism than by social-scientific imperatives. It is the project articulated by Robyn Wiegman (2000) as 'feminism in the meantime' – living alongside others in a moment of loss of anticipatory futures. Although we have now initiated a series of book projects, Meridian 180 is not activity that aims in the first instance to result in a text. Rather, our hope is that, like Donna Haraway's cat's cradle (Haraway 1994), participants will take the work we do together and make of it what they will, in their own contexts and in response to their own problems. For all these reasons, knowledge is not cumulative, but unfolding, and always returning to prior points of origination.

As Keane suggests, recognition, as a source of authority, depends upon being 'true to form': activity must be recognizable as one of 'certain types' (1997: 14). Because we are deploying ethnographic techniques and aspirations in ways that fail to register immediately as outputs of the 'scholarly type', our activity has fallen into being described and recognized as an 'organization' with 'meetings'. Rather than rebel against this (in the mould of the rebellious 'experiment'), we have taken it as an opportunity to work within a given form. In my case, this involves returning to a form I have long studied in conventional ethnographic terms: the ongoing global meeting powered by the tools of the information age.

In March 2015, I, together with a Korean colleague, convened a public meeting in Seoul. Professor Cho Haejong, a cultural anthropologist and prominent public intellectual, described the meeting in her weekly column in one of Seoul's daily newspapers:

> The topic of the seminar held on March 31 was 'Democracy in Aging Societies', with the Korean economist Sung-In Jun leading the discussion. The participating researchers read Professor Jeon's write-up of the topic and uploaded texts of up to 1650 words on the Web, at which point these comments would be translated immediately into Korean, Chinese, Japanese, and English to be sent to over 700 members and archived on the Web platform. On March 31 the 25 members around the world who had commented gathered to present their thoughts for five minutes each, by sub-topic groupings such as values and ethics, redistribution policies, and the politics of fairness. Afterward the participants discussed the issues freely. Professor Jun in his topic write-up pointed out that at no prior period in history has the proportion of senior citizens increased by such high rates and so rapidly, and that attention must be given to the rise of the senior citizen generation in the realm of politics to a highly influential interest group. He pointed out that if senior citizens, who are distanced from the realm of production, should become the political majority, the vote would not guarantee the principles of democracy. Furthermore, democracy itself may have to be questioned in light of the older generations' leaving enormous budget deficits and a polluted environment to later generations, and taking risks such as pushing forward with nuclear experiments whose safety is uncertain (Cho 2015).

Participants hailed from different communities of language and expertise, and much of the ethnographic work of staging the event involved creating the conditions under which others could be heard. The meeting was ethnographic also because of the leap of faith required in ceding 'the problem' to others: the question of how an ageing society might impact on democracy emerged from the membership in Seoul, in the aftermath of a political election in which elderly people, exercising their superior electoral power, had elected a conservative government over the wishes of youth. For our interlocutors in Seoul, here was an intellectual problem that was a true political problem, as well as an ethical conundrum for a Confucian society. It was something they were desperate to talk about. Yet it made little sense to North Atlantic members. For other Asian members, in contrast, the excitement of the meeting was about mutual recognition. For participants from countries that are used to relating to one another in an adversarial mode, in which cultural, political, or historical differences are emphasized, the discovery of a common point of genuine confusion was, for them, surprising and hopeful. Ultimately, it was an experience of respite, a kind of pause to be savoured. As Professor Cho (2015) wrote, 'I missed many of my colleagues at the forum; it is an unfortunate reality that many Korean professors are so worn down in universities reduced to vocational training schools that they do not have the time to stop by a forum for such timely and relevant intellectual innovation'. What I want to focus on here is not the experience of the meeting *per se* but the problem that emerged around the imperative of meeting outputs. My hope is that this focus will illuminate both the character of the meeting and some challenges they pose to the ethnographer.

The imperative of outputs

Our members experienced the post-Fukushima moment as a profound crisis of their own expertise; indeed, what they shared was their loss of a confident vision about how they might usefully intervene in the world. Our challenge, as I saw it, was to exist as a kind of collectivity in which claims about effects, outcomes, and potentialities could disappear so that the unanticipated could reappear at some later stage in more powerful form (Strathern 1988). Now one can easily imagine the standard academic ways in which we were told one cannot do this. The usual reaction went as follows: this is not research since it does not result in a text or even in knowledge claims. If it is not research, it must be some form of activism. But activism without a purpose is nonsense.

This line of dismissal is to be expected. But what tripped up the project far more profoundly was a corresponding bureaucratic need: since this is not scholarship, it must be an organization, with meetings. But meetings without outputs do not produce 'no meeting' – they produce an illegitimate (i.e. pointless) meeting.

I mentioned earlier that documents emerged for me and other ethnographers as a solution, as a way of reimagining ethnographic futures. They opened up possibilities for us as ethnographers and social theorists. Yet this time the same artefacts, refigured as outputs, emerged as a problem, a stumbling block on the way to an open-ended feminist meantime of risk-taking alongside others confronting the limits of their knowledge. In documents, the ethnographer can see a future; outputs in contrast seem to shut that future down. When seen as documents, the artefact can be analysed with our tools: materiality, aesthetics, agency, historicity, and so on. When seen as outputs, the artefact seems anathema to those same tools.

My first impulse was to shield our conversations from such bureaucratic demands. I was inspired in this by the parallel efforts of economic historian David Moss to reorientate his own and his colleagues' professional trajectory methodologically, towards a vision of collective rather than individualized intellectual contribution, and to re-create the scholarly infrastructure for progressive social policy that in his view had been purposely dismantled in support of a neoliberal political agenda over the last thirty-odd years.[1] Moss's group had in fact generated some important policy ideas leading to regulatory changes after the financial crisis of 2008. Yet he often went out of his way to downplay these in conversations with foundations and other institutions to which he was accountable. For him one aspect of the danger of the output was its temporality. He often referenced the anthropologist Franz Boas's work on race, which, he argued, had had little impact at the time of its writing but served as the intellectual infrastructure for a political movement for racial equality a generation later. This somewhat romantic idea of the long-term scholarly legacy as opposed to the short-term bureaucratic impact was by no means novel or outside the discourse of organizational action. On the contrary, it was exactly what funding agencies, with their demands for demonstrable outputs, sought to displace.

Journal of the Royal Anthropological Institute (N.S.), 182-197
© Royal Anthropological Institute 2017

I thought I had a solution to this challenge in the anthropological repertoire's celebration of As If practices (Leach 1982; Strathern 1988; Vaihinger 2000 [1924]; Wagner 1986). As I had learned in prior work, the As If is a powerful legal and bureaucratic tool for bringing open-ended futures into being (Riles 2011). It remained only to operationalize that insight: contrary to the organizational ideal in which meetings have a clear purpose, vindicated in the outputs, we would focus on the means, not the ends, allowing the ends to remain unformed, undefined (Riles 2013).

Yet this approach quickly ran into problems. Upon reading a draft of another academic article in which I had articulated the project as anti-instrumentalist, a consultant hired through my university to help us explore sources of outside funding admonished me to remove that language from my article, as it would be read as problematic by foundation staff. He framed the problem of the project as a 'tension between process and products', and although he expressed sympathy for the value of the kinds of intellectual and personal relations flourishing within the project, he emphasized that in the eyes of potential donors 'process alone' was illegitimate. Sympathetic but sceptical university administrators likewise demanded 'metrics' to demonstrate the 'impact' of the project, while less sympathetic administrators politely dismissed the entire project as a disorganized fantasy, a waste of money and time.

Those most committed to Meridian 180 also expressed concerns. For some, the problem was that they needed something to show for the project to justify their own institutions' demands for accountability for their professional time. They recognized that outputs were not ends in themselves but means of legitimizing the project, but they insisted, nevertheless, that these were necessary. A small number of members raised some concern that a lack of outputs reflected a genuine weakness of the initiative. Still others argued that certain forms of public communication that I had rejected out of hand, such as social media, in fact were more complex and generative than I appreciated, and could be ways of extending or enriching our actual project.

I consider the failure of my own attempts to sidestep the output to be a first ethnographic finding of this project. Without outputs, a meeting is just 'talk for its own sake'. It is not fundable, and, worse yet, it is 'untransparent', 'elitist', insiders excluding outsiders. The challenge of producing outputs, then, is the indigenous counterpart to the sociological question concerning how meetings constitute and act on external contexts (see the Introduction to this volume). Sociologists define organizations (as against publics, for example) in terms of the existence of an 'outside or environment made up of either individuals or other organizations which are cast in the role of the client, consumer, customer, patron, citizen, competitor, stakeholder, user' (Fish, Murillo, Nguyen, Panofsky & Kelty 2011: 160). In this view, there is an imagined world outside the organization that serves as its context (Riles 2001). What this standard sociological definition of the organization is doing is formalizing an indigenous obsession with the difference between the organization's 'inside' and 'outside'. If sociologists define the boundary of the organization as constitutive, those on both the inside and the outside notice the very same conventional definition of boundary as something potentially problematic, a site of illegitimacy.

What our experiment in engaging in activity without outputs demonstrated is that when framed as a meeting, a set of relations become secrets generative of anxious para-sociological descriptions of what is inside and outside.[2] For example, at the conclusion of the Seoul meeting, when I asked the group to whom we thought our outputs should be addressed, participants enthusiastically suggested 'policy-makers' and 'youth' – the

Journal of the Royal Anthropological Institute (N.S.), 182-197
© Royal Anthropological Institute 2017

two categories most underrepresented, in participants' view, at the meeting itself. What our own struggles against and with outputs demonstrate, then, is a set of anxieties about communication within meetings that define what we might call the ideology of the meeting. Meetings are, foremost, sites of talk, and talk should be spontaneous, disruptible, open-ended. Yet at the same time, talk itself is never enough. It is always incomplete by virtue of the fact that it happens only on the inside. Outputs – what crosses the boundary between inside and outside – are necessary to rectify this problematic condition.

The temporality of the output

A focus on outputs reveals that the simple opposition of inside and outside, and with it, the ethically charged boundary between inside and outside, is a fundamental folk category of the meeting. To this, the output adds an equally simple folk temporality of the meeting as comprised of two key moments: the first moment, what happens during the meeting's present; and the second moment, the output that is after the fact.

Hence, outputs pose an inherent temporal challenge: by definition, they come after the event. As such, they are *anticipated* prior to and during the event – it is the possibility of the output that gives the meeting its 'orientation toward the future' (Keane 1997: 12) as participants can imagine the future value of their present work in the form of outputs to come. Yet by virtue of this temporality, outputs are also 'after the fact' (Miyazaki 2006), somewhat superfluous, a headache for those in charge and a responsibility that other participants are often quite happy to shirk.

It was this temporality that ultimately defeated my efforts to treat the instrumentalism of meetings in an As If modality. In the organizational planning for the Seoul meeting, one of the Korean organizers – a professor newly recruited to the project – urged us to use the final session of the meeting to draft a 'communiqué' to be released to the press and to policy-makers. In his view, the conference would have greater 'meaning' if something 'concrete' 'came out of it'. Eager to follow the lead of our Korean collaborators, I agreed but suggested that we be explicit about the 'As If' quality of this exercise: most likely there would be no outside press or policy-makers eager to receive this document (Riles 2001), and yet the exercise of thinking as if there were such an outside to our activities might nevertheless be generative.

During the conference, I noted the ideas that emerged, and in the final session, I presented the participants with my notes (Fig. 1) and asked them to comment on which ideas seemed most salient or appropriate for a communiqué. Participants tried to muster the energy to engage in good faith in this exercise. We highlighted suggestions in red, added new topics in green, and posited linkages between ideas. Yet the excitement that had pervaded our earlier discussions was missing. We had already experienced together the moment of the meeting; there was no need to revisit it retrospectively.

What this exercise demonstrated was that the As If was the wrong tool for the meeting form. It is not that it is too epistemologically adventurous – participants had no problem appreciating the idea of a virtual exercise in output production since organizations do this all the time (Riles 2001). The problem, conversely, was that As If thinking is not *temporally* adventurous enough: it cannot convert a retrospective moment into a prospective one.

In order to see how this is the case, compare my failed effort to produce a conference output with my co-organizer's equally virtual but far more successful initiative. Prior to the conference, she simply gathered together all the on-line forum

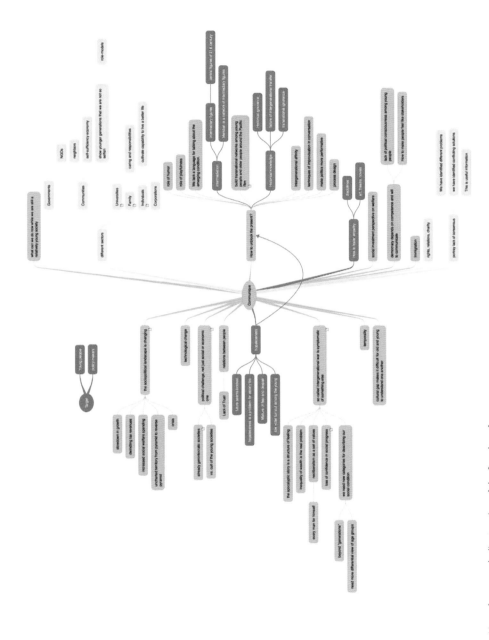

Figure 1. Notes from concluding session of the Seoul conference.

comments by conference participants that had *preceded* the meeting, themselves written in anticipation of the meeting itself, and reprinted those in beautifully bound form. The bound volume was distributed to participants as they arrived at the conference site for the meeting. When participants saw their own words collected together, they experienced their conversation as *already* highly substantial and successful. This output also circulated after the conference among representatives of our patron institutions as evidence of the scholarly seriousness of the deliberations. What my co-organizer had done was to prospectively create the retrospective moment of the meeting output. It was a clever solution to a fundamental temporal problem.

Self-objectification as an anticipatory problem

Just as our team returned from the Seoul meeting, we were asked by the foundations relations staff at our university if we would be willing to undergo an exercise in 'telling our story'. The impetus for the request was that the Rockefeller Foundation had asked the university to identify groups that would use a 'tool' it had funded called 'Hatch for Good'.[3] The tool, a website with simple but engaging graphics envisioned as something to be used in team meetings *about* outputs, aimed to help organizations to *produce* outputs, reframed as 'stories' – as the website put it, to 'tell stories with a purpose'. An organizational project of its own, Hatch for Good needed outputs to demonstrate its legitimacy, and its sponsor, the Rockefeller Foundation, was marshalling its own relations to bring those outputs into being. The Meridian 180 project manager and I, together with a doctoral student in anthropology who had not attended the Seoul meeting, a freelance writer, and some members of the university's communications team, dutifully sat down in a conference room with the Hatch tool looming on the overhead screen and began to work our way through its scripted questions.

The Hatch tool walked the user through a series of simple fill-in-the-blank questions about one's organization that aimed to objectify the organization to oneself, such as who are its members and what is the problem it seeks to address. Self-objectification, here, as Keane (1997) has suggested, is an exercise in anticipating, or imagining, the response of others. The very need for it is an artefact of a conception of the organization's outside. The entire feel of the exercise was structured, manageable, doable. But the encouraging tone ('Nice Job! You've established your narrative framework and set the stage for creating successful stories. Next up: Capacity') belied the tremendous challenge of reflecting on one's activity from an objectified point of view. If the ideology of the meeting suggests a seamless relationship of cause and effect between meetings and outputs, the very perceived need for this tool on the part of important organizational actors such as the Rockefeller Foundation suggested how the production of outputs is in fact an overwhelming exercise.

Hatch admonished us to take an instrumental view of our outputs: 'What do you hope storytelling will help your organization achieve?' The exercise asked us to identify the persons we served, the problems they faced, the goal we wanted them to attain, and the solution we had identified. The example it offered up was that of an NGO that sought to provide clean water to rural villages. In that example, Hatch told us, the people to be served were the villagers, the problem was the lack of water, the goal was clean water for all, and the solution was the NGO's project to build a pipeline to the village. It all seemed simple and straightforward. But in our organization, the people to be served, the problem, the solution, and the intended outcome were all internal, all 'seen at once' (Miyazaki 2004). The freelance writer expressed admiration for the village water project

The Storytelling Organization

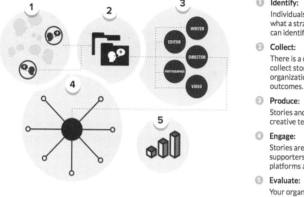

1   2   3

WRITER
EDITOR
DIRECTOR
PHOTOGRAPHER
VIDEO

4   5

① **Identify:**
Individuals at an organization know
what a strategic story looks like and
can identify compelling stories.

② **Collect:**
There is a clear way to submit and
collect stories about your
organization, its beneficiaries or its
outcomes.

③ **Produce:**
Stories and content are produced by a
creative team, using various mediums.

④ **Engage:**
Stories are shared with your
supporters across a variety of
platforms and social networks.

⑤ **Evaluate:**
Your organization regularly evaluates
its storytelling practices to determine
how it can be more effective in the
future.

Figure 2. Graphic from Hatch for Good (available at *https://www.hatchforgood.org/explore/154/ building-a-sustainable-storytelling-organization*).

and bemoaned the fact that our organization could not do something similar. Projected in this way on the conference room overhead, in comparison to the NGO providing clean water to villages, our initiative seemed illegitimate, unimportant. The tool then asked us to envision the organization's 'supporters:' 'Why should your supporters take action now?' This was of course a fantasy exercise – there was no suggestion that we actually consult 'supporters' in producing the outputs. The supporters were treated rather as future consumers of the outputs of the exercise.

As we worked our way through the script, the questions shifted from self-objectification with *outsiders* in mind to reconfiguring the *internal* organization to address its outputs: 'Stories that achieve real and meaningful change don't just materialize – they're strategically conceived, creatively executed and attached to measurable outcomes'.[4] The message was that outputs should be conceived not as afterthoughts but as evidence and effects of robust internal institutional capacities: 'a sustainable storytelling organization'. The script asked leading questions about the responsibilities of staff, or chains of communication, that made specific institutional weaknesses evident to us (the absence of a 'story bank' or a communications manager responsible for producing stories, for example) (Fig. 2).

It is easy to disparage this exercise from an academic point of view in which meaningful scholarly thought is imagined to generate its own *sui generis* effects, without much work after the fact on the part of authors, publishers, or other agents. Yet in light of the previous discussion of output temporality, the Hatch tool had achieved something significant: what it had done was to turn the retrospective problem of producing outputs for a prior meeting into the script for a meeting of its own, with a prospective orientation towards future consumers of the outputs. Moreover, the Hatch tool pinpointed and responded to an actual and present organizational problem: some kind of output needed to be produced, and hence some kinds of institutional relations needed to be activated. Moreover, it responded by turning the problematically retrospective problem of creating an output for a past meeting into a prospective agenda for organizational activity predicated on fostering in participants a sociological vision of the inner workings of their organization. This tool highlighted to participants the internal relational work necessary to produce effects that anthropologists have long emphasized in their work about other kinds of stories of origins or prominent events. As a tool for producing outputs, however, it failed in this case: we could not agree on what outputs to create and in the end abandoned the exercise and moved on.

Extraction

One of our most active members, a high-ranking US government official whom I will refer to as John, had been badgering me for outputs since Meridian 180's inception. What we needed, he repeatedly said, was a set of good 'one-pagers' that could be circulated to policy-makers and to the media. To him, outputs were a matter of a particular kind of expertise. The 'art of the one-pager', as he called it, was learned within the policy community through careful apprenticeship. In stressing these points, he positioned himself as a bureaucrat-outsider – as someone who had expertise that the inside of this 'scholarly' organization lacked.

At the close of the conference, I asked John to help us produce an output. Within merely a couple of days of his return to Washington, he sent me a one-page document (Fig. 3). To my horror, the content of the document, cut and pasted from the on-line forum prior to the conference, ignored the conference discussions entirely. Moreover, the document contained no single statement about the *value* or importance of the event. Why was it significant? Why did it matter? What most offended my academic sensibilities was that there was no trace of sustained thought on the author's part. John responded to concerns about his document in a group email to the leadership with a point of bureaucratic constraint: 'It was unclear that it was my role to put words in anyone's mouth. Should authors now wish to insert their own words, I would have no objection. Thank you very much'.

To an academic, John's text reads like a random collection of quotations that do not add up to any whole; it presents precisely the image of the messy pointless event that we as organizers had hoped to guard against with proper outputs. Yet although on first glance the document appears void of any creative labour, on closer examination it is meticulously formatted and organized with specific points of entry for the reader. 'When, where & how' correspond to a straightforward description of the event itself in a handful of words – the kind our team was unable to produce despite long hours in a conference room with the Hatch tool. Likewise 'Who should engage' has a simple answer: 'human capital officers, welfare policy-makers & researchers'. Organized as 'problem statements', 'issues of concern', 'points & propositions', and 'counterpoints', the document demonstrates, rather than asserts, a message summarized in four of the only words of his own that John inserted into the document: 'state of the art'. As he said to me privately, the conference represented in his view the global 'state of the art' of academic discussions on its topic. As such, there was genuine disagreement among the participants – there was even a debate on certain points. 'We have identified different problems; we have identified conflicting solutions', he said. 'This is *useful information*'.

John's vision of the consumers of this document, in other words, was quite unlike the Hatch tool's imagined consumer of 'stories', someone to be moved to action by a completed, polished artefact. He strongly resisted a retrospective narrative of success.

Journal of the Royal Anthropological Institute (N.S.), 182-197
© Royal Anthropological Institute 2017

> *Draft of 4/12/15*
>
> ### MERIDIAN-180.ORG POLICY OVERVIEW
>
> ### Democracy in an Age of Shifting Demographics
>
> *Keywords*: gerontology; social insurance; youth; hope
> *Who should engage*: human capital officers, welfare policy-makers & researchers
> *When, where & how*: Feb.-Mar. 2015, Meridian-180.org conducted a multi-lingual forum among experts from business, government, and academia, on-line and in person in Seoul, capturing a range of opinion that reflects the state of the art.
>
> #### Problem statements
>
> * How to foster empathy between generations emerges as a major social policy problem where there are limited opportunities for contact between generations outside the traditional family structure: what kinds of intermediary institutions or people can be pinpointed? **(Yuji GENDA, Univ. of Tokyo)**
> * Democracy used to be an efficient institution ... because the institution allocated ultimate right to control social resources upon the people, who mostly overlapped with the productive class of the society. (Sung-In JUN, Hongik Univ.)
> * The relevant question for us is how and to what extent age interacts with other factors such as class, race/ethnicity, and educational status in breeding individual-level political inequality ... (Harris Hyun-soo KIM, Ewha Womans Univ.)
> * [T]he micro dynamics of wealth transference among the meritocratic middle class as defining of the relations of generations in times of aging populations is important to focus upon in all major wealth producing societies today. (George MARCUS, Univ. of Calif. Irvine)
>
> #### Issues of concern
>
> * [T]he rapid evolution of information technology is further alienating the elderly. (Kark-Bum LEE, Future Thinknet)
> * [the question of hope and hopelessness, both for youth and for the elderly, as reflected in low voter turnout among young people] (Hirokazu MIYAZAKI, Cornell Univ.)
>
> #### Points & propositions
>
> * No human society should have the right to cancel the aged people's participation in politics. (Xingzhong YU, Cornell Univ.)
> * [W]hen generations of various historical backgrounds and experiences coexist as contemporaries, they enrich and diversify social and cultural capital. (Sung-Nam CHO, Ewha Womans Univ.)
> * Redistribution policy should ease intergenerational conflicts and guarantee a certain quality of life across all generations. (Masayuki TAKAHASHI, Univ. of Nigata Prefecture)
>
> #### Counterpoints
>
> * [Y]ounger generations do not have the [social or political] status they need to take a lead in designing their society. (Keigo KOMAMURA, Keio Univ.)
>
> Cornell Univ. (USA) ♦ *Transforming the transPacific dialog* ♦ Ewha Womans Univ. (Korea)

Figure 3. 'One-pager'.

Rather, he assumed that users of his one-pager would be savvy enough to expect debate at the meeting and would want to know where the disagreements lay. Indeed, he anticipated that they would want to do the work of weaving the narrative, or determining the bottom line for themselves.

Moreover, John anticipated that the document would be used in a particular way – as 'useful information'. The quotes from particular speakers directed attention not to the event as a whole, but to individual scholars' points of view, presumably to be followed up through direct interviews or consultations with those individuals. This document seemed to anticipate the entire event's decomposition (Strathern 1988: 179-80) into just so many individual academic points of view. And yet on closer analysis, traces of the organization, as the entity that had assembled and offered up all these points of view, were everywhere in the margins – in the names of the sponsoring institutions, the footer with Meridian 180's tag-line 'transforming the transPacific dialog', and the website address of the project. Finally, John's selection of quotations framed the project as a prestigious and international scholarly collectivity – presumably as something quite other, in both its scholarliness and its international orientation, than the domestic policy-makers such as himself whom he took as his target audience.

A few weeks later, a new member of the group, a journalist, suggested she would like to write a story about the condition of youth in East Asia. I decided to test John's one-pager, to see what reactions it would engender, by sending it to her. She responded immediately that this was 'wonderful' and 'exactly what is needed'. Of course, others may have less enthusiastic reactions. But it occurs to me that had John produced a tight laudatory narrative of our meeting, this journalist most likely would have been suspicious, eager to get the real information. This document presented itself merely as 'valuable information' – raw, ready to be used and analysed. John's one-pager memorialized the conference by anticipating its own erasure as it 'impacted' on other conversations and projects in other ways.

In a different ethnographic context, Marilyn Strathern (1988) has described the act of objectifying relations as 'extraction' – a coercive act authored by an exchange partner whereby a part (such as a daughter) in the act of coerced separation is transformed into a metaphor of the whole (such as an affine). To put her point into the terms of this material, a meeting cannot produce outputs for itself – someone or something 'outside' must do that extractive work. In this particular case, what made John and this journalist configurable as 'outsiders' was that they could be imagined as having a different kind of expertise than the conference organizers or participants – the expertise of policy and journalism. This was the lesson of John's intervention, experienced by me and my co-organizer as a semi-jarring appropriation. John's output, moreover, anticipated its own further extraction and appropriation by successive chains of users.

Yet who is the agent of this extraction? John's outsider status to Meridian 180, as a bureaucrat, is certainly one plausible understanding of his relationship to the project – and indeed his credentials and expertise from the world of policy are highly valued by many participants in the project for that reason. On the other hand, this portrayal fails to account for John's many linkages to the academy (he completed all but the dissertation in a prestigious doctoral programme in anthropology; he teaches at a law school on the sidelines of his full-time job; he is the son of two prominent academics). It also fails to account for the way that, notwithstanding John's characterization, Meridian 180 is unrecognizable to many academics as an 'academic' project. The presentation of John as an outsider also omits the fact that he is one of the most active members of Meridian 180, part of the governing body that makes day-to-day decisions for the project, someone who has attended virtually all of our events around the world. Much the same could be said of the journalist who received John's document. From one point of view, she is a professional journalist at a respected international press outlet reporting on our event – the archetype of the organizational 'outside'. Yet from another point of view, she received John's one-pager because she was already a member of the project – and as such was positioned to take it up because she had both an interest and confidence in what its participants had to say.

Journal of the Royal Anthropological Institute (N.S.), 182-197
© Royal Anthropological Institute 2017

Rather than imagine an organization internally and collectively producing outputs for consumption by anonymous outsiders, then, we might imagine a series of singular insiders configured at particular moments as outsiders, so that they may receive the event framed as 'output' and make of it something further of their own. Indeed, one might say that in anticipating that the readers of the one-pager would do the work of synthesis, the real purpose of this document was to bring these imagined 'outsiders' to the inside – to enrol them in the work of producing outputs, which, as the Hatch tool astutely suggests, is the quintessential internal work of the organization. John's contribution was not to objectify the meeting but to create chains of agents imaginable as alternatively inside or outside, each confirming their relations with one another through acts of successive extraction.

Conclusion

At first glance, meetings appear to be another element in the same category as documents, a continuation of an earlier ethnographic response to the collapse of distance between the ethnographer and the ethnographic object. Yet meetings are trickier than documents, ethnographically speaking, because we (both the anthropologists and the ethnographic subjects who spend our lives attending meetings) already have a para-ethnographic take on them. As Douglas Holmes and George Marcus (2006) have observed, we must have such a para-ethnographic sensibility simply to survive and dispense our duties as institutional actors. Moreover, we all have our critiques of meetings – this too is part of the indigenous point of view.

Hence, formalizing these para-ethnographic accounts into an 'actual' ethnography of meetings cannot serve the purpose that ethnographies of documents served for anthropologists, as to do so would be parasitic on a divide between the ethnographer and the site of ethnography that has long ago collapsed. This suggests that ethnographers of meetings would wish to be wary of adopting the folk vocabulary of inside and outside, or of temporally sequenced action and effects, as analytical categories or aesthetic devices of our own, as organizational sociologists have done.

Indeed, the ethnographic experiment described above was possible only because these simple tropes, like the larger problematic of outputs, are key analytical and professional frames for anthropology as well. Outputs are not just an obsession of bureaucrats. Academics, too, are constantly called upon to produce outputs for their scholarly activity, and we have a certain knee-jerk antipathy towards them. We associate them with the privileging of 'form over substance', as in the case in which our own scholarship is evaluated within the structures of meetings in the only way a meeting can: that is, as if it were an output of some work of our own. We tend to respond in a modality of critique (Strathern 2000). We see this most clearly in the parallels between the way the folk ideology of meetings and the academic critique of meetings treat outputs. In the folk ideology, the meeting should naturally result in outputs. In the academic common sense, meetings result in nothing because they are meaningless, while meaningful academic work for its part *naturally* gains attention, changes minds, and so on. In both cases there is little attention to the relational work entailed in turning events into artefacts. In this sense the humble Hatch tool was ironically more anthropological in the conventional sense of its attention to the social grounding of knowledge.

Likewise, the simple two-step of text and context, inside and outside, grafted onto a straightforward temporality of two moments – the moment of doing and the moment of retrospective reflection – is a temporal framework and organizational aesthetic that

Journal of the Royal Anthropological Institute (N.S.), 182-197
© Royal Anthropological Institute 2017

still pervades anthropological research. Indeed, the reason Meridian 180 does not qualify as scholarship in the conventional anthropological sensibility is that it confounds the distinction between the moment of the field, in which one set of relations is activated, and the moment of the academy, when another set of relations is activated, and between the internal text of scholarship and the context of the world it describes and acts upon.

The experiment here has been one of abandoning these aesthetics as scholarly devices by submitting to them elsewhere, in another register. The difference between apprehending documents ethnographically, as I once did, and responding to the imperative of outputs is this: at the end of the day, I need to work out what kind of outputs Meridian 180 will produce, and to ensure that they do in fact get produced and put into circulation. What to do about outputs is a real and practical conundrum for me.

For me now, these challenges become preconditions for reactivating anthropological knowledge in other forms. I have described one particular experiment in this venture: from the effort to think and act without outputs, to As If instrumentalism, to prospective preparation of retrospective outputs. The value of this exercise was not generated through my analysis but through what was done to me, and to my knowledge. What I have gained is a renewed appreciation of the relational ('extractive') quality of knowledge production. I would claim the language of extraction, over the more enticing prospective orientation of Haraway's cat's cradle, as a vocabulary for talking about feminist futures. That is, cat's cradles are still things to be made, collectively. They are forms of shared expertise. What is important about John's expertise, in contrast, is precisely that I do not share it. Were I to learn his expertise, through ethnographic apprenticeship, the output would become a document once again for me. It would lose its power as a solution.

This is admittedly an orthogonal response to the failures of our international institutions to live up to an earlier generation's hope for dialogue across difference, which I chronicled in earlier ethnographic work. It also requires that anthropologists place enough faith in our long-standing humanist commitment to relationality to do without a now outmoded concept of authorial agency in our definition of scholarly work. I, for one, plan to cede the problem of outputs to others.

NOTES

For comments and suggestions that significantly improved this essay, I am grateful to Hirokazu Miyazaki and Adam Reed, as well as to audiences at the 'Anticipatory Knowledge in the Practice of Law, Finance, and Techno-Science' conference, Swiss Graduate Program in Anthropology, Geneva, Switzerland, 9 October 2015, and the Schneider Lecture Panel at the American Society for Cultural Anthropology Annual Meeting, Ithaca, NY, 14 May 2016. I thank Meg Doherty Bea for her research assistance.

[1] More information about Moss's initiative, the Tobin Project, is available at *http://www.tobinproject.org*.

[2] The anthropology of secrecy has demonstrated, however, that the 'secret' is not a self-evident condition of not being generally known (Crook 2007).

[3] *https://www.hatchforgood.org*.

[4] *https://www.hatchforgood.org/theme/strategy*.

REFERENCES

BRENNEIS, D. 2006. Reforming promise. In *Documents: artifacts of modern knowledge* (ed.) A. Riles, 41-70. Ann Arbor: University of Michigan Press.

CHO, H. 2015. Meridian 180 and innovation by global universities. (In Korean.) The Hankyoreh, 7 April (available on-line: *http://www.hani.co.kr/arti/opinion/column/685832.html*, accessed 26 January 2017.)

CROOK, T. 2007. *Exchanging skin: anthropological knowledge, secrecy and Bolivip, Papua New Guinea*. Oxford: University Press.

FISH, A., L.F.R. MURILLO, L. NGUYEN, A. PANOFSKY & C.M. KELTY 2011. Birds of the Internet: towards a field guide to the organization and governance of participation. *Journal of Cultural Economy* **4**, 157-87.

HARAWAY, D.J. 1994. A game of cat's cradle: science studies, feminist theory, cultural studies. *Configurations* **2**, 59-71.

HOLMES, D.R. & G.E. MARCUS 2006. Fast-capitalism: para-ethnography and the rise of the symbolic analyst. In *Frontiers of capital: ethnographic perspectives on the new economy* (eds) M. Fisher & G. Downey, 34-57. Durham, N.C.: Duke University Press.

KEANE, W. 1997. *Signs of recognition: powers and hazards of representation in an Indonesian society.* Berkeley: University of California Press.

LEACH, E.R. 1982. *Social anthropology.* New York: Oxford University Press.

MIYAZAKI, H. 2004. *The method of hope: anthropology, philosophy, and Fijian knowledge.* Stanford: University Press.

——— 2006. Documenting the present. In *Documents: artifacts of modern knowledge* (ed.) A. Riles, 206-26. Ann Arbor: University of Michigan Press.

RILES, A. 2001. *The network inside out.* Ann Arbor: University of Michigan Press.

——— 2006. Introduction: in response. In *Documents: artifacts of modern knowledge* (ed.) A. Riles, 1-40. Ann Arbor: University of Michigan Press.

——— 2011. *Collateral knowledge: legal reasoning in the global financial markets.* Chicago: University Press.

——— 2013. Market collaboration: finance, culture, and ethnography after neoliberalism. *American Anthropologist* **115**, 555-69.

STRATHERN, M. 1988. *The gender of the gift: problems with women and problems with society in Melanesia.* Berkeley: University of California Press.

——— (ed.) 2000. *Audit cultures: anthropological studies in accountability, ethics, and the academy.* London: Routledge.

——— 2006. Bullet-proofing: a tale from the United Kingdom. In *Documents: artifacts of modern knowledge* (ed.) A. Riles, 181-205. Ann Arbor: University of Michigan Press.

VAIHINGER, H. 2000 [1924]. *The philosophy of As If: a system of the theoretical, practical and religious fictions of mankind* (trans. C.K. Ogden). New York: Routledge.

WAGNER, R. 1986. *Symbols that stand for themselves.* Chicago: University Press.

WIEGMAN, R. 2000. Feminism's apocalyptic futures. *New Literary History* **31**, 805-25.

Résultats : promesses et périls de l'engagement ethnographique après la perte de la foi dans le dialogue transnational

Résumé

Cet essai étudie un artefact important de la production de connaissances par les réunions : les résultats. Pour cela, il s'intéresse à l'exemple les activités des Meridian 180, une communauté d'intellectuels des pays bordant l'océan Pacifique, qui travaillent ensemble sur les questions de législation et de politiques transnationales. Pour les membres de Meridian 180, le type particulier de production de connaissances rendu possible par le groupe constitue une réponse à l'incapacité de la bureaucratie internationale de produire et de maintenir un tissu de relations mondiales. Les différentes tentatives du groupe de satisfaire l'exigence de « résultats » éclaire à la fois les aspects de la réunion comme forme d'organisation et les défis et opportunités que les réunions présentent à l'ethnographie. Plus largement, le thème sous-jacent de cet essai concerne les buts et promesses éthiques des styles d'engagement ethnographiques, à présent que la foi dans le dialogue transnational s'est éteinte.

Afterword

MARILYN STRATHERN *University of Cambridge*

As central to the workings of bureaucracies, meetings emerge from this arresting set of essays in diverse guises but quintessentially as miniaturizations of bureaucratic process itself. Indeed, they seem a highly imitable or exportable part of bureaucracy – quite as much as certificated paperwork or the office of chairperson – carrying with them resonances of self-acknowledged 'organization'; it is (an) organization that knows itself through a certain kind of controlled deliberative collective action. Despite the range of circumstances embraced here, the essays do not lose sight of this epitomizing potential. And the contributors have themselves created something of an epitomizing effect in the way that 'meetings', like documents, emerge as an ethnographic object.

Yet as soon as the object is captured, it wonderfully enacts the multiplicity of its ethnographic locations. For between them the instances described in these pages seem to upturn attempts at description. No sooner has one settled with a sense of the formality implied in the concept of a meeting than in the very first chapter Abram refers to the way in which administrative procedures may be 'insulted' (as just ritual or tedious bureaucracy) – the importance of the business in hand being located outside them. On its heels comes the next chapter (Brown and Green), describing two types of meeting, markedly contrasted in the minds of the actors, and articulated in the following account (Lamp) as a functional difference, here between the formal and informal. This divide is deepened by Alexander (chapter 4), who finds that a similar division at the back of people's minds at home (in Britain) fails to translate elsewhere: only some things are imitable, after all. And then chapter 5 (Yarrow) suggests that, beyond a contrast between site meetings and office meetings, the organization in question already has a common purpose that the differential expertise of those at the meeting threaten to unpick – the organization knows itself by other means. Meetings regarded as informal may, furthermore, lack chairpersons, minute-taking, and, even it would seem, the performance of controlled deliberative collective action.

Journal of the Royal Anthropological Institute (N.S.), 198-203
© Royal Anthropological Institute 2017

Ethnographic complexity cannot be shrugged off. What to do with the duplication of arenas on which these chapters remark? With Brown and Green's comment that each type of meeting (the more formal, stakeholder meeting/the less formal, team meeting) itself has a double role – both demonstrating delivery and delivering process – and Alexander's that, in British meetings, the formal and informal each contain elements of the other, we see something else. The forms are playing off against one another: informal meetings are as much 'about' formality as the formal meeting is a set-aside from other kinds of interactions. It was that very play, that relationship, which in chapter 4 proved intractable to imitation. Lamp's contrast between official and unofficial documents at the World Trade Organization or the ever-aspirational hope of the heritage agency described by Yarrow (the hope that different perspectives might add up to a whole) can be taken as manifestations of a similar relationship. Something like that doubling is also ('formally') written into democratic process, as Abram implies, when the separation of administrators and politicians (and their respective kinds of meetings) is rewritten within the administrative meeting as a self-consciousness about procedure that at once declares the legitimacy of the meeting and its confinement, its internal rituals, with respect to a world beyond.

Curtailment

There is, then, an ethnographic object here: the way bureaucratic milieux produce dialogues about the effectiveness of formalization. To dismiss meetings as ritualistic or pointless is another way of evaluating expectations about their efficiency. To expedite things efficiently is what controlled deliberative collective action is purportedly about. The question these essays ask – and Yarrow makes the question deliberately neutral – is just how that formality is practised.

A formally composed meeting is regarded as an instrument for getting things done with maximum efficiency. Potential distractions that arise while it is in session (however and whenever they occur) are edited out: all the appurtenances of agenda-setting, time-keeping, recording, and so forth, imply well-defined matters well in hand. Indeed, the curtailing of issues – as in the way items are intended to occupy designated time-slots – must be regarded as one of the achievements of meetings of this kind. A scholar might see some resonances with what he or she would probably otherwise regard as a very different type of activity, namely classifying and defining issues to produce objects of knowledge, or that a politician might recognize in the need to simplify matters for public consumption. These are familiar ordering practices, routine in a world that takes itself to be complicated in all its processes of life, abundant in artefacts and techniques, rich in informational flow and overflow. Cutting off bits at a time makes things governable. The proliferation of protocols observed by Brown and Green, as Kenyan health managers document their professionalism within a specific 'development architecture', is precisely in the service of ever more curtailment ('control').

Under those social conditions where the acting out of an imagined relation between formality and informality, between control and what escapes from it, makes the bureaucratic meeting a reference-point for meetings of all kinds, what, we might ask, is bureaucracy itself miniaturizing? Perhaps we should be looking for the cosmic dimensions of this miniature. What larger curtailments are made present? What holistic vision do practices of curtailment bring? That bureaucracies may elide official and unofficial meetings with the proper and improper exercise of power, as described in chapter 3 (Lamp), is suggestive. These contrasts flow into the old Euro-American channelling of dualisms between faces in public and in private, between norms impersonal and interpersonal, when it is a question not (as it often is) of power and its lack, but rather of differential sources of social empowerment. Social power has many manifestations; the dialogue about formality and informality imagines a pairing of organizational possibilities where each is specifically open to curtailment from the other.

Scaling up

An epitomizing moment comes in chapter 6 (Corsín Jiménez and Estalella), with the sense in which meetings miniaturize 'society' as such. Here is a scaled-up, cosmic object! In embracing divisions, such as between formal and informal power, society is also more than them. Its own limitation in turn is seen clearest from – is instantiated in – the view from afar. One view is prefigured in Alexander's discussion of Anglophone assumptions about common sense and fact creation: it is in a thoroughly modernist/Euro-American manner that, as devices for (efficient) (ordering) curtailment, meetings mimic larger apprehensions of a scaled-up object. People are often made aware of society as a force or conglomerate beyond themselves when what they see in those with whom they consort is something controlled, deliberative, and collective – observing etiquette, exchanging views, and being as doing-things-together. But this is also a particular kind of 'society', describable in its parts (taken apart for descriptive purposes), actionable indeed a bit at a time, and forever curtailing what lies beyond it.

Yet no sooner had I had settled into a familiar denouement (as chapter 6 also generously notes) than came chapter 7: Evans makes it clear that the suggestive analogy of meetings and society already has a long history. By the same token, the idea of the meeting-ization of society is even more specific than I had analogized. Understood, then, in terms of the historical formation of the nation-state, and in anticipation of chapter 8 (Nielsen), it seems that the society at issue is as the state and its agencies imagine it. In part that imagination persistently dwells on resistance to the state itself, resistance, that is, in terms of organizational ingenuity. The Spanish experimentation in assemblies as they were devolved from the Occupy movement is radical and exemplary. But then there is the battle of the East London allotment gardeners to get around the authorities, and the domesticated confrontation of client and judge in the persons of solicitor and barrister. Liberal political-legal processes have to acknowledge spaces for alternative positionings, now internalized, now externalized. And power is attributed to consensus and to dissent alike. Corsín Jiménez and Estallela refer to the assemblies' blurring of the formal and informal, the meetings in open air that at once challenged and reproduced standard procedures. This was less, one might hazard, for delight in paradox than in order to exhaust – draw the life out of – contrasting techniques for action. (And is it that the more that is taken out of the individual, the more has been given to social process?) Elation and weariness: Evans in turn observes the blurring of the personal and impersonal in minutes suffused with emotion, while the contrast of two allotment schemes was precisely a contrast between the power of personable relationships, on the one hand, and the power of impersonal formality, on the other.

The invocation of early modern antecedents lends an interesting perspective to Nielsen's discussion from Mozambique, where people's local meetings enact a history of organizational practices that took a quite divergent route. The nation-state had to sacrifice a specifically socialist experiment in modernity, thereby keeping 'what might have been' in its pristine revolutionary form. This form suspends scaling. The

Journal of the Royal Anthropological Institute (N.S.), *198-203*
© Royal Anthropological Institute 2017

unchanging aesthetic of what might have been gives it a larger-than-life presence; or, rather, Nielsen argues, it appears unchanged to the extent that it keeps pace with whatever is happening. That this might apply to meetings more generally is underscored by those occasions through which the law must act upon itself. Keenan and Pottage (chapter 9) dwell on what is, so to speak, equally scale-insensitive – not because it never materialized but because it will inevitably materialize. Whatever is happening in a refugee's case, the rubric of documentary inconsistency can keep pace with it. Inconsistency has the incontrovertibility (unscalability) of an aesthetic; the lawyers have no choice but to deal with its anticipation.

Enactment

The cumulative effect of the volume means that, by their simple placement at the end, the last two chapters have something of an epitomizing effect in relation to what has gone before. I dwell on them for the way in which they draw together two strands that have run throughout, namely what meetings do with persons and with time.

Bureaucratic meetings require people's presence in a very specific way: face-to-face. (Given the excoriation that often greets anthropologists' concerns with so-called 'face-to-face' societies, the format is intriguing; or, rather, it gives the lie to what face-to-face could possibly mean. Mention has already been made both of the co-presence of bodies bearing witness and of meetings technologies that act as third parties of a sort.) Record is likely to be kept of who is present, and who is part of the meeting through acknowledged absence. In a world that thinks of itself in terms of anonymous masses or faceless functionaries, on the one hand, and networks of personalized consumers or constant communicators, on the other, what is a gathering of a handful of people? One visual effect is that of a 'group'; here the meeting enacts what people sometimes take as a 'building block' of society – the joining of a few as proxy for the joining of many – and thus the modernist apprehension of society as a kind of super-group, a gathering of persons as individuals. In this familiar framework, turning individuals into social persons ('members' of society curtailed by identity, role, and arena of action) leaves intact the ever-present potential of personalization on an individual basis. Reed (chapter 10) takes us through diverse permutations of orientation, people acting from now impersonal-formal and now personal-informal subject positions. While a changing emphasis on these positions can be charted against the fluctuations of their organization, each person also holds them, in changing proportion, within. The contrast that elsewhere in the volume plays out through different organizational styles is here, in this ethically orientated body, ethicized into the way individuals relate to their selves.

However much they are also 'interactions between roles', the charity meetings described by Reed seemingly imitate an intimacy of sorts, where being able to see the face or expression of a person is taken to be information-rich. Chair's tricks aside, more than one author has touched on the identification of 'personal' responses, and on the role of visible emotion as a sign of the person as an individual. The charity's re-ascription of roles from office to campaign is something like an 'expersonation' of this aspect of the face-to-face encounter. The meeting itself becomes an impersonation of the larger and more diverse population to be caught up in the self-fashioning ethical movement it now supports.

At several moments the chapters have also given glimpses into the management of time, from the iterative presumption that any meeting is but one of a series, to the vital legal encounter squeezed in before a court hearing, to the set-aside timelessness of a repeated event. That meetings are also expected to have a before and after, typically visible in the process of reporting on themselves, was the subject of the experimentation with forms conducted by Riles (chapter 11). How might one create a global institutional vehicle for discussion that avoided performance and accountability? The experiment ran up against time.

Wherever they are held, formal meetings enact the governance of argumentative or political opinion evident in chambers of deliberation such as parliament (in the phrase of one of the authors, we are all parliamentarians). Discussion must be generated, but talk must be controlled. This is typically done through the persons present being regarded as mouthpieces of specific points of view, as representatives or as otherwise recognized members. Time is made an issue within the meeting, with the hazard that talk will bring in distracting or inadmissible verbiage. But time is another kind of issue when even the most spontaneous and free-flowing talk must anticipate what happens after the talking has stopped. There seems no way round the expectation that 'discussion' has to be seen to have happened. Moreover, in the contexts Riles describes, it seems that a discussion can lack retrospective conviction if it does not also remain in some sense prospective, even perhaps (an ideal for some) as a prospective agenda for more organizational activity. Whether as a conditional form or as a rehearsal, figures we have already met, the directionality of this kind of meeting, like the bureaucratic meeting, is invariably to a point beyond or outside. To experiment with, and to that extent question, the parallel and indicative imperative to convert time (time spent in discussion) into an output turns out to be a challenge for anthropological knowledge-making – and to what we mean by ethnographic skill.

Endnote

Let's arrive at where it all began. The elicitation of ethnographic skill was one of Brown, Reed, and Yarrow's aspirations for this volume. They aimed to show the possibilities inherent in 'field'-based description – entailing observation and interpretation – when attention is directed to the practices and occurrences of holding meetings rather than (say) to the textual-visual self-descriptions such meetings generate. In their words, the matter of concern is not just what meetings set out to achieve but what is entailed in doing so. Their aspirations have surely been more than fulfilled. One index lies in the fact that in several instances contributors have produced the reverse, 'ethnographic', effect of apprehending other issues through the lens of the meeting. This can only work if the phenomenon in question, here the meeting, is first taken as itself a social (material, semiotic) entity. It is the specific dimension of certain kinds of meetings, for example, that yields the analogy with a certain concept of society.

Early in their comprehensive and thoughtful introduction, the editors themselves bring in this reference to society. Indeed, many of the points I have seemingly 'made' are ones they had already highlighted. Thus they comment on the circumstances under which formal and informal meetings speak to each other, even require each other to reproduce; they remark that one needs bodies to make meetings happen, though I inflected this in terms of persons and face; and they have given weight to the social and material production of modern time, and to much else besides. Areas of concern also emerge from the introduction to which I have not referred, though one might in retrospect highlight their comments on context. These include the observation that the attention previous studies have often given to contexts generated and represented through meetings deflects attention away from the routine practices through which the meeting also creates its own context. But then, as the editors imply, the concept of context itself disappears and reappears in the realization that participants' investment in the (indigenous) difference between an inside and outside is itself contextualized.

The end result of these provocations and equivocations is not that description becomes impossible. To the contrary, they strengthen the descriptive enterprise by providing, in an exemplary manner, key configurations that make evident the application and limitation of any supporting theoretical-analytical vocabulary. It is not trivial that these applications and limitations become thus evident through an artefact that in the anthropologist's world appears mundane and routine, indeed to the extent that the bureaucratically modulated meeting ordinarily escapes scrutiny. This means that, whatever vocabulary is used, it is being put to a very particular kind of test. Moreover, if, as one contributor observes, the (political) meeting is to politics as myth is to cosmology, changing as rapidly as the world of which it is part, then these essays clearly show that the formula also holds of ethnographic practice to social inquiry. In any event, after an 'ethnography of meeting', I don't think this previously rather dull-seeming corner of the world will ever appear quite the same.

Journal of the Royal Anthropological Institute (N.S.), 198-203
© Royal Anthropological Institute 2017

Index

Abram, Simone, 7, 16, 17, 19, 27–44, 198, 199

accountability, 29, 42, 46, 48, 57, 81, 202

actor-network theory, 14

aesthetics, 13, 15, 42; political, 138, 139, 146–8; socialist, 139–40, 147, 148

agenda, 10, 13–15, 19, 21, 31, 51, 56, 63, 64, 65, 68, 71, 77, 83, 84, 86, 89, 91, 92, 102, 113, 114, 159–61, 170, 171, 180, 199, 202

Alexander, Catherine, 7, 17, 19, 20, 80–94, 198, 199, 200

allotment society, 127–31, 200

animal welfare, 16, 18, 166–81

annual general meeting (AGM), 125, 127; lack of, 175–6

Annual Social Anthropology conference, 13

anthropology, and bureaucracy, 95–6; and common sense, 88; 'at home', 13, 82; cultural, 88; of development, 57; of planning, 29

Appadurai, Arjun, 85

Arendt, Hannah, 93

As If, 187, 188

assemblies, and consensus, 115; and exhaustion, 110, 111, 112, 115–16; as 'experiments of street', 120, 122; form, 15, 111; in Madrid, 111, 112, 113–15, 122; in

public space, 110, 111, 112, 113, 114, 115, 118, 119, 121; methodology of care, 113–14, 118; performance, 15; 'popular', 118–19; role, 119–20; rules, 29; stranger sociability, 110, 111, 112

assembly politics, 121

asylum case meetings, 16, 18, 20, 153–65; agenda, 159–61; arrangement of people, 156–8; law 'passing', 163–4

asylum process, 155

audience, 10, 20, 63, 65, 85

Austin, J.L., 29, 40

Bateson, Gregory, 146

Boas, Franz, 186

body, 15, 145

Bourdieu, Pierre, 132, 164

Boyle, Robert, 117, 122

Brown, Hannah, 7, 10–26, 45–62, 198, 199, 202

bureaucracy, 10, 11, 12, 16, 17, 18, 22, 23, 28, 31, 107, 124; and anthropologists, 95–6

Cahen, Michel, 146

capacity-building, 16, 45, 46, 48, 50, 52, 57, 58, 59

chairpersons, 19, 21, 39, 40, 41, 63, 64, 66, 67, 68, 70, 71, 74, 78, 82, 89, 102, 104, 125,